Hawthorne's Last Phase

BY

EDWARD HUTCHINS DAVIDSON

ARCHON BOOKS

1967

TO MY MOTHER AND FATHER

PREFACE

AFTER nearly seven years' residence abroad, Hawthorne believed that he had come home to his native land and could find there the quiet he had never known in England or on the Continent. Day after day he climbed to his new Italianate tower at the rear of his house in Concord and tried to spin those magical tales which had made his name so famous ten years before. But everything went wrong. He was worn and ill; his daughter Una suffered recurrent attacks of the Roman fever she had contracted in 1858; he felt driven to publish one more novel—just one—so that his son and daughters might obtain an education and his wife be left in comfort if he should die first; and in his own country he felt lost in the Civil War which broke out within a year after his return. Still he toiled over hundreds of pages of closely written manuscripts and yet, despite the soothing words of his friends and the generosity of his publishers, who stood ready to advance sums for unwritten romances, he could not bring himself to complete a single tale which he would show even to his wife. At his death Mrs. Hawthorne was astounded to discover piles and piles of unfinished romances which she and the children published one by one throughout the next nineteen years:

Title	Composition	Publication
The Ancestral Footstep	April-May, 1858	1882–83
Doctor Grimshawe's Secret	1860–61	1882
Septimius Felton	1861–63	1871–72
The Dolliver Romance	1863–64	1864–76

These are the relics an old man left behind him to testify to his failure in the last phase. It is indeed fortunate that Hawthorne himself did not destroy these fragmentary novels. Only by ignoring his most solemn injunctions against publishing any of his literary effects did the heirs reveal these romances which Hawthorne never intended the world to see.

But their editorial methods have brought with them a most vexing problem of texts. Only The Ancestral Footstep and Septimius Felton were published with any faithfulness to the original draft or with any intention except to conceal from the world the failure of Nathaniel Hawthorne in the last years; and even Septimius Felton exists in two drafts, only one of which has been published. Julian Hawthorne so patched and mangled the romance he titled Doctor Grimshawe's Secret that it bears few resemblances to the tale as Hawthorne wrote it and no reader can be expected to make any sense of it until the full text is someday printed. Lastly, the mystery of *The Dolliver Romance* will doubtless never be solved: either Hawthorne himself or one of the heirs destroyed a number of pages and various paragraphs have been deleted in the published version.

Yet the story is not entirely tragic. Hawthorne left behind him not only unfinished drafts of novels but also numbers of preliminary sketches and studies in which he worked out his plots and characters before he finally came to grips with his romances. These studies have never before been revealed and I have been granted permission by their several owners to publish them for the first time in this book. They are of prime importance in any consideration of Hawthorne's art-method. Now we can watch Hawthorne as he moved step by step in the workshop—sketching his plot, outlining a brief cast of characters, fitting these characters into the action, perhaps stopping to conjecture with himself on the next movement of his tale, and then resolving all these disparate elements in a final draft. With this manifold evidence before us, we can look over a great novelist's shoulder and watch him writing twenty-two experimental studies: six for *Doctor Grimshawe's Secret,* eight for *Septimius Felton,* and eight for *The Dolliver Romance.*

In so far as any evidence remains, Hawthorne never before employed this technique in planning his novels of the major phase. The fact that he had never resorted to these methods in the writing of *The Scarlet Letter* or of *The House of the Seven Gables* does not mean that suddenly, about 1860, he revised his whole craft of fiction. It means that, with these studies now before us, we can at last fill the gap between the germinal idea for a romance and the final composition. The very fortunate survival of these hastily scribbled studies provides us with the basic chemicals in the laboratory of art.

My investigation of Hawthorne's craftmanship is based on these twenty-two preparatory studies which Hawthorne jotted on any loose sheets of paper that came to hand. Sometimes he tore pages from a pocket notebook; sometimes he ripped a single large sheet in half and used both portions; and at other times he entered his notations between the lines and on the backs of letters which he had received from friends and well-wishers. A few studies may still be missing, a few lost forever, but I have reproduced every sketch which, to my knowledge, has survived. If there are any more, they would not add much important testimony; the bulk is sufficiently large to fascinate any student of Hawthorne or anyone interested in the craft of fiction.

In order to allow the reader to watch Hawthorne progressing from the first tentative steps to the final drafts, I have labeled these hitherto unpublished items "studies" and, to distinguish one from the other,

I have arbitrarily given them alphabetical designations. To the long, unfinished manuscripts which Hawthorne penned after roughing out his romances in the studies, I have applied the term "drafts" and I have similarly assigned letter-designations to them in order that the reader may follow the hesitant steps in the workshop of the last phase.

I cannot honestly pretend that I have arranged these studies in the chronological order of their composition. Not one of them bears a date in Hawthorne's hand; a few were written over letters whose dates in a correspondent's hand I have taken as a clue. But two facts have quite happily assisted me in establishing their order and precedence. From the first to the last as I have arranged them, we can watch the story grow from a small germ into a fairly complete tale. There are, of course, backward steps and recapitulations but even with these shifts and hesitations we can see the story develop under Hawthorne's hand. Secondly, there is Hawthorne's penmanship. From the clear, legible handwriting of the major phase, through the English notebooks, and even down to 1860, Hawthorne's chirography remained fairly constant. Even when he began the first studies for Grimshawe in the summer of 1860, his penmanship was clear and precise. Afterward occurred an incredible change. By the opening of 1861 his handwriting had become so small and cramped that the second of two Grimshawe drafts shows a marked deterioration over the first. Throughout the composition of *Septimius Felton* from 1861 to 1863 the letters become increasingly ill-formed and the penmanship tight and almost microscopic. By the summer of 1863 the hand is an old man's, tremulous and enfeebled by age. What is most extraordinary is that the handwriting changed *in only a few months*. Thus while Hawthorne composed a group of studies in a single spring or autumn, the penmanship of the last study shows a marked change or inferiority over that of the first.

With some apologies I have taken the liberty of reproducing these studies in the body of this book. To have placed them at the end would have demanded an appendix of vast proportions; it would likewise have required the reader to keep a finger placed near the end while he fumbled back and forth from my text to Hawthorne's. Furthermore, as a means of facilitating the reader's progress, I have grouped two or three of these studies together. They develop identical characters and show an evolution in the plotting of a romance.

Despite the difficult handwriting, I have attempted to reproduce these studies exactly as Hawthorne wrote them, maintaining the idiosyncrasies of his spelling and punctuation. In a few instances where the manuscript is blurred or the pages have been damaged, I have supplied a reading in square brackets; "[*sic*]" has been used sparingly to denote irregularities which might be taken for typographical errors. Finally I have placed the pagination of each study in square brackets, even when Hawthorne himself did not number the leaves. If he wrote between the lines or in the unused spaces of letters or concluded his jottings on the same side of the leaf on which he had begun, I have followed a similar method of pagination. For a full description of these twenty-two studies and of the last drafts, as well as for their present owners, the reader is referred to the bibliography.

Whenever possible I make references, both in the body of this book and in the notes, to the published texts of these four posthumous novels. But I have naturally restored the drafts to the proper order in which they were written and therefore I have been forced to make elaborate plot summaries, either of several drafts which the heirs have juggled and patched together or of hitherto unpublished manuscripts. I trust that my alphabetical designations of these drafts will make their order clear. In the notes I have made references both to the drafts and to the published texts; when the two versions differ, I have, of course, followed the manuscript reading. But when I quote from hitherto unpublished or partially published drafts, I have not burdened the notes with references which the reader could not be expected to find for himself until the whole corpus of the Hawthorne drafts is someday revealed.

With these important studies and with my restoration of the drafts to their proper sequence in the Hawthorne canon, I should like to outline briefly what I am trying to do with this mass of new material. The first chapter traces Hawthorne's life and writings in the last phase and forms a very necessary introduction to the tangled story which follows. Even though *The Marble Faun* and the essays on England, published in 1863 as *Our Old Home*, come within the chronological frame of my discussion, I make only a few allusions to them because they are both outside the scope of this investigation. *The Marble Faun* was Hawthorne's last successful novel; *Our Old Home* was a revision of the English notebooks which Hawthorne undertook for the *Atlantic Monthly* in order to keep him in funds until he could complete a "Romance of England" or a "Romance of Immortality." In the second chapter I show how Hawthorne while residing in England as United States Consul to Liverpool, stored his notebooks and his imagination for the time when he could return home to Concord and write romances. The latter half of this chapter investigates *The Ancestral Footstep*, in itself hardly more than a preliminary study for *Doctor Grimshawe's Secret*, which Hawthorne undertook in 1860. Each succeeding chapter treats a single romance—*Doctor Grimshawe's Secret, Septimius Felton,* and *The Dolliver Romance*—and each one demands a different approach and reveals different facets of Hawthorne's craftsmanship. The last chapter attempts to weave together all of these diverse threads into some general conclusions on Hawthorne's art-method—conclusions which may very well apply to the novels of the major as well as of the last phase.

My one Appendix has been included in order not to freight the text with matters tangential to the main design. It relates Julian Hawthorne's editing of the Grimshawe drafts, a story I have been able to piece together after much arduous detective work among blasts and counterblasts in a family quarrel after Hawthorne's death, and more especially among the pages of the drafts themselves which have had a very curious history. I might have added further appendices and spread out segments of still unpublished drafts, but in the studies themselves and in the last versions of these fragmentary novels one may find the "moral" writ large and underlined: it is little wonder that Hawthorne never completed a romance in the last phase.

ACKNOWLEDGMENTS

I OWE so many debts for kindness and aid that I can hardly hope to acknowledge them all. First, however, to Miss Belle da Costa Greene of the Pierpont Morgan Library, New York City, I wish to express my deepest appreciation for permission to study and copy the Hawthorne items in that collection; in addition, Miss Greene supplied me with photostats at the expense of the Library and entrusted to my care valuable manuscripts which I found essential to my study. I wish that Mr. W. T. H. Howe were still alive so that I might thank him for his favors and for his charming entertainment at his country home in Kentucky. Fortunately, his collection was purchased for the Henry W. and Albert A. Berg Collection of the New York Public Library, and the officers and trustees of that institution have given me full permission to reveal the manuscript items deposited there. A special debt of gratitude is due Mr. John D. Gordan, Curator of the Berg Collection, who gave me much excellent advice in the mere business of getting permissions to publish this manuscript material; I should like further to add that Mr. Gordan offered me a clear right to use one brief Hawthorne manuscript item, the only one which I could not include in this book, but the lack of inclusion is not in any way Mr. Gordan's fault.

To the Henry E. Huntington Library in San Marino, California, and especially to Mr. Leslie Edgar Bliss, I am grateful for permission to publish material which that notable institution has acquired and makes ever available to students of American literature. The Massachusetts Historical Society and the Yale Collection of American Literature supplied me with several indispensable items. I also recall pleasant memories of working in the Sterling Memorial Library at Yale University; there my special obligations are due Mr. Andrew Keogh and Miss Anne Pratt, who offered helpful bibliographical suggestions. Miss Sarah R. Bartlett, Librarian of the Concord Free Public Library, Concord, Massachusetts, worked ably in my behalf and obtained for me a photostat of the first chapter of *The Dolliver Romance,* the manuscript of which is deposited in that library. Lastly, Mr. Manning Hawthorne, as representative of Nathaniel Hawthorne's heirs, granted me the final and very necessary permission to reveal these manuscript studies for the first time in this book.

To others I owe just as much: Professor Randall Stewart of Brown University, who allowed me to read and make extracts from Hawthorne's English Notebooks before they were published; Professor

Norman Holmes Pearson, who stood always ready with advice and encouragement; Professor Benjamin C. Nangle, editor of the Yale Studies in English, who guided this book through the press; Mr. Robert H. Haynes, Assistant Librarian of the Harvard College Library, who supervised the photostating of one manuscript; Mrs. Robert S. Heath of Titusville, Pennsylvania, who generously waived her prior claim to an important Hawthorne manuscript item and allowed me to use it in this book; President John C. Baker of Ohio University, who made smooth the way for partial financing of this work; my colleagues, Dr. Joseph B. Heidler, Mr. Paul Murray Kendall, and Mr. Charles Allen Smart, who read the book in manuscript and offered many necessary corrections and improvements; the staff of the Edwin Watts Chubb Library and its librarian, Miss Anne Keating; the Research Committee of Ohio University, which readily supplied funds for photostats; and the Ohio University Fund, Incorporated, which voted me a grant without which I could not have published this book.

I reserve a special paragraph for Professor Stanley T. Williams of Yale University, in whose graduate course in American Literature I initiated this study. He enabled me to obtain access to material which might otherwise have remained closed to me; he supervised this study which was presented to the Graduate School of Yale University in partial fulfillment for the degree of Doctor of Philosophy; and, best of all, he has always remained the good friend.

My wife, Ann S. Davidson, helped me prepare the final copy and the index and laughed to scorn my scholarly groans and wails.

EDWARD H. DAVIDSON

Athens, Ohio
November 4, 1948

BIBLIOGRAPHICAL NOTES

Citations of manuscript material are short-title references to items fully described in the "Bibilography—Preliminary Studies and Manuscripts." Thus a page reference to "Grimshawe G" will be to the particular recto or verso number of the draft in the Morgan, Huntington, or Berg Collections.

All references to Hawthorne's writings are to be found in the respective volumes of *The Complete Works of Nathaniel Hawthorne,* with Introductory Notes by George Parsons Lathrop (Riverside ed., Boston and New York, 1883, 12 vols.). Obvious abbreviations for individual works are used in the footnotes. References to *The Ancestral Footstep, Septimius Felton,* and *The Dolliver Romance* are to be found in Vol. XI of this edition, except that the exact wording is that of the original autograph, not of the published edition. When citations are made from *Doctor Grimshawe's Secret,* the page number refers to Vol. XIII of the Riverside Edition, but the wording is likewise that of Draft "G" or "H," not that of Julian Hawthorne's edition. *Passages from the American Notebooks* is occasionally employed only for portions of Hawthorne's journals not included in Professor Stewart's edition.

The following is a list of abbreviations:

American Notebooks
Stewart, Randall, ed., *The American Notebooks by Nathaniel Hawthorne.* New Haven, Yale University Press, 1932.

English Notebooks
Stewart, Randall, ed., *The English Notebooks by Nathaniel Hawthorne.* New York and London, Modern Language Association of America and Oxford University Press, 1941.

Hawthorne and His Wife
Hawthorne, Julian, *Nathaniel Hawthorne and His Wife.* Boston and New York, Houghton, Mifflin and Company, 1884. 2 vols.

Yesterdays
Fields, James T., *Yesterdays with Authors.* Boston, Fields and Osgood, 1890.

Letters to Ticknor
Letters of Hawthorne to William D. Ticknor. Newark, N. J., published for the Carteret Book Club, 1910. 2 vols.

CONTENTS

HAWTHORNE'S LAST PHASE

I

Nathaniel Hawthorne: 1858–64

1

EVER since Hawthorne had accepted President Franklin Pierce's appointment to the Liverpool consulate in 1853, he had looked forward to the day when he would again be able to take up his pen and write another romance. His tenure of office had been chiefly for the purpose of acquiring sufficient funds to permit him to resume those artistic tasks which had made him famous. Thus, when his resignation was finally accepted after the inauguration of President Buchanan and a successor had been installed in the consulate in October, 1857, he "drew the long delightful breath" of escape.[1] For several months he roamed through Warwickshire and London; then shortly after the New Year of 1858 the Hawthornes sailed across the Channel and arrived in Paris on January 5.[2] A leisurely journey southward brought them to Genoa on the eighteenth and two days later they arrived in Rome.[3]

The ancient capital offered so many new places of interest even to a practiced tourist like Hawthorne that literary work was almost impossible. Yet he was able to write daily entries in his journal and finally, on April 1, to begin a brief experimental draft of an English romance which was published many years later as *The Ancestral Footstep*.[4] Its theme was one which had struck Hawthorne almost as soon as he had arrived in Liverpool: the return of an American to England for the purpose of solving an old mystery in his family. The work went so slowly and proved to be so unsatisfactory that Hawthorne was content to abandon it on May 19. He had already found the faun of Praxiteles in the Villa Borghese and resolved to write a romance on the appearance of an innocent, primitive man in a world of sin.

At the end of May the Hawthornes were in Florence where they met more noteworthy people than they had ever seen in England. Browning called during the first week to invite Hawthorne and his wife to spend an evening at Casa Guidi and soon the two families were

1. *Our Old Home*, II, 55. See also *Hawthorne and His Wife*, II, 163.
2. *Hawthorne and His Wife*, II, 169; *Letters to Ticknor*, II, 70.
3. *Hawthorne and His Wife*, II, 176.
4. See Chapter II.

on the friendliest terms. Nearby lived others who made Hawthorne's residence exceptionally pleasant: the Bryants, who soon departed for Venice; T. Adolphus Trollope, the brother of the more famous Anthony; Miss Isa Blagden, a friend of the Brownings', and the American sculptor, Hiram Powers. Indeed, life in Florence was more delightful than Hawthorne had ever imagined it could be but the round of social engagements did not prevent his beginning, in late July, a new romance, *The Marble Faun*.[5]

Early in October, however, the Hawthornes returned to Rome and, by the middle of that month, were in "a comfortable, cosey little house" in the Piazza Poli.[6] On the twenty-fourth an insignificant event took place which was to change the course of Hawthorne's last years: his daughter Una and Ada Shepard, the governess, visited the Palace of the Caesars and Una caught a cold which, within a week, had turned from an ordinary cough into the dreaded Roman fever. During the four subsequent months Hawthorne could do nothing but watch the ravages of disease; he abandoned his journal and the projected romance while his daughter lay for weeks in a stupor. At last in April, 1859, Una sank lower and lower until Hawthorne gave up all hope.[7]

The burden of illness was lifted by the end of April and Hawthorne began to breathe more freely. *The Marble Faun* had been so long laid aside that he felt the need for a more invigorating climate than Italy offered. Accordingly, he bade Rome farewell in late May and sailed with his family to Marseilles; from thence they passed northward, pausing at Avignon and Geneva, until they arrived in England. By mid-July they had settled at Redcar on the coast of Yorkshire and Hawthorne resumed work on the Italian romance.[8] The novel was finished in Leamington some time in October and published by Smith and Elder on February 28, 1860.[9] When the first edition was almost immediately exhausted, Hawthorne knew that he had reestablished himself as one of the leading novelists of the day. The remaining three months in England were spent in short tours to London and Oxford and bidding farewell to the few friends he had acquired during his tenure of the Liverpool consulate.[1]

5. *Italian Notebooks*, p. 373.
6. *Idem*, pp. 432, 478–9.
7. *Hawthorne and His Wife*, II, 206–07.
8. *Idem*, pp. 225–6.
9. *Yesterdays*, p. 88; *Letters to Ticknor*, II, 91; Caroline Ticknor, *Hawthorne and His Publisher* (Boston and New York, 1913), pp. 234–5. Julian Hawthorne (*Hawthorne and His Wife*, II, 233) mistakenly asserts that the romance was finished "early in the spring of 1860."
1. *Yesterdays*, pp. 88–91.

2

It was on June 16, 1860, after a seven years' residence abroad, that
Hawthorne sailed with his family from Liverpool to Boston. Aboard
the "Europa" were James T. Fields, editor of the *Atlantic Monthly*
and partner in the publishing house of Ticknor and Fields, Mrs. Fields,
and Harriet Beecher Stowe with her husband and children. On the
twenty-eighth the ship docked at Boston and the passengers disem-
barked. A few hours later the Hawthornes arrived in Concord to
make their home once more in the Wayside, which they had purchased from Alcott in 1852.[2]

The village was quiet and rural compared to the great Continental
cities but it was merely a calm between a small and a great storm.
Only six months before, the John Brown uprising had taken place at
Harper's Ferry and the townspeople had risen with all New England
to protest against any harm which might be done to the conspirators.
When the news had arrived that Brown and some of his companions
were hanged, Emerson had declared that the gallows would be made
as glorious as the cross.[3] Frank Sanborn, principal of the Concord private school, had been rescued in the preceding April by an angry mob
of the citizenry who prevented his being forcibly carried to Boston
where he was to stand trial for his part in the rebellion.[4] By June 28
the village was quiet, but there were sounds throughout the country
which foretold a national calamity.

For a time Hawthorne enjoyed a reunion with his friends who were
all eager to welcome him. Alcott resided in the Hillside, just over the
hedge from Hawthorne's house,[5] and less than a mile away Thoreau
shared a house with his sister Sophia.[6] William Ellery Channing, the
"Concord poet," had been one of Hawthorne's associates in the
Brook Farm days; he too was happy to greet Hawthorne. Emerson
was one of the first to welcome Hawthorne with a call on the first day
of his return to Concord.[7] Several weeks later Emerson gave a summer evening party and the old friends were all presented to Hawthorne. Thoreau afterward admitted that he could see no change in

2. Mrs. Annie Adams Fields, *James T. Fields; Biographical Notes and Personal
Sketches* (Boston, 1881), p. 83. See *Boston Daily Advertiser*, xcv (29 June 1860), 3.

3. J. E. Cabot, *A Memoir of Ralph Waldo Emerson* (Boston and New York, 1887),
p. 597.

4. F. B. Sanborn, *Hawthorne and His Friends, Reminiscence and Tribute* (Cedar
Rapids, Iowa, 1908), p. 8.

5. Rose Hawthorne Lathrop, *Memories of Hawthorne* (Boston and New York,
1923), pp. 414–18.

6. *Idem*, pp. 420–21.

7. Ticknor, *op. cit.*, p. 244.

Hawthorne's manner. "He is as simple and childlike as ever."[8] Sanborn, however, thought him ". . . less shy, more accustomed to meet his fellow mortals gracefully,—but, too, less simple and agreeable in intimate manner and general character."[9] Lowell saw him at about this time and agreed with Sanborn. "He looks no older than when I saw him last, eight years ago, wears a moustache, and is easier in society than formerly."[1] The only change which Hawthorne himself would admit was ". . . a moustache of Italian growth" which he had acquired the previous year.[2]

In that summer of 1860 there was quiet in Concord, the last peace Hawthorne was ever to know, and life for him settled into the pleasant routine of reading, walking, and writing. He engaged some carpenters to erect a private study or tower, like Miriam's, at the rear of his house, and there he began two literary tasks. The first was a revision of his voluminous English notebooks for the purpose of publishing a series of essays on England in the *Atlantic Monthly*. The earliest of these articles he completed shortly after his return to Concord and during the next three years he submitted ten essays which Fields happily accepted. For each of these he received $150 or $200 with which, in addition to his savings from the consulate, he was able to provide his family with the ordinary comforts of life. But they were mere hackwork, designed to supply Hawthorne with a steady income until he could complete another romance.[3]

The second task was the more important one—the writing of that English novel which he had begun and then put aside in Italy. Once again in the summer of 1860 he returned to his initial plan of an English romance and began to compose the various studies for a novel later to be known as *Doctor Grimshawe's Secret*. But nothing went well; he labored to complete one large draft, thrust it aside, and began all over. The Confederate bombardment of Fort Sumter was the final disruption of Hawthorne's work on the romance and he never returned to complete it.[4]

If Hawthorne were unsuccessful as a writer, the literary world, and particularly the young world of William Dean Howells, was not the wiser. One day in August, 1860, Howells asked Oliver Wendell Holmes how to become acquainted with Hawthorne. Holmes replied dryly, "Ah, well! I don't know that you will ever feel that you have

8. H. D. Thoreau, *Writings* (Riverside ed., Boston and New York, 1906), xi, 420.
9. Sanborn, *op. cit.*, p. 51.
1. C. E. Norton, ed., *Letters of James Russell Lowell* (New York, 1894), 1, 302. The letter from which this quotation is taken is misdated "June 12, 1860."
2. Horatio Bridge, *Personal Recollections of Nathaniel Hawthorne* (New York, 1893), p. 164.
3. *Hawthorne and His Wife*, II, 303–04.
4. See Chapter III.

really met him. He is like a dim room with a little taper of personality burning on the corner of the mantel."[5] Nevertheless, several days later, Howells walked boldly up the main street of Concord until he found himself before the door of the Wayside. He presented a letter of introduction from Lowell and Hawthorne shyly asked him to come in. They talked for a time as they walked along the hill at the rear of the house. Later Hawthorne wrote, "I find this young man worthy," on a card which the delighted bearer could present to Emerson.[6]

3

The opening of the Civil War found Hawthorne dispirited and lost. He had left England in order to find a place in Concord where he believed he might once more write romances. Now he realized that a vigorous patriotism was in the air and that he had to explain to his son Julian, as well as rationalize the fact for himself, that the South was attempting to free itself from Northern rule. Southern pretensions were arousing in his mind, during these early months of the conflict, a hearty antipathy to the slaveowners. "I hope," he frequently said, "that we shall give them a terrible thrashing, and then kick them out."[7] But as the struggle wore on, he began to be nostalgic for England. "It is odd," he confided to his friend, William D. Ticknor, ". . . that I have never felt so earnest a desire to go back to England as now that I have irrevocably planted myself at home."[8] In the end the war shook loose the institutions on which he had based his whole life and which, when once they were gone, were replaced only by the hollow platitudes of fanatics repeated ceaselessly in the newspapers. When he again wrote to Ticknor, in an attempt at wry humor, that he wished "they would push on the war a little more briskly," for the "excitement had an invigorating effect"[9] on him, he was merely concealing his private conviction of the tragic waste which the conflict wrought. For him there was no hope. Thus he spent the rest of his days in fear and misgiving for his country which had given evidences of such greatness in the days of Andrew Jackson.

Yet the war was a challenge and offered promise of a better work than the abandoned English romance. Hawthorne had often found his mind recurring to a legend which Thoreau had told him of a man, once a resident in the Wayside, who thought that he should never die. Furthermore, a curious historical coincidence suggested to him the

5. William Dean Howells, "My First Visit to New England," *Literary Friends and Acquaintance* (New York and London, 1911), p. 38.
6. Mildred Howells, *The Life and Letters of William Dean Howells* (New York, 1928), I, 30.
7. *Hawthorne and His Wife*, II, 270.
8. *Letters to Ticknor*, II, 114.
9. *Idem*, p. 116.

locale of Concord and the opening of the Revolutionary War. On April 19, 1861, the first volunteers from the village had marched away to join the Union forces near Washington; on that day in 1775, eighty-six years before, the British had entered Concord to destroy the stores in the possession of the colonists. It was a parallel which Hawthorne could not escape: between the Civil War and the Revolutionary War he saw enough resemblances to set his hand again at work on a romance. He would take a vital subject of his own day and, by throwing the whole thing back to the days when the minutemen fired the famous shot, he would draw deep in men's hearts all of those "moral" suggestions and meanings which had made his name justly famous. He wrote steadily on the fragment, later published as *Septimius Felton*, throughout those dark days of late 1861 and 1862 when everyone thought that the Confederates might take Washington.[1]

The war may have inspired Hawthorne but it also made him restless and in the early months of 1862 he felt a great need to see the conflict for himself. Accordingly, in March he persuaded Ticknor to go with him to Washington and to the scenes of the struggle.

The two friends left Boston on March 6 and arrived in New York, where for two days they were pleasantly entertained by "various artists and literary people."[2] They departed for Philadelphia on the ninth and the next day completed their journey to Washington as the first reports of a naval engagement between the "Merrimac" and the "Monitor" were trickling in. The succeeding period in the capital city was filled with sight-seeing and with conversations in Willard's Hotel, where everyone was mingling in the frenzied excitement of war. Then on March 13 Hawthorne and Ticknor were introduced to President Lincoln at the White House. In some respects the occasion was amusing, for they had accompanied a deputation which solemnly presented a whip to the Chief Executive. Lincoln handled the situation with a simple tact that convinced Hawthorne of the strength and dignity of this man to lead the nation through the war.[3]

For the remainder of the month Hawthorne was busily engaged in making tours to General McClellan's headquarters at Fairfax Seminary, Virginia,[4] to Harper's Ferry on the first train of the recently

1. See Chapter IV.
2. *Love Letters of Nathaniel Hawthorne*, published for The Society of the Dofobs (Chicago, 1907), II, 277.
3. For the date of Hawthorne's meeting Lincoln, see *Philadelphia Inquirer* (March 15, 1862), p. 4. For Hawthorne's impressions of Lincoln, see "Chiefly about War Matters," *Works*, XII, 308-12.
4. Hawthorne calls this place "Fairfield Seminary" ("Chiefly about War Matters," p. 321) but he is obviously mistaken. *The New York Times* (March 30, 1862, p. 1) carries the following note, "Fairfax Seminary, quite recently the headquarters of General McClellan, . . . is a very large institution, on a commanding site, about two miles west of Alexandria."

reopened Baltimore and Ohio Railroad,[5] and to Newport News, where the first modern naval battle had taken place just a short time before.[6] Early in April Hawthorne was at home in Concord and in better health and spirits than at his departure.

This pleasant sense of vitality was only temporary and the mood of despair seized him again when the disasters of McClellan's peninsular campaign proved that the war was not to be ended by a change of the battlefront. Hawthorne was only expressing a general disquietude when he confessed to Horatio Bridge on April 19, "I feel a tremendous anxiety about our affairs at Yorktown. It will not at all surprise me if we come to grief."[7] Then, as if the pattern of personal and national distress were not complete, Thoreau died on May 6. On the day of the funeral Hawthorne and his wife walked to Thoreau's house and up the hill to Sleepy Hollow Cemetery. Several months later Hawthorne was still brooding over his friend's death; he thought he might write a memorial for Thoreau as an introduction to his next novel.[8]

Yet while Henry Thoreau's legend of the deathless man still haunted Hawthorne, there were the essays on England which he must continue to send to the *Atlantic Monthly;* in addition to these, he had completed an article which summed up his impressions of the war but all of them were mere potboilers. He could idle away the summer of 1862 and fulfill his contract with Fields, but as the autumn drew on he tried to take up again the romance of immortality which he had sketched out in the spring. But there was "something preternatural" in his "reluctance to begin."[9] Every month the war was striking at the very homes of his friends and neighbors: Lowell had lost a favorite nephew in the early engagements;[1] young Holmes was wounded at Antietam;[2] and Louisa May Alcott, who had spent her strength nursing soldiers, returned home early in 1863, scarred with a fever which sapped her vitality and probably shortened her days.[3] There was little hope to be gained from scanning the newspapers and Hawthorne at times stopped reading them for fear of learning some new disaster to a friend or to the nation. He took up instead the vol-

5. *Hawthorne and His Wife,* II, 309–10.
6. "Chiefly about War Matters," p. 332. For additional details concerning this excursion, see Howard M. Ticknor, "Hawthorne as Seen by His Publisher," *The Critic,* XLV (July, 1904), 54.
7. Letter to Horatio Bridge, April 19, 1862, in the Maurice Collection.
8. F. B. Sanborn, *The Life of Henry D. Thoreau* (Boston and New York, 1917), p. 492 n.; R. H. Lathrop, *op. cit.,* pp. 431–2.
9. *Hawthorne and His Wife,* II, 323.
1. H. E. Scudder, *James Russell Lowell, A Biography* (Boston and New York, 1901), II, 82.
2. O. W. Holmes, "My Hunt after the Captain," *Works* (Riverside ed., Boston and New York, 1894), VIII, 16–77.
3. F. P. Stearns, *Sketches from Concord and Appledore* (New York, 1895), p. 78.

umes of Sir Walter Scott's works and each night read aloud from those marvelous tales until he had communicated nearly all of them to his family. To Hawthorne, however, the reading was far easier than the writing of romances; yet he still locked himself in his tower during the morning and came out for dinner with only a look of haggard disappointment on his face. No matter how resolutely he sat before the old desk and tried to tell the story of Septimius Felton, whom Thoreau had suggested to him, he saw that he could bring no resolution to the romance and, sometime early in 1863, put it aside after composing two long drafts, as well as numerous preliminary sketches and studies.[4]

At the opening of 1863 he was sick in body and apathetic in mind. Una's second attack of Roman fever left him with the same fears and sleeplessness which he had known in Italy. His own affliction was not so much the ravages of an easily diagnosed illness as a languid decay; he seemed to grow weaker and thinner as the days passed; he spent most of the daylight hours indoors and, when he did walk out, he could summon hardly enough strength to climb his favorite hill at the rear of his home. He suffered from nameless aches, not so painful as annoying, and accompanied by attacks of chills which made him wish to seek out the sunny side of his house and bask there. Old age, he said, was like having a cold for the rest of one's life.[5] If it were only a quiet and gentlemanly thinning of the hair and weakening of the will, he might find some consolation in the devotion which a loving family bestowed on him; but he was afflicted with ridiculous attacks of nosebleeding, one of which lasted twenty-four hours and almost drained his last strength in one unstanched flow. No wonder he cared little for companionship or for the casual visits of friends throughout the spring of 1863, when even the war itself failed to arouse his interest. He came to believe that his end was near, for he wrote to Ticknor expressing a doubt that they should ever meet again: he had been shut in the Wayside so long that he felt rusted in a hole "and could not get out even if [he] wished."[6] And of Fields he asked wearily, "I wonder how many people there are in the world who would keep their nerves in tolerably good order through such a length of solitary imprisonment."[7]

Still the remunerative hackwork must go on and when he had completed the tenth essay on England, he contracted with Ticknor and Fields to issue the series in a volume entitled *Our Old Home*. This book he intended to dedicate, despite the warnings of his friends, to

4. See Chapter IV.
5. Septimius "L," "25 (additional)," p. 1.
6. *Letters to Ticknor*, II, 120; Caroline Ticknor, *op. cit.*, p. 301.
7. *Yesterdays*, p. 104.

his old college mate Franklin Pierce, who had made possible the consular experiences. Unhappily for Hawthorne, his friends were right: Pierce was extremely unpopular in the North but Hawthorne, aware that old ties meant more than transient politics, was not to be overruled.[8] As a measure of his esteem for Pierce, he traveled to Concord, New Hampshire, to hear the ex-President deliver the Bunker Hill address on July 4. He sat on the platform while Pierce attacked Lincoln and the conduct of the war. As he spoke, the audience was suddenly stirred to excitement by reports of a great battle at Gettysburg.[9]

It was unfortunate that Pierce should have been so outspoken as he was on this occasion. For more than a year the abolitionist writers had been lashing him unmercifully. Now, with the triumph of Gettysburg as confirmation of their views, they gave him one of the most outrageous castigations any man could receive in the public press of the Union. Hawthorne, nevertheless, remained faithful to the promise of his dedication and, when *Our Old Home* was published on September 19, the critics included the writer in the same political class with the "traitorous" ex-President.[1]

4

The winter of 1863 made apparent the alarming state of Hawthorne's undefined illness and for the first time his family refused to be put aside with flippant excuses that he had only a cold in the head. At times he tried to work; the acrimonious notices of *Our Old Home* spurred him forward in October to begin the second romance of immortality and, further to give himself a much-needed stimulus, he contracted with Fields to issue the novel serially in the *Atlantic Monthly*. He planned to write a sketch of Thoreau as a preface to this new romance—"the duty of a live literary man to perpetuate the memory of a dead one"—but his mysteriously failing health made composition more difficult than ever before. By the first of December he had completed only one of the three chapters which were later given to the world as *The Dolliver Romance*.[2]

8. For more complete treatments of Pierce and the Civil War, see R. F. Nichols, *Franklin Pierce, Young Hickory of the Granite State* (Philadelphia, University of Pennsylvania Press, 1927), p. 197 ff.; for Hawthorne and Pierce during these years, see Randall Stewart, "Hawthorne and the Civil War," *Studies in Philology*, xxxiv (January, 1937), 91–106.

9. Sanborn, *Hawthorne and His Friends*, p. 61; Nichols, *op. cit.*, p. 523.

1. These slurs on Hawthorne were all made in reviews of *Our Old Home*. See *Boston Daily Advertiser*, cii (September 30, 1863), 2; *Boston Liberator*, xxxiii (October 2, 1863), 158; and *New York Evening Post*, lxii (October 7, 1863), 1. See also Stewart, *op. cit.*, p. 103. It is amusing to recall that Emerson ripped out the pages of the dedication in his volume; see M. A. DeWolfe Howe, ed., *Memories of a Hostess* (Boston, 1922), p. 15 n.

2. *Yesterdays*, pp. 109–10.

On December 2, Mrs. Franklin Pierce died in Andover, New Hampshire, and Hawthorne immediately left Concord to be at his friend's side. Mrs. Pierce's death struck Hawthorne with strange poignancy. He knew her only as his friend's wife but as he looked at her body he saw "a remote expression about it as if it had nothing to do with things present."[3] When the two men stood together at the edge of the grave, Pierce, forgetting his own private sorrow for the care of his friend, drew up the collar of Hawthorne's coat to protect his shivering face from the cold. It was a gesture which drew the two old college mates together in the hour of their mutual loss. On the evening of the funeral he was back in Boston and spent the night with Fields, who expressed delight over the first chapter of the new romance; but Hawthorne was beyond encouragement. The burden of the present seemed intolerable and he began to talk quietly about his happy childhood in Maine when he had roamed the woods or skated at night on Lake Sebago. "Everything is beautiful in youth," he said, "for all things are allowed to it then."[4]

The next day found him again at the Wayside to continue his life and to submit for the first time to the obvious enfeeblement of his condition. He would sit for a whole afternoon wrapped in a shawl and looking at the winter snow which encrusted each branch and twig with "a weight of icy splendor."[5] Trying to hide his private anxiety behind a mask of cheerful playfulness, he would laugh at his own debility and irresolution; nevertheless, he could not conceal from his wife that the "pride of strength in him" had succumbed to the touch of old age.[6] He tried to read but his enjoyment was limited to the rollicking verses of Longfellow's *Tales of a Wayside Inn*—"the grand old strains," as he wrote to the poet, "that have been sounding on all through my life."[7] His own creative work was ended forever and the *Atlantic* would never receive more than one chapter of *The Dolliver Romance*. His last days could never again be easy after the loss of his artistic powers. Old age had brought him the triple misery of loneliness, ill-health, and a burdensome reputation which he felt he must maintain. He had lived long enough to see some of his friends go before him and leave him solitary; physically he weakened perceptibly until his last day; and his hopes for a satisfactory bank account had been dissipated in numerous expenses.

By the first of March, 1864, it was apparent that a change of scene

3. Howe, *op. cit.*, p. 58. See *Yesterdays*, pp. 112–13.
4. *Yesterdays*, p. 113; Howe, *op. cit.*, p. 59.
5. *Hawthorne and His Wife*, II, 333.
6. *Ibid.*
7. Samuel Longfellow, *Life of Henry Wadsworth Longfellow* (Boston and New York, 1891), III, 28.

was imperative in order to revive his rapidly failing health. Ticknor came once more to his rescue and the two friends set forth on the twenty-eighth to make another slow journey South, perhaps as far as Washington.[8] They passed the first night in Boston in the company of old acquaintances; Mrs. Fields recorded her impressions of Hawthorne's wasted figure:

He shocked us by his invalid appearance. He has become quite deaf, too. His limbs are shrunken but his great eyes still burn with their lambent fire. He said, "Why does Nature treat us so like children! I think we could bear it if we knew our fate. At least I think it would not make much difference to me now what became of me."[9]

On the next day they left for New York, where they took rooms in the Astor House, and by April 4 Hawthorne had gained enough strength to proceed to Philadelphia, where Ticknor was suddenly seized with "a bilious attack." Without any warning to his companion who stood watching throughout a day and a night, Ticknor died on April 10, leaving Hawthorne stunned and scarcely able to make his way back to Concord.[1]

On the fifteenth Ticknor was buried and it immediately became evident that Hawthorne could no longer remain in Concord. At this point Pierce suggested that they undertake together a leisurely journey which would carry them as far as New Hampshire.[2] In the middle of May Hawthorne left to join Pierce in Boston. He seemed to know that he would never return and, standing at the gate of his home, he looked "Like a snow image of an unbending but an old, old man. . . ." He glanced back for one last glimpse of his family and was gone.[3]

The two companions left Boston and proceeded by easy stages to Plymouth, New Hampshire, where they arrived on May 19. That night in a room in the Pemigewasset House, Hawthorne slipped quietly out of life, troubled by no return to consciousness, undiscovered by Pierce until the early hours of the next morning.[4]

The funeral service was held on the twenty-third in the Concord village church. James Freeman Clarke, who had married Hawthorne to Sophia Peabody twenty-two years before, preached the funeral sermon. The manuscript of the first chapter of *The Dolliver Romance* lay on the coffin throughout the service and remained there while

8. Bridge, *op. cit.*, pp. 190–1.
9. Howe, *op. cit.*, pp. 62–3.
1. Caroline Ticknor, *op. cit.*, p. 324; *Hawthorne and His Wife*, II, 343.
2. *Hawthorne and His Wife*, II, 344.
3. R. H. Lathrop, *op. cit.*, p. 480.
4. *Hawthorne and His Wife*, II, 346.

Longfellow, Emerson, Channing, Agassiz, Lowell, Alcott, Whipple, Holmes, Hilliard, and Pierce walked at its side up the hill to the Sleepy Hollow Cemetery.[5] The grave was beneath a cluster of pines where Hawthorne and his wife, like Lilias Fay and Adam Forrester, had often dreamed of an ideal pleasure house.

5. *Yesterdays,* p. 124.

II

The Romance of England and "The Ancestral Footstep"

I. The Seeds of Romance

1

IN his early years Hawthorne had assumed the tedious responsibilities of the Boston and Salem customhouses in order that he might tide himself over the ill-paid times of short-story writing. His acceptance of the Liverpool consulate in 1853 had been governed by a similar wish: to save enough money and thereby maintain his family in the latter years of his life and to insure a period during which he would never be forced to worry over bills, no matter how small might be the return from future novels. His intention was to accumulate $20,000, as a saving both from his annual salary of $10,000 and from the fees he received by affixing his signature to invoice certificates on cargoes. In neither respect was he successful; his income was so drastically reduced by a Congressional enactment of 1855 that he came to abandon any hope of an easy retirement during his last years. In addition, he engaged in two hapless speculations. The first was a loan of $10,000 to his old friend John O'Sullivan, who bought a worthless Spanish copper mine.[1] The second occurred in 1856 when he wrote a preface to and paid for the publication of Delia Bacon's *Philosophy of Shakespeare's Plays Solved.*[2] In the end, the costs of living and of travel, together with these two expenditures from which he never gained any return, seriously diminished the capital he desired to accumulate. It is indeed a sad commentary on these last four and posthumously published novels that Hawthorne struggled so valiantly and so hopelessly for the sheer purpose of earning money.

Yet there was another and, perhaps, more important reason why Hawthorne accepted President Pierce's appointment to the Liverpool consulate. He wished to live in England for at least four years while he sedulously kept the notebook, so long a repository of ideas for tales,

1. Julian Hawthorne, *Hawthorne and His Circle* (New York and London, 1903), p. 135; R. H. Lathrop, *Memories of Hawthorne*, p. 478. For Hawthorne's friendship with O'Sullivan, see *Hawthorne and His Wife*, I, 160–3, II, 47–102 *passim*. For Hawthorne's salary at the consulate, see Lawrence Sargent Hall, *Hawthorne, Critic of Society* (New Haven, Yale University Press, 1944), pp. 50–5.
2. Caroline Ticknor, *Hawthorne and His Publisher*, p. 182 ff.; Theodore Bacon, *Delia Bacon, A Biographical Sketch* (Boston and New York, 1888), pp. 164–317.

and gathered material and impressions for novels he would write when he returned to the Wayside. From almost the first day of his arrival in England he kept this journal, an amazing collection of studies of people, of descrptions and minutiae which only Hawthorne's mind would notice and record. Some were brief; some covered a dozen pages in one day's harvest; many seemed to stray far from any importance as commentaries on the English and the English scene. Yet all of them might be the rough plans, the suggestive details, the tantalizing mesh and chaos of life which Hawthorne's imagination might one day transform into an English romance.

Literary criticism is almost completely absent from the English journals. Furthermore, Hawthorne was unwilling or too shy to seek out the great writers of his day; perhaps they had nothing to tell him. He had more interesting and important things to do than to follow the conventional literary pilgrimage to shrines and famous homes. He knew, moreover, that a careful delineation of the landscape, of the architecture of English villages, and of anecdotes pertaining to odd, out-of-the-way burroughs would be of special help to him in the composition of a future romance. A ghost story about an old castle, a tree with a hollow trunk, an immense spider in the British Museum, a beautifully preserved asylum dating from Queen Elizabeth's day— these were the staple of his interest which assumed far greater space in the notebook than did any of the foreign policies of English and American diplomats. After he had been two years in the consulate, he wrote Ticknor, "I think my Journals (which are getting to be voluminous) would already enable me to give you a book. . . ."[3] In the third year he remarked to his publisher, "I keep a journal of all my travels and adventures, and I could easily make up a couple of nice volumes for you. . . ."[4] To watch the patient storing of many insignificant details is to find the groundwork which Hawthorne laid for the romances of the last phase.

2

Despite the sudden depletion of his salary in 1855, Hawthorne never seems to have denied himself the necessary funds to pay for his numerous excursions up and down the English countryside. To prepare himself for these tours, he read as many guidebooks and county histories as he could find; but he read them with his pen always ready to note the legends connected with old castles and the biographies of saints and martyrs who lay buried in the churchyards. These works suited his taste as happily as had the books of Cotton

3. *Letters to Ticknor*, II, 100–01.
4. *Idem*, II, 15.

Mather and the narratives of witchcraft in Salem during the years of his apprenticeship, for they suggested themes for romances. For example, just a few months after his arrival in England, he was reading a history of Chester in which he discovered the account of an English raid into Wales. His afterthought is typical: "It is a good theme for a legend."[5] Throughout the winter evenings he pored over these curious books and put away into his mind and into his notebook the oddities of English history and English legend.

There was one particular impulse—half whimsical, half serious— which made his hand reach for these antiquarian works; and though he seems to have discounted most of the information he gleaned, he nevertheless pursued the subject until he finally admitted that he was marching along a blind alley. He wished to discover the exact origins of his family and the precise spot from which his forefathers had emigrated to the New World. He knew that William Hathorne, because of some impelling religious motive, had abandoned a home in England, but Hawthorne wanted to find the old county, a few sunken graves, or (what might be better still) some legend which the natives might still be telling of his ancestor. Perhaps in some weed-grown cemetery he could ponder the strange beginnings of his family—of the witch-hunting Hawthornes, of the seafaring Hawthornes, of the novelist Hawthorne.

First of all, he wanted facts; the fiction would come later. Accordingly, within two months after his arrival, he wrote Fields an amusing request:

I wish you would call on Mr. Savage, the antiquarian . . . and ask him whether he can inform me on what part of England the original William Hawthorne came from. He came over, I think, in 1634. . . . Of all things, I should like to find a gravestone in one of these old churchyards, with my own name upon it; although, for myself, I should wish to be buried in America. The graves are too devilish damp here.[6]

Hawthorne's search for genealogical facts was in vain.[7] Yet this lack of positive information was no real hindrance to him. From his initial hopes that he might find an ancestral home or grave came a fantasy of romance in which he might identify his ancestor with any English county that best suited his purpose. As the months passed by and as the learned Mr. Savage could do nothing to put the roots of his family

5. *English Notebooks*, p. 34. Hawthorne was reading George Ormerod, *The History of the County Palatine and City of Chester* (London, 1819).
6. This letter, in the Huntington Library, is partially reproduced in *Yesterdays*, pp. 73–4.
7. The origins of Hawthorne's family do not seem to have been known until about 1880. See J. A. Emmerton and H. F. Waters, "Gleanings from English Records about New England Families," *Historical Collections of the Essex Institute*, xvii (January, 1880), 33–5.

tree deep in the English soil, he began to toy with the idea that he was the last surviving male heir of a family long absent from the old home. In himself, he became the living, visible symbol of a link between England and America.

My ancestor left England in 1635. I return in 1853. I sometimes feel as if I myself had been absent these two hundred and eighteen years—leaving England emerging from the feudal system, and finding it on the verge of Republicanism. It brings the two far separated points of time very closely together, to view the matter thus.[8]

For this reason his pilgrimages to scenes of historic or legendary interest were the result of a homing instinct. The baffling inheritance of family traits and the influences of blood ties, of sins and good works, might be focused on his own person.

Throughout Hawthorne's years in England these ideas were slowly crystallizing in his mind and assuming that nebulous form which would result in important works of romance. His reading in local histories, his whimsical investigations of his own family, and his increasing distaste for the English themselves, whom he found more annoying than his own countrymen—all these were germinating in his mind and awaited only a proper subject around which they would cluster as magically as coral growth on the bottom of a warm sea. He waited two years for the germinal idea to come but it came surely at last.

In the first week of April, 1855, he was dining at the home of his friends, Mr. and Mrs. J. P. Heywood. The other guests included Mr. and Mrs. Ainsworth of Smithell's Hall in Lancashire. At some point in the conversation Mrs. Ainsworth began to tell Hawthorne about the manor house which she and her husband had recently purchased and were in the process of repairing. Then she recounted a legend. Hawthorne later wrote in his journal:

The tradition is that a certain martyr, in Bloody Mary's time, being examined before the then occupant of the Hall, and committed to prison, stamped his foot in earnest protest against the injustice with which he was treated. Blood issued from his foot, which slid along the stone pavement of the hall, leaving a long footmark printed in blood; and there it has remained ever since, in spite of the scrubbings of all after generations.[9]

Here indeed was a subject which made his fingers tingle to be holding a pen again. First he must verify the details. What did the antiquaries say about the legend? On the following night Hawthorne read in a history of Lancashire that ". . . the footstep is not a bloody one, but is a slight cavity or inequality in the surface of the stone,

8. *English Notebooks*, p. 92.
9. *Idem*, p. 106.

somewhat in the shape of a man's foot with a peaked shoe."[1] To any other man the reason for the impression in stone might have aroused a gentle laughter but Hawthorne read on. "The martyr's name was George Marsh," a Nonconformist clergyman who had been tried for heresy in Smithell's Hall, condemned, and burned at the stake in April, 1555.[2] It was an odd circumstance which found Hawthorne reading the history of a martyr three hundred years after the event and, on a mind always aware of historical correspondences, the legend impressed itself with remarkable force.

Acting on Mrs. Ainsworth's invitation to see the bloody footstep for himself, Hawthorne, in August, went to Smithell's Hall in order to investigate the prodigy. Shortly after his arrival, his host conducted him through the house and grounds. Of course, the most fascinating item was the stone on which George Marsh was reputed to have stamped his foot. "This miraculous footprint is still extant," Hawthorne afterward noted in his journal. "It is almost at the threshold of the door opening from the rear of the house, a stone two or three feet square, set among similar ones, that seem to have been worn by the tread of many generations. The footprint is a dark-brown stain in the smooth gray surface of the flag-stone. . . ."[3] He proceeded to enumerate several reasons for the phenomenon: George Marsh's adherents might have worn the depression during many pilgrimages to the hallowed spot, or the stone might have come from the earth bearing the amazing blood-red mark. But he could not dismiss the tale as mere humbug and Hawthorne's own conclusion is important, "At any rate, the legend is a good one."[4]

Throughout Hawthorne's consular residence the subject of the romance was never developed beyond this point. Yet the subsidiary details, the variations on the main theme, were taking shape in his mind by a process of gradual and selective accretion. A legend had supplied him with the general outline; legends were likewise to fill in the background and supply many of the characters.

3

Another old manor house came to play an important part in Hawthorne's last phase. In August, 1854, he went with Mrs. Hawthorne and George P. Bradford, an old friend of his Brook Farm days, to

1. *Ibid.*
2. *Ibid.* For additional information on the martyr, George Marsh, see John Foxe, *Book of Martyrs* (Hartford, Conn., 1833), pp. 319–23; Thomas Fuller, *The History of the Worthies of England* (London, 1840), II, 193–4; Robert Halley, *Lancashire: Its Puritanism and Nonconformity* (Manchester, England, 1869), I, 76–85, 88–9.
3. *English Notebooks*, p. 194.
4. *Idem*, p. 195.

Eaton Hall, in Cheshire. The most remarkable event of the trip was a tour of the greenhouses on the estate and just before their departure a gardener who had acted as a guide presented Mrs. Hawthorne with "a purple everlasting flower . . . as a memento of [their] visit."[5] This flower had little to do with the English romance but it came to full bloom in the two romances of immortality.

The English countryside—especially its churches, ancestral seats, and villages—was redolent of the past and a particular delight to Hawthorne. His chief pleasures were reserved for Warwickshire and more especially for Leamington and Stratford. The rare springtime beauty of the English scene struck him more forcibly than it could the ordinary tourist who made a literary pilgrimage to the homes of Shakespeare and the Earl of Leicester, for it represented to him the perfect balance between man and nature. This balance was conspicuously absent in the untamed forests of the United States, where man was busily engaged in subduing nature and dominating a continent. Precisely for this reason an American was peculiarly fitted to appreciate these new-found beauties. "It is only an American who can feel it," Hawthorne noted;[6] for here was a portion of the earth which would supply the ideal locale for a romance. His first tour through Warwickshire was in June and July, 1855;[7] in September and October, 1857, he rented a house in Leamington. The county was filled with sites of great historical interest and called forth in Hawthorne memories of England's glorious past—Drayton's " 'high-complexioned Leam,' " Warwick, and Cumnor Castle where Amy Robsart had met her tragic end.[8]

For Hawthorne's purposes, however, the most important result of these two visits was an excursion to Leicester's Hospital, an institution bristling with all sorts of legendary and historic memories. It had been "the seat of a religious fraternity far back in the Middle Ages, and continued so till Henry VIII turned all the priesthood of England out of doors."[9] Later it became the property of the famous Earl of Leicester, who "devoted the ancient religious precinct to a charitable use,

5. *Idem*, p. 175. George P. Bradford (1807–80) had been one of the leaders at Brook Farm, where he had been in charge of the department of belles lettres. After the collapse of that venture he undertook to sell vegetables to the housewives of Plymouth, Mass. At that time (1842) Hawthorne considered him to be "a perfect original . . . a character to be felt and understood, but almost impossible to describe." *American Notebooks*, p. 163. While a resident of the Old Manse, Hawthorne invited Bradford to come and live with the "new Adam and Eve" but Bradford declined. *Ibid.* Thereafter their friendship waned, for Hawthorne remarked in 1854 that Bradford's ". . . conscientiousness seems to be a kind of itch, keeping him always uneasy and inclined to scratch!" *Hawthorne and His Wife*, II, 43.
6. *Our Old Home*, p. 78.
7. *English Notebooks*, pp. 119–43; *Hawthorne and His Wife*, II, 62–5.
8. *Our Old Home*, pp. 63–105 *passim*.
9. *Idem*, p. 92.

endowing it with ample revenue, and making it the perpetual home of twelve poor, honest, and war-broken soldiers." Its halls and doorways were carved with the Earl's own insignia, the bear and the ragged staff, and each of the resident pensioners wore the same badge on his cloak. Inside, the institution preserved "the identical modes that were established for it in the reign of Queen Elizabeth"; and the great dining hall still seemed to echo a Latin oration delivered by James I.[1]

Warwickshire opened other delightful views for the eye of an avid tourist. There were roads leading to the outskirts of Leamington and particularly one road which Hawthorne preferred, of all others, to take. "It pursues a straight and level course, bordered by wide gravel-walks and overhung by the frequent elm, with here a cottage and there a villa. . . ."[2] Down this or a similar road was the Church of Whitnash in front of which was "a very ancient tree, with a huge, hollow trunk";[3] at one side stood "the village-stocks" which the vicar had dragged out and set up to enthrall the curious.[4] Still another road led to Coventry, where Hawthorne found a splendid old building, St. Mary's Hall, in which the local mayor entertained his guests at an annual feast.[5] These small details, recorded in the everbulging notebooks, might someday become the bright pigments on the canvas of romance.

The onerous duties of the consulate did not prevent Hawthorne from making other tours through Lancashire and Cheshire. Poulton Hall was within easy reach of his house and he found other places almost as interesting as those in Warwickshire. As early as his first month of residence he walked to Lower Bebington and saw St. Andrew's Church and heard a prophecy concerning this ancient structure, ". . . when the ivy should reach the top of [the] spire, the tower was doomed to fall."[6] Another attraction not far from Liverpool was Eastham—"the finest old English village I have ever seen," Hawthorne noted. In the center of the churchyard stood another old yew tree like that at Whitnash; it was so decayed by age that there was left only a hollow trunk into which a man could crawl and look upward to the sky. "This tree was noted as the Old Yew of Eastham, 600 years ago." The tree symbolized the tiresome endurance of old institutions and old families in England. "And, after all, what a weary life it must have been for the old tree! Tedious beyond imagination!"[7]

1. *English Notebooks*, pp. 141–2; 583–5.
2. *Idem*, p. 388.
3. *Idem*, p. 589.
4. *Our Old Home*, p. 77.
5. *English Notebooks*, p. 578.
6. *Idem*, p. 27.
7. *Idem*, p. 57; *Our Old Home*, p. 78.

Not all of Hawthorne's memorable English experiences were associated with fair and quiet countrysides. The consular office required him to interview dying American sailors in cheap hospitals or to attend courts in which his countrymen were on trial. One day in 1856 he visited the West Derby Workhouse in Liverpool, an asylum for the poor and deformed of all ages. Here he discovered a sickly, dirty boy who had ulcerous sores all over his body. The little urchin groped along the floor and Hawthorne, stooping to pick him up, felt a strange sense of kinship as if the two of them belonged to the same family. "If it were within the limits of possibility," Hawthorne remarked, "I should have certainly set down its affection to the score of blood-recognition. . . ."8

A few guests came to visit the Hawthornes. Of course, Herman Melville passed by on his way to Palestine and stayed several days. When John O'Sullivan and his family were on their way to occupy the United States Embassy in Lisbon, they stopped for a week or two before resuming their journey. The most memorable detail of their visit was a tale told by Mrs. O'Sullivan. After her grandmother had been buried for many years, the tomb was opened and the coffin was "found to be filled with beautiful, glossy, living chestnut ringlets, into which her whole substance seems to have been transformed." Here was a strand which could be woven into the main subject of the bloody footprint: "An old man, with a ringlet of his youthful mistress treasured on his heart," Hawthorne concluded, "might be supposed to witness this wonderful thing."9

Hawthorne's few appearances in public were as an after-dinner speaker at formal banquets. The first occasion was at the Liverpool Town Hall in August, 1853, and he was again asked to speak in February, 1855.1 His greatest success came in April, 1856, when he addressed the Lord Mayor's dinner in London. By the time he attended another banquet of the Lord Mayor's, he had begun to realize the suitability of these experiences for a romance. "I want to preserve all the characteristic traits of such banquets; because, being peculiar to England, these municipal feasts may do well to picture in a novel."2

For all the time Hawthorne spent in London, there are only a few entries in the notebook which later found their way into the novels. The circumstance is odd in view of the fact that Hawthorne "already knew London well" before he arrived for his first extensive visit in September, 1855. Soon after settling his family, he "had trodden the thronged thoroughfares, the broad, lonely squares, the lanes, alleys,

8. *Hawthorne and His Wife*, II, 104–05; *English Notebooks*, pp. 275–6.
9. *Idem*, p. 60.
1. *Idem*, pp. 101–03.
2. *Idem*, p. 440.

and strange labyrinthine courts"; and these "aimless wanderings" confirmed all that he had read.[3] He soon entered into society, attended the Milton Club dinner, the Reform Club banquet, and many another lesser function. In Park Lane he met Charles Reade, who did not strike Hawthorne as anything more than a self-satisfied gentleman.[4] He was, on the other hand, profoundly awed in the presence of Leigh Hunt, "a beautiful and venerable old man," whose manners and speech were so perfect that they must have been derived from "his American blood."[5] Yet only two quite unimportant events had any bearing on the English romances. One was his visit to Ford's Hospital, in Grey Friar's Street, an institution so similar to Leicester's Hospital that he was moved to comment:

A collection of sombre and lifelike tales might be written on the idea of giving the experience of these Hospitallers, male and female; and they might be supposed to be written down by the Matron of one—who had acquired literary taste and practice as a Governess—and the Master of the other, a retired school-usher.[6]

The other, and more important, incident occurred during a visit to the British Museum. In one of the side rooms he saw some "immense hairy spiders, covering with the whole circumference of their legs a space as big as a saucer."[7]

Hawthorne's peculiar artistic nature could find little in London that might be of any use in a future romance. A large city, constantly turbulent and subject to unpredictable changes, afforded no haven for a mind in search of ancestral relics and traditions. Hawthorne inevitably turned to the quiet countryside and to old manor houses which remained unaltered amid the destruction of nineteenth-century life. He was interested only in a country which might give him a vivid sense of the past and England was able to perform this service for him. It provided him with Smithell's Hall and its legend of the bloody footprint to form the theme of a romance; it supplied the colors and descriptive details which he wove into the fabric of these later tales. The Norman church, with its sable tower, its dim and quiet interior, was, he wrote, "impressed into the minds of my long-ago forefathers . . . so deep that I have inherited it";[8] the Elizabethan villages, with houses of brick and oak, fronted by luxuriant and well-trimmed hedges, their gardens full of bright flowers and shrubs of box—here was the English scene, prefigured in his youthful reading, and now

3. *Our Old Home,* p. 256.
4. *Hawthorne and His Wife,* II, 118; *English Notebooks,* p. 317.
5. *Idem,* pp. 254–5; *Our Old Home,* p. 322.
6. *English Notebooks,* p. 579.
7. *Idem,* p. 610.
8. *Idem,* p. 124.

made real and living. Like the quaintly gowned pensioners of Leicester's Hospital who were "shouting across the gulf between our age and Queen Elizabeth's," the passages in the notebook were demanding that they be given life in a romance.

II. The Ancestral Footstep

Although Hawthorne long had in mind the theme of a new romance and had even set down a few tentative paragraphs in his English notebook, he did not at once begin work on a novel until after his arrival in Rome in January, 1858. He must needs settle his family and begin tours of the Eternal City; yet he could not long delay the practice of creative writing after the four long years in the Liverpool consulate.

Almost from the first day after his arrival in Rome, Hawthorne was busily engaged in visiting the important sites and in recording his impressions in the Italian journal. Finally, on April 1, he took a new paper-bound notebook and began an experimental draft of his English romance.[9] For six weeks he worked steadily, recording his daily life in the Italian journal and at the same time filling page after page of this other notebook until he reached May 19. On that date he abandoned his tale, later known as *The Ancestral Footstep*, and never again returned to complete it.[1]

Nearly a month before Hawthorne found a pertinent reason for discontinuing this romance. On April 22 he had visited the Villa Borghese where he saw the faun of Praxiteles. A few hours later he recorded this significant germ in the Italian notebook, "a story, with all sorts of fun and pathos in it, might be contrived on the idea of [the faun's] species having become intermingled with the human race."[2] Not long afterward he set to work on *The Marble Faun* and for nearly two years the novel on the Italian subject entirely displaced the tentative English romance, which he would not take up again until he reached Concord in the summer of 1860.

The Ancestral Footstep is a painter's sketch in preparation for a greater work to come. Twice the plot breaks off before the story has reached any real stage of development. In outline it may well be one of Hawthorne's own tours of Warwickshire, embellished with a cast of characters and with a few scenes drawn from other counties in the west of England. Lathrop, the first editor, divided the fragment into three convenient sections, for the beginning of each part of the story resumes at an entirely different point from where it had broken off.

9. *Ancestral Footstep*, pp. 434, 437.
1. *Idem*, pp. 435, 518.
2. *Italian Notebooks*, p. 172.

The first part opens with Middleton, a young American lawyer, who has come to England in order to find the roots of his ancestry. Arriving at a Midland town, he finds a charitable asylum for old men; there he becomes acquainted with Hammond, an aged pensioner, and Hammond's daughter Alice. The old man tells Middleton the strange legend of the bloody footprint at nearby Smithell's Hall and likewise alludes darkly to a lost American branch of the same family. One afternoon not long afterward Middleton walks to the Hall with the purpose of seeing the footprint for himself. Quite unexpectedly he meets Squire Eldredge, the present owner of Smithell's, who in a fit of anger over Middleton's intrusion strikes the American with the butt of a gun; the blow jars the hammer and sends a bullet through Eldredge's heart. At this point the narrative broke off; Hawthorne decided to ignore Eldredge's death and the tale resumed on a different course.

Part Two opens with Middleton again at the asylum. There we learn that Hammond had left the United States after a series of fraudulent speculations in which many people were ruined. The two men decide to visit Smithell's Hall, which is still in possession of Squire Eldredge, but that worthy gentleman is a very commonplace landowner who appears to have no intentions of shooting vagrants. They are cordially shown through the mansion and see the haunted chamber and the bloody footstep on the threshold. Throughout the tour there are vague hints that malevolent influences are at work to thwart Middleton's search for his ancestry but these are never disclosed.

At the opening of Part Three Middleton is again happily established at the hospital. Soon he accepts an invitation to dine and spend the night at Smithell's Hall. His room is "a chamber in the oldest part of the house" where he finds a mysterious cabinet. Yielding to a natural curiosity, he opens a secret compartment and finds some documents which appear to establish his rightful claim to the estate. For a time he plans to disclose his ancestral connections with the Eldredge family but the squire anticipates him by plotting his murder. These evil designs never materialize; the fragment closes with a meditative paragraph on the proper arrangement of these disjointed scenes.

1

So closely do these narrative and descriptive elements of the romance parallel Hawthorne's own experiences in and record of England that it is suggestive to compare certain passages of the fragmentary novel with their counterparts in the English journal.

Smithell's Hall is obviously the same manor house which Hawthorne himself had visited in 1855. In the romance it is ". . . one of

those old wood and plaster mansions which are among the most ancient specimens of domestic architecture in England";[3] less than three
years earlier Hawthorne had written in his notebook, "The house is
. . . timber-framed throughout, and is overlaid with plaister [sic]."[4]
On entering the house Middleton notices "a dark oaken-panelled
room . . . with many doors opening into it. There was a fire burning
on the hearth; indeed, it was the custom of the house to keep it up
from morning to night. . . ."[5] For these two items Hawthorne need
only turn back the pages of his notebook to his entry for August 25,
1855, "This fire is always kept up, throughout summer and winter;
and it seemed to me an excellent plan. . . ."[6] Finally, for the colorful
detail of the bloody footprint Hawthorne leaned heavily on his notebook, "Middleton looked down and saw something, indeed, very like
the shape of a footprint, with a hue very like that of blood. . . . It
might have been blood; but he rather thought, in his wicked skepticism, that it was a natural, reddish stain in the stone."[7] Even Middleton's "wicked skepticism" is amusingly similar to Hawthorne's own
confession that he thought it was all a "humbug."[8]

When Hawthorne brought Middleton into an unnamed Midland
county, he could hardly resist the chance to use his extensive notebook
entries on Warwickshire and, more especially, to make important
levies on his sketch of Leicester's Hospital. The almshouse for old men
in *The Ancestral Footstep* is patently a reproduction of that famous
charity dating from Queen Elizabeth's time:

The Eldredge Hospital was founded for the benefit of twelve old men, who
should have been wanderers upon the face of the earth; men, they should
be, of some education, but defeated and hopeless, cast off by the world for
misfortune, but not for crime. And this charity had subsisted, on terms vary-
ing little or nothing from the original ones, from that day to this; and, at this
very time, twelve old men . . . had centred here, to live on the poor pit-
tance that had been assigned to them, three hundred years ago.[9]

The limits of a romance in embryo did not permit an extended description of this remarkable structure. After changing the name to
the "Eldredge Hospital," Hawthorne was content to draw a brief
sketch and let it stand as it was.

Middleton's walks in the neighborhood of the hospital are nearly
identical with Hawthorne's own excursions through Warwickshire.
The young American visits "every little church that raised its square

3. *Ancestral Footstep*, p. 472.
4. *English Notebooks*, p. 193.
5. *Ancestral Footstep*, p. 477.
6. *English Notebooks*, p. 194.
7. *Ancestral Footstep*, p. 482.
8. *English Notebooks*, p. 194.
9. *Ancestral Footstep*, p. 463.

battlemented Norman tower of gray stone, . . . making himself acquainted with each little village and hamlet that surrounded these churches."[1] Again, Hawthorne's attendance at civic banquets is reflected in an undeveloped memorandum: Middleton is a guest "at the Mayor's dinner in St. Mary's Hall."[2] That Hawthorne himself had never been present at a function in this old edifice did not make it any the less suitable in a romance; he was simply choosing St. Mary's Hall as a model and he planned to use it as the setting of a dinner similar to those he had attended in London and Liverpool. This molding into one locality of many details selected from different parts of England is typical of Hawthorne's method in the last phase. Warwickshire, especially the section around Leicester's Hospital, would be the particular scene of action, but incidents which had taken place during Hawthorne's residence in other parts of the island were to be blended together to form the mise en scène of the romance. Smithell's Hall in Lancashire, an old church in Chester, a charitable institution in Warwickshire, a Lord Mayor's dinner in London—all these were sketched in this fragment and awaited a more complete treatment in *Doctor Grimshawe's Secret.*

2

The characters in this notebook-romance reveal the same shifts and revisions as do the incidents of plot. Only Middleton is consistently drawn throughout the three parts of the study, perhaps because he is a pale reflection of Hawthorne himself: he is sensitive and shy; he enjoys reading county histories and ferreting out the genealogies of ancient families. But he finds his greatest delight in wandering through the lovely scenes of the English countryside and in browsing aimlessly through graveyards or the misty lands surrounding famous manor houses.

Alice, on the other hand, maintains little consistency and goes through several transformations under Hawthorne's pen. Early in the fragment she is one of those spirited New England girls who had come down through the novels of the 'fifties. Middleton exclaims appropriately during one of his conversations with her: " '. . . you are my country-woman. That wild, free spirit was never born in the breast of an English-woman; that slight frame, that slender beauty, that frail development of a quick, piercing, yet stubborn and patient spirit,—are those the properties of an English maiden?' "[3] In Part Two Hawthorne elaborated these hints: she has the same slight figure of

1. *Idem,* p. 467.
2. *Idem,* p. 512.
3. *Idem,* p. 458.

the preceding sketch but she is set apart from English women by her "singular freedom," by her lack of "the ruddy complexion, which . . . is believed the great charm of English beauty," and by her "elasticity" and "irregularity, so to speak, that made her memorable from first sight."[4] Hawthorne paused later in this section to consider these last qualities and for a brief moment she becomes a fay creature, mysterious beyond Middleton's comprehension, "singing and dancing through the whole" romance, "in a way that makes her seem like a beautiful devil."[5] She might be satisfactory amid the rarefied air and Old World charm of Leicester's Hospital but, as Middleton's future bride, she would never do in this guise. Therefore, in Part Three, Hawthorne came back to his original and clearly stated intention to make her a New England girl transplanted into a foreign land. In one instance, moreover, she comes alive as a precursor of Hilda in *The Marble Faun*, for she had been "born and bred in America, but . . . had resided two or three years in Rome in the study of her art . . . ; she makes busts and little statues, and is free, wild, tender, proud, domestic, strange, natural, artistic; and has at bottom the characteristics of an American woman."[6]

In depicting the other characters in *The Ancestral Footstep*, Hawthorne exhibited even less precision than he had with Middleton and Alice. For example, he intended to draw a figure of an old man who, in part one, had all the qualities of a harmless mendicant. He is first introduced as Rothermel, Middleton's walking companion—"one of those itinerants, such as Wordsworth represented in 'The Excursion.' "[7] Next he appears as Hospitaller Hammond in the Eldredge Hospital, although for one day he is called Wentworth.[8] As Hammond, he is a pleasant old antiquary who takes delight in exhibiting to Middleton the ancient relics of the neighborhood and in explaining the history of noteworthy landmarks. Toward the end of the narrative he undergoes an unexplained metamorphosis: he had been an American financier who risked his fortune in illegal speculations and was forced to flee to England; there he became a malicious and crafty agent for Squire Eldredge.[9]

To give Hammond a place in the story, Hawthorne saw that he could leave the old hospitaler with his evil past as a manipulator and, at the same time, make him the agent who ruined Middleton's father. Thus there would be the strands of old times stretching down into the present; there would be the doubt in Middleton's mind whether

4. *Idem*, p. 467.
5. *Idem*, p. 490.
6. *Idem*, p. 519.
7. *Idem*, pp. 438–9.
8. *Idem*, pp. 457–9.
9. *Idem*, pp. 485–6, 518.

or not he could trust Hammond. In the end the tale would be stronger for this twofold problem which Middleton must face—the enmity of Squire Eldredge and the mysterious connivings of Hammond. Yet Hawthorne proceeded no further than to throw out these hints for later elaboration and to conclude with the mystery of Hammond still unsolved.

The characteristic life of the Hospital is brought out, and the individual character of this old man, vegetating here after an active career, melancholy and miserable; sometimes torpid with the slow approach of utmost age; sometimes feeble, peevish, wavering. . . . The character must not be allowed to get vague, but, with gleams of romance, must yet be kept homely and natural by little touches of his daily life.[1]

Squire Eldredge, Middleton's rival for the possession of the estate, suffers as many changes as Hammond. At his first appearance he is "a frank, free, friendly sort of a person enough, who had travelled on the Continent [and] employed himself much in field-sports"; and again, he is ". . . reasonably well-educated, and with few ideas beyond his estate and neighborhood, though he had once held a seat in Parliament for part of a term."[2] This brief portrait owes not a little to Mr. Peter Ainsworth, the owner of Smithell's Hall, whom Hawthorne had met in 1855. Ainsworth, like Eldredge, was ". . . a good specimen enough of the old English country gentleman, not highly polished, pretty sensible, loving his land and his trees, and his dog and his game, doing a little justice-business, and showing a kind of fitness for his position, so that you feel rather satisfied than otherwise to have him keep it."[3] Suddenly and without warning, Eldredge is transformed into an Italianate villain, sinister, crafty, though cultured and with excellent manners. Although in this guise he invites obvious comparisons with those other villains, Chillingworth and the hypocritical Judge Pyncheon, he is certainly more fit to be Middleton's enemy in his search for the ancestral home.

Even though the delineation of these characters is weakened by the obvious limitations of the form of the journal—its lack of cohesion and its random composition from one day to another—yet Middleton, Alice, and Eldredge reappear in *Doctor Grimshawe's Secret* with very little change. By the same method of trial and error with which he maneuvered his plot, Hawthorne was attempting to put his dramatis personae in order so that, in some later romance, they would emerge complete and lifelike. These figures, as they appear in the tentative notebook jottings of *The Ancestral Footstep*, were never intended to have assumed their final form but, like the painter's initial

1. *Idem*, pp. 518-9.
2. *Idem*, pp. 474, 478.
3. *English Notebooks*, p. 196.

pencil sketches, they were to receive color and strong lines of individuality in a more finished composition to come. They began as abstractions—the American spectator of the English scene, the sensitive New England girl, and the Italianate villain—and they never progressed beyond the vague limits of their types. Their actions and their appearance were governed by their allegorical meaning and, unfortunately, they never stepped from allegory into life.

3

On two occasions Hawthorne brought Middleton before an old cabinet which would establish the young American's inheritance of Smithell's Hall. In one instance Middleton never dares open the documents which he finds in a drawer; at another time, however, he presses a mosaic in the floor of the cabinet and finds only a pinch of ugly dust in a secret compartment.[4] It was here that Hawthorne intended to draw the moral of his tale. The legend of the bloody footprint would symbolize "the baneful influence of the past as represented by family traditions and by old houses" and the futility of seeking wealth which had been stained by the sins of elder generations.[5] Long ago in the American notebooks, in the early tales, and especially in *The House of the Seven Gables,* Hawthorne had submitted ample testimony to the conviction "that the disintegration of old families is for the good of society."[6] The first duty of the present was to throw off the weight of the past. As early as 1846 he had written in his notebook a paragraph beginning, "To represent the influence which Dead Men have among living affairs. . . ."[7] In *The House of the Seven Gables* this notation was dramatically reflected in Holgrave's exclamation, " 'Shall we never, never get rid of this Past? . . . It lies upon the Present like a giant's dead body!' "[8] The possession of ancestral wealth is a hindrance rather than a blessing and, after Hawthorne had visited the British Museum, he concluded that "The present is burthened too much with the past."[9] In *The Ancestral Footstep* Hawthorne compares the recovery of ancient wealth to the opening of an old grave out of which, as from Pandora's box, swarms a host of sins to plague the new generations of men; and he explicitly states the lesson to be drawn from Middleton's search for ancestral wealth: " 'Let the past alone: do not seek to renew it; press on to higher and better things,— at all events, to other things; and be assured that the right way can

4. *Ancestral Footstep,* pp. 480, 511, 482.
5. *American Notebooks,* p. lxxvi.
6. *Idem,* p. lxxx.
7. *Idem,* p. 106.
8. *Seven Gables,* p. 219. Cf. *American Notebooks,* p. lxxxi.
9. *English Notebooks,* p. 294.

never be that which leads you back to the identical shapes that you long ago left behind. Onward, onward, onward!' "[1]

Thus in *The Ancestral Footstep* Hawthorne took the mysterious discoloration on the threshold of Smithell's Hall as a symbol of a thought which had been haunting him for a large part of his life. It was his conviction that the present age of man is of far greater importance than the past; no matter how much he himself was attracted by the old legends, gravestones, and ruins of bygone times, his interest was that of a dreamer who allows himself to indulge his dreams but whose rational faculties insist that he keep his fancies only as a luxury for moments of a colorless existence. His attitude toward England, both in *The Ancestral Footstep* and in *Doctor Grimshawe's Secret*, reveals this curious paradox in his thinking: although he loved the relics of ancient story and tradition and spent the happiest hours of his consular office investigating them, he could never love them for themselves alone; he must always peer through the ivy and lichens which covered them to the "moral truth" they represented. To him they were obstacles in the path of a new race springing forth in America, a new and stronger breed of men who ever cried, "Onward!" while their English cousins stagnated in their storied world of tradition and romance.

1. *Idem,* pp. 488–9.

III

"Doctor Grimshawe's Secret"

1

HAWTHORNE had abandoned the fragmentary *Ancestral Footstep* in favor of the more tempting subject which grew into *The Marble Faun;* but as soon as that latter novel was published in February and March, 1860,[1] he turned once more to the idea for a romance of England which had been waiting for his pen and hand throughout the years of the English consulate.

This new work would be more than a revision of *The Ancestral Footstep;* it must be a wholly new romance. Perhaps even before he came back to Concord in the summer of that year, he had set to work on the first preliminary studies for his tale. Then, probably in the late summer of 1860, he began serious composition of his long romance which should become, as he later said, "the crowning achievement" of his literary career.[2] The work moved rapidly forward throughout the remainder of that year and into the early months of 1861.

But something had gone wrong. The old magic was lost; Hawthorne could not bring his pen to spin effortlessly those stories which had once been so captivating; time and again he stopped his narrative and paused for hours, even days, while he conjectured, planned, sketched, shifted characters and scenes in an effort to make some sense of his tale and then finally, in a fit of anger and despondency, rushed his first draft to a conclusion and then started all over again. This revision he never finished. The piles of manuscripts, some of which were published twenty years afterward as *Doctor Grimshawe's Secret,*[3] were forever laid aside. The romance which he hoped might be the crowning achievement of his life had become, as he confessed despondently in 1863, an "abortive project,"[4] and the best he could do to ease his conscience was to reduce his English notebooks into the form of essays for the *Atlantic Monthly.* These ephemera were, he

1. The first English edition, entitled *Transformation,* was published on February 28 (Caroline Ticknor, *Hawthorne and His Publisher,* p. 234); the first American edition, entitled *The Marble Faun,* was published on March 8 (*Boston Daily Advertiser,* xcv, March 8, 1860, 2).
2. *Grimshawe,* p. vi. Cf. *Our Old Home,* i, 15–16.
3. The title was Julian Hawthorne's. For a complete discussion of the editing and publication of *Grimshawe,* see Appendix.
4. *Our Old Home,* i, 16.

admitted, a poor substitute for a full-blown novel on the differences between Englishmen and Americans.

2

As *The Ancestral Footstep* already bears witness, Hawthorne intended from the outset to write a romance based on two major ideas: first, the story of an American who came back to his forefathers' home in England and there busied himself with proving that he was the rightful heir to an old manor house; secondly, the legend of the bloody footprint which Hawthorne had heard from Mrs. Ainsworth of Smithell's Hall. In his mind these seminal ideas were already joined; the American's search for his lost patrimony would be symbolized in the bloody footstep, an emblem of crime committed long ago.

In addition to the two long drafts which were later used as the basis of the text of *Doctor Grimshawe's Secret,* there are six preliminary studies which bear on the romance; these sketches were written, probably in the summer of 1860, on any loose sheets of paper which Hawthorne had at hand. Some of them show the tale progressing in a fairly straightforward manner, while others are jottings and brief asides on characters, scenes, and the direction the romance must take.

The most convenient way to present these studies is to divide them into two groups of three each; sketches "A," "B," and "C" form the first section and studies "D," "E," and "F" constitute the latter group. This division is quite easily marked. Hawthorne meditated throughout the first three studies on an American who comes "to England, to search after his ancestry"; then as he moved his story forward, he tentatively sketched a few of the chief characters and stated his theme or moral. In the second group he shifted his whole scene to Salem, Massachusetts, and to an investigation of the ancestry and background of this American who went to England.

Throughout the first three studies Hawthorne did not go very far beyond what he had already outlined in *The Ancestral Footstep.* The identical characters—an American tourist, a young Englishwoman, and an unnamed squire of Smithell's Hall—reappeared without any change in their appearance. By the time he reached the third sketch, he began to leaf through the English notebooks and to borrow his own description of Leicester's Hospital in Warwickshire.

Study "A," which consists of two leaves written on both sides, first projects the "central thought" of the romance and briefly outlines the cast of characters. Each of the succeeding two sketches is written over only one leaf; together they add further conjectures and details of plotting which will become apparent as the romance grows under Hawthorne's hand.

STUDY A

[1] An American comes over to England, to search after his ancestry; there has been a family history of interest in the new world; and there are traditions with respect to the family in England, at the distance of more than two centuries, which are very dim and interesting. These look wild and strange. Endeavor to give the effect of a man's leaving England 200 years ago, and coming back to see it so changed. The American shall be a person of high rank, who has reached eminence early: a Governor, a congressman, a gentleman; give him the characteristics and imperfections of an American gentleman. He shall, I think, be unmarried. He searches for relatives, browses in books of records, consults heraldry; for there is a misty idea, as in so many cases, that a great estate and perhaps title is due to him. Bring out the American strongly among old English scenes and manners; make all that he sees objective, as it seems to a new American. There must be a young lady, an Englishwoman—to whom, unflinchingly, give English characteristics, as contrasted with the American. She shall turn out to be one of his relatives; he shall find another in a factory person; another descendant of an old family in a groom; another in a rich mendicant. There shall be a vein of wildness and romance in the American, at which the English shall smile and be puzzled; and this, too, shall be characteristic of his country. His researches shall produce effects, by bringing to light facts, which neither he himself nor anyone else expected.

[2] Among the personages introduced shall be an American defalcator, or other criminal, of some years ago, who shall be living here in England, either with his family, or in solitude—the latter, I think. Take Schuyler[5] for a model of this figure. One nobleman must likewise be introduced;—yes—a member of the family. The American's researches must bring about results, unexpected by himself, and not such as he had at all aimed at—overturning whatever seemed fixed. The nobleman's title and estate, for instance.

The first emigrant to America (200 years ago) shall have carried with him a family secret, which shall have been retained in the American branch, though latterly it shall have been looked on as an idle tradition. The English heir shall have lost this secret. At the time of the American's appearance in England, the family shall be at some

---

5. Philip John Schuyler (1733–1804), was an American patriot and major general in the Revolutionary War. Hawthorne's plan to model the "defalcator" on Schuyler may have been owing to the antagonism of New England to certain of Schuyler's military acts in the war.

crisis; and by means of this secret, the American shall find himself empowered to influence the result. He shall keep himself unknown to the family—at least, till the denouement. Perhaps he shall decide to let the old family go to ruin; perhaps otherwise.

The scene of an old gentleman walking through the streets, in a state of mania.[6]

[3] The English and American ideas to be brought strikingly into contrast and contact. The American comes back to England, somewhat with the sense of a wronged person; for there shall have been a tradition of his ancestors having been driven away with wrong and contumely. He returns to find them in a state of apparently greater prosperity than ever, but yet on the verge of a crisis, which he perhaps discovers through his researches into old records and estimates by his legal knowledge. There shall, on the other hand, be a tradition in the English family of a vanished heir, who, if he were alive, would take all the land and estates; and this on comparison shall coincide with the American tradition. It shall be a story told in the castle, as far back as James I's reign, with all the medieval romance to it; and the American may learn it, at the family-seat, which is a modern mansion built upon the foundation and taking in some of the walls of an old castle. Feeling himself the heir, the American shall consider himself entitled to dispose as he pleases of the estate and honors and so shall, in exercise of his judgment, let the title and estate pass away. Some terrific action must, at this time, be going on in the English family; greatly in debt; an hereditary madness in the English branch; a gambler, a man on the turf. It must be shown, I think, throughout, that there is an essential difference between English and American character, and that the former must assimilate itself to the latter, if there is to be any union. Throw it into more extravagant eminence, and make the coloring deep and sombre, in order to bear it out;— there may be scenes and passages of the strongest reality interspersed. The noble must have some mark upon him; some fatality; something inherited, which shall represent the craft, the bloody force, the wrong, by which the honors of his race have been obtained. The difficulty is, in this state of non-adventurousness, to introduce any crime. I must think and seek for evil, such as a gentleman and a nobleman can commit.

[4] This nobleman; what is his condition [?] He has something on his conscience—what? Something that nullifies all his advantages; and it must be something in the common course of things, only made to seem strange by the imaginative associations that I shall cluster about it. A noble outside, but something mean within. With all his grandeur and state, there must be some mean thing that he does, or

6. See *English Notebooks*, p. 97.

some mean tendency. I think he should be one of the old Catholic families of Lancashire. He must do something strange and grotesque, that nobody would expect a noble to do; go as a scissor-grinder about the country; operate as a horse-doctor; in short, live in two entirely different characters at once. There must be some thing in this nobleman's heart, that shall push him into the wildest extravagances,—he shall walk on the verge of lunacy, and at last step over. Something in the state of his affairs that shall compel him to do these things; or else some malignant influence impelling him. Something that tends towards murder. But that is an old story. No; there shall be a terrible ridicule and satire in what this nobleman is compelled to do and suffer, that shall become tragic by its grotesque aptitude.

STUDY B

[1] Thus around this American of to-day will be made to diffuse itself a romantic, if not a preternatural interest; and the feelings of the Democrat and Aristocrat will be brought out in all the stronger contrast. There shall have [been] a wonderment of ages as to what has become of the lost heir of the family; and all sorts of stories shall be told at the firesides about him; and it shall seem, after awhile, as if he had re-appeared in the person of the American—who, also, shall have the feeling that he is the identical one. A murder shall have been committed; a bloodstain, that keeps freshening out of the floor yet, at due times. But then the family secret, partially lost, but to which the American brings the lost part;—what can that be? Something, I am afraid, that has reference to property; no this secret must typify the hereditary disposition of the family. It shall seem as if dead men still were active agents. How? how? how? I don't know, really. How in heaven? Mrs. Stowe; authoress of "Uncle Tom's Cabin." The American is of course a lawyer, and might too have been a soldier in the Mexican War;—yes, he shall. And since a politician, and governor of a state; and still quite a young man; therefore capable in affairs. He shall by and by feel himself the master of this nobleman's fate; who shall have confided in him what he would not have confided to a countryman of his own. The great gist of the story ought to be the natural hatred of men—and the particular hatred of Americans—to an Aristocra-[2]cy; at the same time doing a good deal of justice to the aristocratic system by respecting its grand, beautiful, and noble characteristics. At last, I think, the American must have it in his power to put an end to the nobility of the man; and shall do so, not without reluctance and pain. He shall have proof of something, long ago, that shall have given him this power. The scene need not be entirely in England; it can be carried to the Continent;—perhaps

back to America. The present nobleman—there shall be something in the past that may have impelled him to a present crime or meanness, unworthy of his rank; and which he shall daily feel. He must die in some way, most probably by suicide. No; there may be some tremendous error, but no petty vice or meanness in his character. I think he should be drawn with a natural generosity and nobleness, doing credit to the best influences of his position; but some misfortune must unavoidably grow out of his position, and ruin him, through the means of the American, who must make amends to the reader's feelings by marrying an Englishwoman, with every prospect of happiness. How'll that do? It may be his daughter that the American marries;—but how shall she be drawn[?] She can hardly be made the type of the English maiden. The end must be the ruin of the nobleman, at all counts, the absorption of his property, the concealment of his title. Perhaps he shall all along have had a secret knowledge that he is, as a person, a humbug. I don't make this out.

STUDY C

[1] The ancestor of Chatsworth emigrated to America 200 years ago, being an outlaw from his family, and desiring to conceal his existence from them. He carried with him certain family heirlooms, records, traditions, and especially some fragment of a thing. The first emigrant was a younger son of a noble family; but by the extinction of the elder branch, his descendants have become, at this time, in reality, the heirs to the estate and title. In the long lapse of years, however, this looks dreamlike and fabulous; so that when Chatsworth comes over, he does not really expect anything. He finds his visions, his traditions, his hereditary descriptions of the estate, the title &. singularly agreeing with the reality; and, in fact, satisfies himself that he is really the rightful heir. Meanwhile, he has established an acquaintance, or at least, has obtained the facility of looking into the family, of the nobleman. Here will be ample opportunity of giving all the good and picturesque points of English ancestral homes, English rank, and high society; with the American view of them. By and by, through his close and earnest inspection of the family affairs, Chatsworth.discovers a secret connected with them—a secret, to which he has the clue by his ancestral traditions—it has lasted all this time, ulcerating into the heart of the family, and the present nobleman, a man of high honor and admirable qualities, is as much distressed by it as any of his ancestors have been. Now here is the rub; and it seems impossible to get over it. It cannot well be something shameful that has happened long ago—a hereditary insanity—a murder—a blue-beard closet—

perhaps what was a mere trifle, in the American's traditions, has come in [the] course of ages to be a terrible impending calamity. Some debt then contracted, and never paid off; some claim, the clue of which the American ancestor carried off. Oh, how strange!

[2] A hospital for poor travellers to have been endowed by the family in ancient times; and Chatsworth, on his first visit to the family house, gets admittance as a poor traveller into this hospital; and there meets with other personages of the story. Here, too, some member of the family might see and talk with him—the heroine, for instance— while visiting the poor people.

After completing his first group of three studies, Hawthorne realized that the restricted English scene would not suffice to give the requisite scope and meaning to his romance. One element was certainly lacking: a valid reason why an American should come to England to seek his ancestral home. To follow the symbol of the bloody footprint through two hundred years of English history was not enough; the mysterious token should have made its track even to the forests of New England. Accordingly, Hawthorne temporarily abandoned his sketching of the English scene—the hospital, Smithell's Hall, and the Warwickshire countryside—and, in Study "D," took his story to America.

This four-page sketch suggests that when, in the summer of 1860, Hawthorne was noting his random meditations on the English romance, he returned to those days in the 'forties and to his courtship of Miss Sophia in the house of Dr. Nathaniel Peabody in Salem. Not only was it a fashionable house in the town but it was also situated next to the Charter Street Cemetery where Col. John Hathorne, the witch judge, and others of Hawthorne's forefathers lay buried.[7] As a young man Hawthorne had often wandered through that graveyard, read the gravestones, and mused on the lives of those who, like young Fanshawe, were interred there.[8] And always in his thinking a cemetery had important meanings. It would illustrate the relationship of man's contemporary affairs with the times of long ago. This symbolic connection was uppermost in Hawthorne's mind as he wrestled with the problem of supplying an American scene for his romance. The cemetery would be the symbol; the house of Dr. Peabody, adjoining the graveyard, would be the home of a small boy who grew to manhood and eventually went to England in search of his ancestors. These ideas are implicit in the fourth and most complete sketch of the novel.

7. *Passages from the American Notebooks*, p. 118. Cf. T. F. Hunt, *Visitors Guide to Salem* (Salem, Essex Institute, 1927), pp. 14, 62.

8. Hawthorne used the grave of Nathaniel Mather as a model for the grave of Fanshawe. *American Notebooks*, p. xliv.

Study "E," a one-page sketch, did not move the story forward nor did it introduce any new elements or surprises into the narrative. Hawthorne was still not certain what use he would make of Leicester's Hospital. It might be an excellent symbol to illustrate the endurance of old traditions in a modern world of change and social revolution; it might likewise serve to bring before the reader the English characters who must cluster about the young American. With this second purpose in mind, Hawthorne turned to draw a hasty sketch of his secondary men and women—the warden of the hospital, the owner of Smithell's Hall, the poor pensioner, and the heroine. In addition, Hawthorne assigned a new name, "Etherege," to the youthful wayfarer in England.

But Study "E" breaks off before Hawthorne has even roughly sketched his cast of characters. He will let these people assume their final shape when he really comes to grips with his romance. He had already decided on the American and English locales for the tale and the symbolic meaning of the bloody footprint he had stated and restated. There remained for him only the staggering problem of joining together these oddly varied elements: the house in Charter Street in Salem; the old apothecary; the boy who grew to be a politician and sought the roots of his ancestry in England; Leicester's Hospital; and, above all, the haunting legend of Smithell's Hall with its symbol of the bloody footprint to illustrate those widely differing national characteristics of Englishmen and Americans.

Unfortunately, Hawthorne could not rely on his own creative powers effortlessly to weave the skein of his narrative from the maze of threads in the studies. Sitting in Concord during that summer of 1860, he must look far across the Atlantic to visualize his English scenes; and, even as he gazed, the outlines were blurred, the hills assumed strange shapes, and the people he had met assumed odd guises. There was, however, one way to stimulate his waning energies and to guide his hand through the long travail: he would go to his English notebooks in which were recorded more impressions and descriptions than he could ever make into the stuff of fiction. Thus he composed his final sketch.

This last study, "F," was Hawthorne's private index to his English notebooks; it is likewise an index to Hawthorne's own mind in the last phase. So little reliance could he place on his own habits of old and on his creative artistry that, on a small sheet of notepaper about five and one-half inches square, he jotted thirty-six separate items, some with page references to the journals and others merely with dates which in either case would readily direct him to his own notebooks. There was little order or coherence in the way he made this index; sometimes the items followed each other in the chronological sequence of his consular life; otherwise they were far-separated in time and place and came disjointedly as one incident or impression recalled another in Hawthorne's memory. To some he had already alluded in the preceding studies; others refreshed his mind and sent him to the journals for material which he had so far not considered worth using; and still others, because great chunks of the notebooks could never be "romanced," were left on the dustheap.

STUDY D

[1] The story opens at Salem, the old house in Charterstreet, on the edge of the grave-yard. There dwells an old gentleman, a scholar, a peculiar sort of man, marked by mild eccentricities. He has a young girl in his gloomy old house; and for some unknown reason, he has noticed a boy, the son of poor and obscure parents, and is instructing him in the languages, paying attention to his morals and manners, and bringing out the graces of a fine and noble character which seem to exist in him. The life in this gloomy old house, of these three persons, should be strikingly presented, with occasional glimpses, out of [a] window as it were, of the New England life of the little town, done in a homely, vivid way.

The old gentleman is not to be rich, but it is seen in him that he comes of a gentle and genial blood; and in a remarkable way, he shall draw out similar tokens in the boy.

The little girl shall be elvish and sprite-like; but yet the reader's prevailing impression of her shall be of a sweet and kindly creature; she shall be sportive, through the shadow of that old house, and as something dark in her lot shall be upon her. She must not be too strongly defined, either; she starts ever and anon, in a vivid presentment, out of a surrounding vagueness and obscurity. Her relationship or connection with the old gentleman shall not be defined, though he shall often manifest affection and pity for her.

A youthful Arcadian life, bright and sweet, though curtained round by gloom, shall be led by this boy and girl, in the gloomy old house; sporting in the grave-yard, hand in hand with ghosts.

The old gentleman's chief business shall seem to be [2] of an antiquarian nature, and to hunt up old genealogies for his own pleasure; and he shall often show a certain family pride, his own family having a historic name, and having been loyalists and sacrificed thereto a large part of their property. In pursuit of this taste, as well as by inheritance, he shall have gathered around him a great deal of curious colonial lore, and also a large variety of articles, interesting from some connection with noted individuals. The effect [of] all this must be to gather a certain grim atmosphere of mystery round the kindly and genial individual. It [is] well to present him to the reader as seen through the observations and conjectures of an imaginative boy. He shall also practise experiments in natural science, and shall have a tradition of medical knowledge from having been originally intended for a doctor. This quaint and queer household shall, in the narrative, be continually brought into relief by contrast with the practical, modern life about them.

It shall be surmised, from casual observations and from certain incidents, that the young girl [is] not a native of New England; perhaps there [may] be room to suppose that she was born in Old England. Some dim reminiscences she shall have of other modes of life; other scenery; of old, ivy-grown edifices; and there shall be a vague pride in her chaaracter, such as the English have of themselves; a looking down upon the Americans, a holding herself above them.

The boy shall appear to be a dependent on the bounty of the old gentleman; yet, whenever he seeks to express his gratitude, the latter shall decline, seeming to feel pain at such expressions.

In this early part of the Romance hints must be given of the family history on which the Romance hinges; and the boy shall have a strong passion to go to England to search out certain riddles that propound themselves to him.

When a sufficient impression on the reader has been made, and a good deal of mystery compelled into a cloud, the old gentleman shall suddenly die; and the other two characters shall vanish for a term of years.

[3] This part of the Romance closes, & after an interval of many years, the story is resumed. A gentleman is introduced as rambling in England, scarcely a gentleman he might seem, being in very humble guise. But the reader shall be suffered to perceive that this is the boy whom he already knows. In the interim, he has gone through great vicissitudes; the old gentleman left him the means of obtaining an education, and he began life as a political adventurer, and met with great success. Still a very young man, he has been in Congress, has displayed brilliant eloquence, has been disappointed in some aspiration, and has thrown up public life in disgust with the abuse, the brutal violence with which it is carried on.

Under these circumstances, in the illness and collapse after great excitement, he has remembered the old gentleman's brief hints and vague expressions, and has come to England, he hardly knows for what—to search out the family abode. He is giving rein to the imaginative tendency which he used to indulge in his boyhood, with the more enjoyment, because the hard, hot practical life of America has so long made his life arid & dusty. And so he goes wandering about England on foot, guided by the wildest signs, which he will not acknowledge to himself as being his guiding signals. In this way, he by and by comes to an old town, where there is a hospital; but he is robbed about this time, and left for dead, and taken into the hospital, where several people, who are of use in the succeeding parts of the Romance, immediately group themselves around him.

In the first place, however, I think he should be removed into the Warden's house, who proves to be a clergyman of the Church of England, a little stiff at first, but genial and gentlemanly, living in comfort, a bachelor. Of him he learns much about the constitution of the hospital, and when he gets well enough to go out, he becomes acquainted with one of the pensioners, a reserved, stately sort of an old man, who has evidently seen better days.

[4] Before leaving the old house by the grave-yard, it must be mentioned that, one day, two strangers—apparently from foreign parts—come, and are very earnest to find a certain ancient grave. They seek for it, apply to the old gentleman for information; he seems not exactly surprised to meet them. They retire, at last, and as it should seem, without success. Afterwards, the boy meets one or both (if there be more than one) of these men in England.

Among the old gentleman's pictures is one of a man of striking appearance, but in the habit of a bond-servant—coarse, and perhaps with some badge of servitude upon him. Afterwards, in England, the boy finds the same face, but [it] is in an old family portrait gallery, and splendidly apparelled. He inquires about this latter portrait, and finds the original had mysteriously disappeared. Perhaps his guardian tells him the servitor's portrait is the likeness of [an] ancestor of his. It might afterwards come out that he had been transported after the battle of Worcester.[9]

The brother of the American old gentleman was a man of great ability, whose financial operations had been on a vast scale; so that even national events had depended on his action. Possibly, the action of the story may be thrown back fifty years; and he be a partaker in Burr's treasonable projects. Having had the direction of great affairs, here he is in this seclusion, and in his forced idleness, he takes upon himself to influence everything in a secret manner, by a touch as it were with the remnants of his faculty; and in this way, he intermeddles with our hero's fortunes, more especially as he once ruined his father in America. He shall have made a great impression of sagacity on the Warden, and on all that come in contact with him. As of a man who knew the world and how to guide it, though now so retired and fallen. Or he may have been a wild political reformer, having run

9. King Charles I and his Royalist army were disastrously defeated at the battle of Worcester on September 3, 1651. See G. M. Trevelyan, *England under the Stuarts* (14th ed., London, 1928), p. 299.

into all extravagances of Pantisocracy, & was ending his days in dependence on this queer incident of feudal and old-world customs.

[1] The old hereditary hospital for poor people—to be described from a real scene. Etherege has the tradition of it dimly in his memory and he finds it, perhaps, more perfectly realized than any other of his traditionary reminiscences. He is taken ill here; and, being temporarily without resources, he obtains admission into the hospital. Here, perhaps, he has his first interview with the heroine. Possibly, he may already have become known to his relatives by rumor, and may be an object of interest to them. But, at all counts, that may enable him to get acquainted with the localities and persons of the family, in a way he otherwise could not, and thus he shall see them in a picturesque and in some sense [MS. blurred] at the same time wandering all round their domicile, sometimes admitted into it, but still as of an alien order. The gentleman may perhaps be seen accidentally through his disguise. Sometimes he may surprise the inhabitants by his knowledge of circumstances respecting the family, supposed to be known only to themselves, or by his explanation of what had been immemorially a mystery to those most interested in it. In this way, I think he shall become acquainted with the nobleman himself. Afterwards, they shall meet in society, the American in his own distinguished position. Perhaps he may revisit the ancestral seat, at a feast; or possibly there may be a coolness between him and the nobleman. Etherege must of course be distant and haughty, and their intercourse will be embarrassed by the terms on which they first meet, and by what then passed between them.

Etherege, after his first introduction to the family through his hospital experience, might be represented as searching into old houses at Chester—at the chapter house in the Cathedral there;—or wherever deeds are registered. The American must in his own consciousness, and also in the conviction of the nobleman, be the rightful heir of the estate and the earliest title; but his democracy, and his generosity, and a feeling of shame, must prevail with him not to claim his rights. The general tenor of the book must illustrate the sympathy and the difference between Americans and Englishmen.

Perhaps his second meeting with the nobleman may be at a banquet, or other public dinner, where the American is called up to speak to a group as a distinguished politician.

STUDY F

[1] Description of City Plate ——— March 26th [25th]   '56[1]
A thatched cottage, June 17th   " [2]
Vagabond musicians &c.   June 20th   '54[3]
Growth of hair in the grave, page 164   '54[4]
Woman in hand-wagon   Novr 14th   '54 ['53][5]
Earl lying unburied, page 98   '54[6]
The profane swearer in Lancashire, whose
    horrible fit of swearing caused a plane-tree
    before his house to wither away.[7]
Paralytic old lady. Page 257.—   May   22^d   '57[8]
Southport Police Station   March 1st   '57[9]
Character of Mr Scarisbrooke, March 1st   '57[10]
Coroner's Office Page 200 ——————   '57[11]
Inspector of Nuisances—page 194   '57[12]
Warwick & Hospital &c October 30   '57[13]
Whitnash Church Novr 8th   '57[14]
The Bloody Footstep. August 25th   '55[15]
Kirk Bradden, August 10th   '54[16]
Judge Platt. August 21   '54[17]
St John's Church August 24   '54[18]
Rhuddlan Castle, Sept 20th   '54[19]
Welsh Cottage   do.   do.[20]
Fat women   Sept 26th   '54[21]
    (Mem. Look for an earlier passage on this subject) [22]

1. *English Notebooks*, p. 288.
2. *Idem*, p. 362.
3. *Idem*, p. 63.
4. *Idem*, pp. 59–60.
5. *Idem*, pp. 38–9.
6. *Idem*, p. 37.
7. *Idem*, p. 278.
8. *Idem*, p. 463.
9. *Idem*, pp. 442–4.
10. *Idem*, p. 442. The name was properly "Scarisbrick."
11. *Ibid.*
12. *Idem*, p. 439.
13. *Idem*, pp. 583–9.
14. *Idem*, p. 589.
15. *Idem*, pp. 193–5.
16. *Idem*, p. 70.
17. *Idem*, pp. 71–2.
18. *Idem*, pp. 72–3.
19. *Idem*, pp 83–5.
20. *Idem*, pp. 86–7.
21. *Idem*, pp. 88–9.
22. *Idem*, pp. 27–8.

Capt Gibson October 19th   '54[23]
Crazy old man in the street Nov[r] 14th   '54[24]
Tranmere Hall March 7th   '55[25]
[2] American lady in Liverpool almshouse unknown
    Sept 12th   '53[26]
Man with the plague burying himself Oct[r] 22[d] '53[27]
Claimants of the Booth estate—royal blood Dec[r] 31st '53[28]
Eastham church-yard April 3[d] '54[29]
Hospital, May 20th '54. Do. Nov[r] 16th '55[30]
Length of English day, June 17th '54[31]
Musicians June 20th '54[32]
English stone-walls & parasitical growth, July 13th '55[33]
English eating, March 6th '56[34]
Loving cup, March 25th '56[35]
Pew in Battle Church April 1st '56[36]
Rusty arrow-head, dug up in the church yard of Radford
    Semele July 2[d] '55[37]

The small index shows Hawthorne's infatuation for his notebooks
—that tempting array of persons, places, and observations on the English scene, in short, the whole panoply of his consular experiences—
and these he hoped to weave into the tale of Etherege's search for his
ancestors. The other studies had resulted only in a hasty and constantly shifting arrangement of these autobiographical details; Study
"F" would provide the clearinghouse through which he could work,
backward and forward, into the piles of notebooks which lay on his
desk in the Italian tower.

23. *Idem*, pp. 93–6.
24. *Idem*, p. 97.
25. *Idem*, pp. 104–05. The date was actually March 4.
26. *Idem*, p. 25.
27. *Idem*, p. 37. This refers to the same entry as "Earl lying unburied."
28. *Idem*, p. 43.
29. *Idem*, p. 57.
30. *Idem*, pp. 60–1, 266–7.
31. *Idem*, pp. 62–3.
32. *Idem*, p. 63.
33. *Idem*, p. 159.
34. *Idem*, p. 278.
35. *Idem*, p. 322. The date was actually April 13.
36. *Idem*, p. 308.
37. *Idem*, p. 143.

3

Perhaps in the late summer or early fall of 1860[2] Hawthorne began to write his first draft which I have designated as "G." He worked with great rapidity and probably completed it before the end of the year. Even though the handwriting is firm and clear, the evidences of haste are everywhere present. When Hawthorne was not satisfied that he had properly treated a character or clearly described a scene, he paused momentarily to insert a jotting in the margin, at the top of a leaf, or even between the lines of his sentences. In no wise was this draft to be a finished narrative; from the first page there are liberally sprinkled notes and asides which point to Hawthorne's intention to return and rewrite the whole story at a later time. What makes this draft a most extraordinary document in Hawthorne's workshop is the fact that it consists of narrative—the fairly straightforward movement of the tale—alternating with long meditative asides on the next development of the romance. For a few pages Hawthorne would compose his story quite smoothly, then suddenly break it off, and engage himself for a number of leaves in plotting his next step, meditating on his characters, and cursing himself for his inability to know where he was going or what he would do with the people he had spawned. One third of "G" consists of these tortured questions and meditations on the next movement of the romance.

Fortunately for Julian Hawthorne, one of the most interesting features of this draft is that, when Hawthorne paused in the onward rush of his narrative for an extended section of planning, he returned to pick up the threads of his story almost exactly where he had dropped them. Thus, when Julian Hawthorne came to edit "G," he discovered that he could break it into clearly divided parts: the meditative passages, lifted bodily from the manuscript, formed a complete and quite interesting unit; and the narrative sections could be joined one to the other and form a fairly coherent tale.

But there was a further complication. In addition to "G"—two-thirds narrative and one-third planning and conjecture—Julian Hawthorne later discovered a revision, Draft "H," which was a rewriting of the *first half* of "G" but did not bring the tale to the conclusion which Draft "G" did. Therefore, Julian Hawthorne performed a clever piece of literary sleight of hand: taking "H" as the basis of his edition of the novel, he added to the end of "H" the narrative portions from the latter half of "G" and, by shifting one chapter of "G" from the end to the middle, he sent to the publisher what still remains as Haw-

2. This date is based on an allusion in the draft to "President Buchanan" (p. 39[a]), who went out of office in March, 1861.

thorne's *Doctor Grimshawe's Secret.* (For a full discussion of Julian Hawthorne's editorial methods, see the Appendix.)

What, Julian Hawthorne's contemporaries and we may well ask, happened to the digressive passages lifted from "G"? As a partial answer to his critics, some of whom penetrated the mystery, Hawthorne's son published a few extracts in the *Century Magazine* for January, 1883, a month after the romance had come off the press.[3] But revealed in this chopped-up manner the novel does not look anything like the story as Hawthorne wrote it. These intercalary asides, the most vivid glimpses into Hawthorne's workshop, must for the first time be considered as an integral part of Draft "G." A discussion of the revision "H" we may postpone for a later page.

Therefore, in order to give the reader some glimpse into the mysteries of Draft "G," which in Hawthorne's handwriting covered both rectos and versos of seventy-four sheets of paper, I shall submit an extended outline, with narrative and meditative passages alternating with each other just as Hawthorne composed them. While all of the intercalary jottings cannot be included, yet the major digressions may be briefly summarized; these I shall designate by italics.

The story opens in Salem sometime after the Revolution. Beside the Charter Street Cemetery there lives an old apothecary, Dr. Etherege, half quack and half true scientist, who has engaged himself in a lifelong study of spiders and of magical nostrums which might be extracted from cobwebs. The gloom of the household is partially relieved by Ned and Elsie, two happy children whom the Doctor has adopted. Their only nurse is the Doctor's housekeeper, Sukey, but their lack of a mother's love is more than filled by the wonderful stories which the Doctor tells. He describes faraway places in England, lovely gardens, old churches and gravestones, and an old estate with a bloody footstep on a stone entranceway. *Hawthorne stops abruptly to plan for the visit of an Englishman who will come to Salem in order to find an American descendant of an old English family.*

Amid these romancings, there arrives one day an English lawyer, Mr. Mountford, who is in search of a lost heir of the very estate the Doctor has been describing. Mountford's quest is fruitless, for even in the cemetery next door there is not a sign that a lost American heir was buried long ago in New England soil. *Hawthorne sketches the legend of Smithell's Hall and tentatively proposes various crimes which may have been committed two hundred years ago. Then he outlines the reasons why an heir came to America, perhaps even be-*

---

3. "A Look into Hawthorne's Workshop. Being Notes for a Posthumous Romance," *The Century Magazine,* xxv (January, 1883), 433–48. Hereafter cited as *Century Notes.*

fore the Puritans arrived. None of these conjectures satisfies him and he returns to his narrative.

The Doctor, now grown old in his pseudoscientific pursuits and failing to discover the magic brew in spiders' webs, dies suddenly, and Ned and Elsie are left to make their way as best they can. *Hawthorne now turns to outline a number of important matters which he must treat in the next section of the novel: the Doctor's brother, once a manipulator in affairs of state and now a resident in a charitable asylum; the legend of the bloody footprint and its place in the story; and the English girl whom the Doctor may once have loved and who, years after her death, was found to have been transformed into masses of golden ringlets.*

A number of years later a young American is on a walking tour of the Midland counties of England. The purpose of his excursion is veiled in mystery; in fact, we scarcely recognize him as little Ned, now Edward Etherege, a successful lawyer, politician, and disappointed job seeker in the United States Government. Strolling down a lovely bypath, he is suddenly attacked by an unknown assailant, beaten into unconsciousness, and left for dead. Only the happy chance that pensioner Pearson of the nearby Braithwaite Hospital is passing and administers first aid saves Etherege's life; and the young man is carried to the asylum where the good offices of a surgeon effect a quick recovery. Throughout his convalescence Etherege engages in polite talks with the warden of the institution concerning the founding of the hospital, the history of the county, and especially the legends pertaining to the manor house, Braithwaite Hall, only a few miles away. As he begins to move about and study the asylum, Etherege is continually puzzled by strange relics which the Doctor had long ago described in Salem. Stories of spiders, a tale about a secret chamber, and the monotonously repetitious design of the dragon's head everywhere about the hospital make Etherege feel that the papers he carries may establish his ancestral claim to Braithwaite Hall. The mystery deepens still further when he meets Elsie Cheltenham, the old pensioner's daughter; Etherege is positive that she is the Elsie whom he had known in the spider-infested house of his boyhood. When he charges her with failure to recognize him, she feigns either ignorance of him or an unwillingness to recall their childhood together. *Hawthorne has apparently let his narrative get out of hand. He pauses to conjecture the best use he can make of the bloody-footprint legend; the influence the Doctor, even after his death, may have on persons and events in England and the early history of the pensioner. This last character troubles Hawthorne more than any other figure and he spends pages and pages of the draft to fit the old man into the tale.*

It is an established custom at the hospital for the warden to give an annual banquet for the indigent old men and for the well-to-do squires who are the trustees of the institution. *Hawthorne breaks off suddenly to revise again the old pensioner. The plan is now to make Pearson the true heir of Braithwaite Hall when the coffin of the lady with the golden tresses is opened. Thereupon, because he has grown more than Hawthorne had anticipated, Pearson is made the Doctor's brother and definitely linked with the Doctor's attempt to get revenge on the Braithwaites by presenting Ned Etherege as a false claimant to the estate. Then Hawthorne reviews what he has already written and takes up his narrative again.*

At the annual banquet in the hospital Etherege meets the present Mr. Braithwaite, a half-Italian, half-English gentleman whom his neighbors in the county regard with suspicion. Despite this enmity, the banquet goes well; there is much old ceremony to amuse the American; the heavy, beef-eating Englishmen take delight in jibing him on the primitive state of his country; but particularly there is the fantastic ritual of drinking wine from a loving cup which is passed down the line of celebrants in accordance with a centuries' old tradition. During the meal Mr. Braithwaite invites Etherege to pay him a visit at the old hall. A few days later, when he is about to leave the hospital, the pensioner and Elsie warn him of the evil which will befall him if he steps across the fated entrance with the bloody footmark. *Hawthorne appends a number of random conjectures on the symbolism of the coffin full of golden hair, the history and meaning of the footstep, and the character of Mr. Braithwaite.*

When Etherege arrives at the hall, the master is absent but he is courteously entertained by a Catholic priest, Father Angelo, who breeds spiders for the magical properties of their cobwebs. *Hawthorne sketches ahead to the climax in Braithwaite Hall. There are frequent suggestions that someone has long been imprisoned in the dungeon and that Dr. Etherege was somehow connected with this prisoner.*

On the first night of his visit Etherege rashly drinks two glasses of Braithwaite's favorite wine into which a drug has been introduced. Hours later he regains consciousness and finds himself in a dungeon cell with a silent, insane-looking old man. Happily, however, Pearson and Elsie are so much concerned for Etherege's safety that they force the warden to accompany them to the hall. They insist on seeing Etherege but Mr. Braithwaite protests that the American has that very morning departed for London. From some knowledge of the hall, the pensioner presses a stone in the wall, a door opens, and they all descend to a secret chamber where Etherege is rescued, still dazed from the effects of the drug. But at such a sudden burst of sunlight, the mysterious, insane prisoner dies immediately and Pearson points to a secret coffin to which he has a key. As he throws back the lid of the coffin to reveal the gold and jewels of ages long ago, everyone gasps in astonishment: the coffin is filled with beautiful golden ringlets, masses of golden hair into which some dead woman has been totally transformed. The illusion is gone; the dream is broken; the folly of seeking lost wealth makes Etherege feel so ridiculous that he is glad to leave the county and journey to his new ambassadorial post at the court of Hohen-Linden. *Obviously dissatisfied with his romance, Hawthorne wrote a brief résumé of the whole plot and tried to straighten out the characters of the Doctor, the pensioner, and Elsie, all of whom had suffered inexplicable changes throughout the draft. Then he turned to a sketch of the prisoner long kept in the dungeon. (This scene Julian Hawthorne shifted bodily into the center of his edition.) Only a brief conversation takes place between the prisoner and an unnamed person and the draft ends.*

If this synopsis has seemed strange and incoherent, it is no more so than Draft "G" itself. The story had reached no conclusion at all; nothing had gone well. The narrative, by Hawthorne's own admission, was pitched in a tone of the wildest absurdity;[4] the Doctor's postmortem influences on events in Warwickshire had been absolutely without sense or preparation; and no provision had been made for the incredible revelation of the golden locks nor for the pensioner's inheritance of the estate. The story was so disjointed and unbelievable that nothing remained for Hawthorne but to "Try back again."

This revision "H" is, however, later—perhaps as late as the opening months of 1861. For the present we may well investigate this huge Draft "G" and watch Hawthorne in artistic undress. The following section treats, first, Hawthorne's building of scene and narrative (to aid him in this task he had before him the index "F" and the English notebooks themselves in which was deposited enough material to quarry if he lived to be a hundred); secondly, his efforts to breathe life into these characters who began as mere abstractions in the preliminary sketches; here we may peer into the dark corners of the workshop and watch Hawthorne use contemporary men and women as models for his creatures of fancy.

Study "F" contains no items which Hawthorne could use in the early portion of the novel whose locale is Salem. He was on home territory and had no need to refresh his memory of Dr. Peabody's house and the Charter Street Cemetery. Sophia Peabody's girlhood home was obviously the prototype for Dr. Etherege's house. As early as 1838 the proximity of the cemetery to the residence had made its impression on Hawthorne as a curious piece of symbolism:

4. "G," 71b; *Century Notes,* p. 447.

It gives strange ideas, to think how convenient to Dr. P[eabody]'s family this burial ground is,—the monuments standing almost within arm's reach of the side windows of the parlor,—and there being a little gate from the back yard through which we step forth upon these old graves.[5]

The description of Dr. Etherege's house, written twenty-two years later, is not very far from that notebook entry:

Thus rippled, surged, broke almost about the house, this dreary grave-yard, which made the street gloomy, so that people did not like to pass the dark, high wooden fence, with its closed gate, that separated it from the street; and this old house was one that crowded upon it, and took up the ground that would otherwise have been sown as thickly with dead as the rest of the lot; so that it seemed hardly possible but that the dead people should get up out of their graves, and come in there to warm themselves.[6]

Certainly the spiders were never denizens of Dr. Peabody's house, for Hawthorne found their prototype during a visit to the British Museum where he saw "immense hairy spiders, covering with the whole circumference of their legs a space as big as a saucer."[7] The importance of these spiders is not their size but their symbolism; one huge spider became Dr. Etherege's "demon." In the end it was the spider-symbol which vitally changed the old apothecary from a kindly dabbler in science into an evil genius who, having once arranged a chain of events, is able, long after his death, to effect a terrible revenge on the family of Smithell's Hall.

These two items are Hawthorne's only indebtnesses to himself in the early sections of "G" before he takes his young American abroad.

5. *Passages from the American Notebooks*, pp. 118–19.
6. "G," 1ᵇ. Cf. *Grimshawe*, pp. 346–7.
7. *English Notebooks*, p. 610. Initially the spider would signify the queer lore in which the Doctor is interested: ". . . his intimacy with the African spider (to which some oriental pet name shall be assigned) must throw a sort of grotesque awe about him. It shall be considered his demon" (11ᵃ). A few pages later Hawthorne expanded this suggestion into a character portrait of the Doctor. "The Doctor's inventiveness shall be perhaps his one Yankee trait, mixed in with and running through all his cobwebby old hereditary nonsense; and it is so inevitable that, having nothing else to act upon, it deals with cobwebs. . . . The Doctor shall have his absorbing dream of re-generating the world by means of cobweb, and quite restoring it to health; and shall pursue his discovery as an alchymist that of the golden secret; and shall think it within his reach, if he could but live a year, a week, a day longer; nay even to finish the one process that he has now in hand" (2ᵇ). These notations on the spider were only the beginning, for, in page after page in the meditative passages of "G," Hawthorne turned the spider round and round until it became the symbol of the apothecary's evil influences, even after his death. One notation will suffice to show the change in this old man's character: "The Doctor must have a great agency in these doings . . . ; he must have the air, in the Romance, of a sort of magician, without being called so; and even after his death, his influence must still be felt. Hold on to this. . . . He must have travelled over England in his youth, and there have fallen in love, and been jilted by a lady of . . . [the Braithwaite family];—hence his spite against the family, and his determination to ruin it. He shall have sought out . . . an heir, and educated Etherege for that purpose" (40ᵇ).

Despite the undeniable charm of the narrative, much of it is a welter of discordant elements: the English lawyer Mountford fails to come alive and his mission in Salem is never resolved; the spiders have little purpose in the house and the bloody footprint fades away in the babble of a small boy's voice.

But our concern is with Hawthorne's craftsmanship, not his failure. On the very first page Hawthorne initiated a practice which he continued throughout the remaining drafts of the last phase. As his pen moved regularly across the paper, he would pause and hastily insert in the margin, at the end of a paragraph, or at the top of a page, some idea to be elaborated in the subsequent pages. Thus, on the first page he entered the memorandum concerning the spider, "Fanciful theory about its web."[8] Six leaves later he expanded this aside into a complete discussion of the Doctor's belief that "The cobweb was the magic clue by which mankind was to be rescued from all its errors, and guided safely back to the right."[9] Other suggestions were never utilized until the revision "H" was undertaken: "Give vivid pictures of the society of the day, symbolized in street scenes,"[1] or "The Doctor shall be held in great odium in the town, and wicked stories shall be told about him. . . ."[2]

These jottings and meditative passages testify to Hawthorne's dissatisfaction with his tale, but he felt himself impelled to push on with his work and bring it to a conclusion. Therefore, he hastened to the English scene of his romance which he thought he might write with more ease than he had composed the first chapters. These latter sections reveal the extensive levies he made on his own notebooks and the key to his habit and to the material he wished to use is in the Study "F." Passing backward through the index to the notebooks, we shall follow Hawthorne's hand in modeling the stuff of romance on his own English experiences.

The key to the opening of Etherege's walking tour is in the note "Warwick & Hospital &c October 30 '57." Already in Study "D" Hawthorne had briefly outlined how a young American "comes to an old town, where there is a hospital." But the index note for "October 30" referred only to Leicester's Hospital after Hawthorne had gained admittance; consequently, with the same ancient edifice in his memory, he leafed back a few pages in his notebook to the entry for September 11, when, on a stroll with Julian, he had walked along "the Holly Walk" and through "hedge-rows, chiefly of hawthorn, but intermixed with blackberry bushes, on which the berries hung abundantly."[3]

8. "G," 1a.
9. "G," 7a.
1. "G," 1a.
2. Ibid.
3. English Notebooks, p. 567.

When Hawthorne had refreshed his memory of this walk, he expanded the scene into Etherege's stroll through a Midland county:

The path on which he [Etherege] trod was of a character that deserves a word or two of description—a well-trodden, rather broad footpath, running just here along the edge of a field, and bordered on one side by a hedge, which in itself contained materials for a lengthened description . . . such a beautiful impenetrable obstacle, and so did nature luxuriate within its limits, and such a Paradise it was for the birds that built their nests there, in an intricacy and labyrinth where they must have thought themselves as safe as in the first Paradise where they sang for Eve. Flowers, pleasant, homely flowers grew in it; and many creeping plants, that were no contemplated part of the hedge, had come at their own accord and dwelt here, beautifying and enriching the hedge by way of repayment for the shelter and support that it afforded them.[4]

For the hospital itself Hawthorne had already made ample preparation in Study "E": "The old hereditary hospital for poor people— to be described from a real scene," and the index reference to "Warwick & Hospital" sent him back to the full entry for October 30 on Leicester's Hospital. From the main outlines of the large old charity down to the smallest detail, Hawthorne worked over his own notebook description and carried it into the fragmentary romance. One example of the debt of the fictional to the actual hospital will suffice to show this heavy-handed reliance. The journal reads, "All round the quadrangle, which the four sides of the edifice enclose, there are rep[et]itions, large and small, of the Leicester cognizance, the Bear and the Ragged Staff, and escutcheons of the arms of families with which he [the founder] was connected."[5] Even the coat of arms, slightly transformed, came forth in Hawthorne's replica: "All over the interior part of the building was carved in stone the dragon's head, with wearisome iteration; as if the founder were anxious to imprint his device so numerously lest . . . the Omniscient Eye should fail to [be] reminded that Sir Humphrey Braithwaite had done it."[6]

The next segment of the romance occurs after Etherege's recovery from the mysterious assault: the warden and the American take a walk through the countryside and villages around Leicester's (or the Braithwaite) Hospital. Fundamentally, the pictorial matters were of little consequence and Hawthorne found no difficulty in describing a cottage, a church, and an old elm tree because he had little interest in realistic natural scenery. Therefore, he felt no reluctance in referring directly to his English notebooks for the requisite items of landscape.

4. "G," 13ª.
5. *English Notebooks*, p. 584.
6. "G," 21ª; *Grimshawe*, p. 191.

In Study "F" Hawthorne had jotted, "A thatched cottage, June 17ᵗʰ ['56]," but the pertinent notebook passage concerns a cottage which Hawthorne saw near Salisbury Cathedral. The hint was, however, enough to send his mind back to the year before and to some cottages which he had seen in Leamington, near Warwick Hospital.

These houses stood close together in one row . . . with roofs of tiles, and some of thatch; and, in two or three of them, the windows opened on hinges. Several of the houses were good large dwellings . . . ; but others in the same range were the veriest old huts I have seen in England;—the thatch mossy, and in one case covered with a great variety of queer vegetation—tufts of grass, house-leeks, and other plants, all differing in their shade of green.[7]

When Etherege and the warden took their walk, they followed almost the same path Hawthorne had trod.

Approaching nearer, they passed a thatched cottage or two, very plain and simple edifices, though interesting to Etherege from their antique aspect, which denoted that they were probably older than the settlement of his own country, and might very likely have nursed children who had gone, more than two centuries ago, to found the commonwealth of which he was a citizen. If you considered them in one way, prosaically, they were ugly enough; but then there were the old latticed windows, and there the thatch, which was verdant with leek, and strange weeds, possessing a whole botannical growth.[8]

The jotting, "Whitnash Church Novʳ 8 '57," an edifice located near Warwick Castle became the center around which clustered numerous details from several parts of England. In the notebook for 1857 he described Whitnash Church and then mentioned casually that nearby grew an ancient tree with a large, hollow trunk.[9] This tree recalled to him a more important tree, which he mentioned in the index as "Eastham church-yard April 3ᵈ '54"; from that suggestion he leafed back through his journal to a passage which ended, "In the center of the church-yard stood an old yew-tree of immense trunk, which was all decayed within, so that it is a wonder how the tree retained any life— which nevertheless it did. (This tree was noted as the Old Yew of Eastham, 600 years ago.)"[1] Just as Hawthorne had walked around Eastham Church to the graveyard, so did Etherege and the warden, who came upon "a very ancient yew tree, all the heart of which seemed to have been eaten away by time. . . . 'The tree is of un-

7. *English Notebooks*, p. 122.
8. "G," 26ᵃ; *Grimshawe*, p. 215.
9. *English Notebooks*, p. 589.
1. *Idem*, p. 57.

reckonable antiquity' "—the warden concludes—" 'so old, that in the record of the time of Edward IV it is styled the Yew tree of Braithwaite Green.' "[2]

From Whitnash Church in Warwickshire and Eastham Church, five miles from Hawthorne's home in Rock Ferry, Hawthorne moved in recollection to St. Andrew's Church in Lower Bebington for another colorful detail in the idealized countryside through which the American was strolling. Perhaps because the church lingered in his mind as "old, old, old," Hawthorne recalled a legend ". . . the traditional prophecy, that when the ivy reached the top of Bebington-spire, the tower was doomed to fall."[3] In almost identical words the warden of the hospital told Etherege that the ivy of the church they saw near Leamington was carefully kept ". . . from climbing to the battlements, on account of some old prophecy that foretold that the tower would fall, if ever the ivy mantled over its tip-top."[4]

For the banquet in Braithwaite Hall, Hawthorne had noted in Study "F" the significant item "Loving Cup," which recalled the two occasions when, as a representative of the United States Government, he had been invited to make after-dinner speeches. The second of these, in April, 1856, when he was the guest of honor at the Lord Mayor's dinner in the Mansion House, London, became the model for the banquet in Braithwaite Hospital. After the occasion Hawthorne set down in his notebook a careful outline of the ceremony of the loving cup:

The Lord Mayor presents the covered cup to the guest at his elbow, standing up so that the guest should remove the cover; his lordship then drinks, the guest replaces the cover, takes the cup into his own hands, and presents it to his next neighbor, for the cover to be again removed, so that he may take his own draught. His next neighbor goes through the same form with the person below him; and thus the whole company are finally interlinked in one long chain of love. When the cup came to me, I found it to be an old and richly ornamented goblet of silver. . . .[5]

With a few word-changes the ceremony was cast bodily into the English romance:

First, each guest receiving it [the cup] from the next above him, the same took from the silver cup its silver cover; the guest drank with a bow to the Warden and company, took the cover from the preceding guest, covered the cup, handed it to the next below him, then again removed the cover, replaced it after the guest had drunk, who on his part, went through the same

2. "G," 27ᵃ; *Grimshawe*, p. 218.
3. *English Notebooks*, p. 119.
4. "G," 26ᵇ; *Grimshawe*, p. 217.
5. *English Notebooks*, p. 322.

ceremony. . . . The cup was a fine, ancient piece of plate, massive, heavy, curiously wrought with armorial bearings. . . .[6]

For the purposes of his romance, Hawthorne used the loving cup as a symbol of the deadly enmity between Mr. Braithwaite and Etherege, for one holds the cover for the other as a token of their ill-concealed rivalry. Then just a few minutes later, Etherege responds to a toast by rising and delivering a few elegant words on the broader grounds of the relations between England and America. Similarly, at the Lord Mayor's banquet, Hawthorne had discussed the relations between the two countries and then sat down amid general applause.[7]

For the climax of his fragmentary novel, Hawthorne had noted "Bloody Footstep" in Study "F" and he turned back to his notebook entry for August 25, 1855, and to his visit to Smithell's Hall at the invitation of Mr. and Mrs. Ainsworth. After a satisfying dinner, his hosts took Hawthorne to see the bloody footstep, or a dark stain very much like a footprint, in a flagstone at one of the side entrances to the house. Despite Hawthorne's conclusion that the mark might be merely a reddish discoloration in the pavement, he took care in the romance to bring Etherege to the same entranceway and to a view of the miracle.

The foot was issuing from, not entering into, the house. Whoever had impressed it, or on whatever occasion, he had gone forth, and doubtless to return no more. Etherege was impelled to place his own foot on the track; and the action, as it were, suggested in itself strange ideas of what had been the state of mind of the man who planted it there; and he felt a strange, vague, yet strong surmise of some agony, some terror and horror, that had passed here, and would not fade out of the spot.[8]

The last jotting in "F" forms the very climax of the tale when the old pensioner is revealed as the heir of Braithwaite Hall. The notation, "Growth of hair in the grave," led Hawthorne directly to his notebooks and to the story which Mrs. John O'Sullivan one day told Hawthorne in April, 1854.

Mrs. O'Sullivan's grandmother died fifty years ago, at the age of twenty-eight. She had great personal charms, and among them a beautiful head of chestnut hair. After her burial (in a family tomb) the coffin of one of her own children was laid on her own coffin; so that the lid seems to have decayed or been broken, from this cause;—at any rate, this was the case when the tomb was opened, about a year ago. The grandmother's coffin was then found to be filled with beautiful, glossy, living chestnut ringlets, into which her whole substance seems to have been transformed; for there was nothing else but this coffin-full of shining ringlets, the growth of half-a century in

6. "G," 46a; Grimshawe, pp. 254–5.
7. Cf. "G," 47a and Grimshawe, p. 260, with English Notebooks, p. 323.
8. "G," 57b; Grimshawe, pp. 300–01. Cf. English Notebooks, p. 194.

the tomb. An old man, with a ringlet of his youthful mistress treasured on his heart, might be supposed to witness this wonderful thing.[9]

In the subterranean chamber of Braithwaite Hall, when Etherege is rescued by the pensioner and Elsie, a similar coffin is found in a corner; as the old pensioner throws back the lid, they are all stunned by the contents.

The entire, mysterious coffer was full of golden ringlets, abundant, clustering through the whole coffer, and living with elasticity, so as immediately, as it were, to flow over the sides of the coffer, and rise in large abundance from the long compression. Into this . . . had been resolved the whole bodily substance of the fair and unfortunate being, known so long in the legends of the family as the Beauty of the Golden Locks.[1]

The characters in Draft "G" are nearly all duplications of people who have figured before in Hawthorne's fiction: the scholar-idealist Etherege; the dark, villainous Lord Braithwaite; the typical New England girl Elsie; the enfeebled old man, pensioner Pearson; and the kindly sycophant, Dr. Etherege. Yet, for almost the first time, we can watch them grow under Hawthorne's hand from the preliminary studies, through the meditative passages of "G" and to their final, however ineffectual, place in the romance. We can watch Hawthorne exercising several old habits of mind: first, he initiates them in the studies as abstract figures and waits to see them take on personal traits in the long drafts; secondly, he makes them symbols, or ties a symbol to them, and the symbol is the chief formative influence in their development and growth; thirdly, the symbol, if it becomes clear and meaningful, automatically suggests to Hawthorne's mind a model or prototype and in the end it is the combination of the symbol and the model (usually a model in the English notebooks) which at last produces a man behind the shimmering gauze of romance.

Edward Etherege, the young American wayfarer, warrants little study, because Hawthorne paid scant attention to him. He is no more than Middleton from *The Ancestral Footstep* or, for that matter, Hawthorne himself in a youthful disguise. He is drawn with no distinction; he is little more than a bloodless man who represents "the peculiar hatred of Americans to an aristocracy."[2] There is one bright glimmer in Study "F," a notation to the "Claimants to the Booth estate"; Hawthorne was recalling his days at the consulate when he must seriously disabuse some of his foolish countrymen of the idea that they might be heirs of old castles or relatives of Queen Victoria.[3] But nothing

9. *Idem*, pp. 59–60.
1. "G," 67b; *Grimshawe*, p. 342.
2. See above, p. 34.
3. *English Notebooks*, pp. 117–18.

comes of such a jotting and at best Etherege stands weakly in the
long line of scholar-idealists whose good manners, perhaps like Hawthorne's own, impressed such snobs as the warden and Mr. Braithwaite.[4]

Elsie is similarly lacking in substance; she is not even fitted into
the story, for we never know whether or not she was the same Elsie
who lived with the old doctor beside the cemetery in Salem. The most
that can be said for her is that she is one more in Hawthorne's progeny
of New England girls—blonde, spritely, and halfheartedly uncon-
ventional.

The figure of Mr. Braithwaite is our first significant introduction to
Hawthorne's building of character. He grows from an abstract notation (such as the following in "A": "He has something on his conscience—something in the common course of things") to become a
symbol of evil and wily designs. He must be "Italianized throughout,
and Popishfied," Hawthorne noted in a meditative passage of "G,"[5]
but he found great difficulty in particularizing the proper sign of
wickedness which the lord must carry with him. Hawthorne was well
along in the story and fast approaching the denouement and still he
had made no preparation for Braithwaite's place in the romance. One
of many tortured conjectures in "G" will indicate Hawthorne's almost
profane anger with himself:

The life is not yet breathed into this plot, after all my galvanic efforts. Not
a spark of passion as yet. How shall it be attained [?] The Lord of Braithwaite Hall shall be a wretched, dissipated, dishonorable fellow . . . Up to
his death, he must feel as if this American had come to thwart him and ruin
him in everything, and shall hate him accordingly. . . . This won't do;
some marked character must be given to this fellow, as if he were a fiend,
a man sold to the devil, a magician, a poison-breather, a thug, a pirate, a
pickpocket; . . . it must have picturesque characteristics, of course; something that fixes strange and incongruous necessities upon him. . . . Could
I but achieve this, I should feel as if the book were plotted; otherwise, not.
Something monstrous he must be, yet within nature and romantic probabil-
ity—hard conditions. A murder—'twont do at all. A Mahometan?—pish! If
I could only hit right here, he would be the centre of interest. . . . Shall he
be preternatural? . . . A monkey? a Frankenstein? a man of straw? A man
without a heart, made by machinery? . . . A resurrection man? What?
What? What? A worshipper of the sun? A cannibal? a ghoul? a vampire? a
man who lives by sucking the blood of the young and beautiful? . . . A
man with a mortal disease?—a leprosy?—a eunuch?—a cork leg?—a
golden touch?—a dead hand?—a false nose?—a glass eye? . . . Some
damn'd thing is the matter.[6]

4. See *American Notebooks*, pp. xliv–xlix. Throughout this analysis of characters I
rely on Professor Stewart's apt terminology.
5. "G," 35[a].
6. *Idem*, 52[b].

The "matter" was that Hawthorne was looking for an emblem or symbol to particularize the man, just as the "man of straw" had had a brief pipe-smoking life in the story "Feathertop" or the cold "man without a heart" had lived in Ethan Brand. But the right image would not come; the symbols of another day could not be revived in this Italianate-Englishman.

When one symbol failed him, Hawthorne turned to another in order to resolve the evil of the lord. "He must have some peculiarity," Hawthorne repeats, and he goes on desperately to specify what that peculiarity may be; in the end he revived a symbol just as old as the "man of straw" and the "man without a heart"; in a later aside in "G" there comes the clue: "He might . . . have an ice-cold right hand; but this should be only emblematic of something else. . . . He might have a scar, which, in circumstances of desperation, grew blood-red."[7]

In the American notebook for 1842 Hawthorne had entered the germinal seed of this symbol: "A person with an ice-cold hand—his right hand; which people ever afterwards remember, when once they have grasped it."[8] Already he had used this symbol in his earlier fiction: Gervayse Hastings and the Virtuoso were both afflicted with cold hands and the Reverend Mr. Dimmesdale "put forth his hand, chill as death."[9] The scar which grew blood red likewise has its origin far back in the same notebook: "A noted gambler had acquired such self-command, that, in the most desperate circumstances of his game, no change of feature ever betrayed him;—only there was a slight scar upon his forehead, which, at such moments, assumed a deep blood-red hue."[1] The "scar" was never used in the portrait of Mr. Braithwaite but the cold hand came through in the end, though weakened and perhaps subtilized almost beyond recognition: that gentleman greets Etherege with a clasp of the left hand, while he keeps the right hand from any human contact.[2]

Thus from the hasty improvisations in the meditative passages of "G" came one emblem—the suspiciously cold right hand, the symbol of Braithwaite's isolation from mankind as well as his deadly rivalry with Etherege.

But the symbol must be attached to a body, preferably a man who suffered a lifelong isolation and loneliness from his fellowmen. In the index "F" is a clue to the model for the nobleman, "Character of Mr. Scarisbrooke [*sic*]," and from the English notebooks may be extracted one hint of what Hawthorne was trying to do in portraying the man with a cold hand.

7. *Idem*, 53ª; *Century Notes*, p. 440.
8. *American Notebooks*, p. 97.
9. See *Mosses from an Old Manse*, pp. 329, 559, and *Scarlet Letter*, p. 228.
1. *American Notebooks*, p. 102.
2. "G," 56ª; *Grimshawe*, p. 293.

I heard some of the railway passengers talking, yesterday, about Mr. Scaris-brick, of Scarisbrick Hall, who is the landlord of Southport. He is an ec-centric man, they said, and there seems to be an obscurity about the early part of his life. . . . He is a Catholic, but is bringing up his children, they say, in the Protestant faith. He is a very eccentric and nervous man, and spends all his time at this secluded hall, which stands in the midst of mosses and marshes; and sees nobody, not even his own Steward.[3]

But Hawthorne never saw Mr. Scarisbrick and the journal was there-fore barren of those sharp details which he could retrace in the out-lines of his nobleman. Thus, while Mr. Scarisbrick is the vague model for Lord Braithwaite, a close prototype lies in the English notebook in the person of another man, this time one whom Hawthorne met and described in the journals, who likewise suffered from a preternatural estrangement; this model is a direct descendant of John Evelyn, the famous diarist, and Hawthorne recorded after his visit to Wotton:

Mr. Evelyn is a young-looking man, dark, with a moustache, rather small, and of no distinguished aspect, except that his face is rather oddly forlorn and uncomfortable in its expression. He seems to be nervous, and though he has the manners of a man who has seen the world, it evidently requires an effort in him to speak to anybody; and I could see his whole person slightly writhing itself, as it were, while he addressed me.[4]

The physical outlines of Braithwaite somewhat resemble those of Mr. Evelyn: "He was a tall, dark man, with a black moustache, and almost olive skin, a slender, lithe figure, a flexible face, quick, flashing, mo-bile."[5] Although both men are dark and wear moustaches, Mr. Braith-waite bears a few resemblances to Mr. Scarisbrick in his devotion to the Catholic Church, his mysterious early life, and his loneliness in a musty old manor house.

Thus Braithwaite is a composite portrait but he was born as an abstraction in the studies; he passed through a series of transforma-tions as Hawthorne experimented with symbols of cold hands and chill hearts and finally he emerged looking very like Mr. Evelyn of Wotton and hiding his right hand behind his back as a token of his aloofness from all life around him. In Braithwaite the evolution is complete and he lives, a shadowy form, as both symbol and actual man.

If Hawthorne labored to bring some life into Braithwaite, his strug-gles with pensioner Pearson were even more titanic; in the end he followed the identical generative processes—abstract figure, then the search for a symbol, and finally the model—which marked his work in creating the portrait of the villain. In Study "A" we find his origin:

3. *English Notebooks*, p. 442.
4. *Idem*, p. 305.
5. "G," 44ᵇ; *Grimshawe*, pp. 248–9.

"Among the personages introduced shall be an American defalcator, or other criminal, of some years ago, who shall be living here in England, or in solitude—the latter, I think." Hawthorne was planning to introduce a great financier who, like Samuel Insull of another day, carried hundreds of investors down with him in a terrible financial debacle and then fled to Europe to escape the judgment of his countrymen.

By the time he was under way in "G," however, Hawthorne was beginning to play with correspondences and the interrelations between the two countries; he was also laying the groundwork for Etherege's adventures in Warwickshire. Accordingly, early in that draft the "defalcator" was softened into the Doctor's brother for whom a fire was always kept burning and the table laid in the Charter Street house.[6] One significant note begins the shift from an abstract manipulator into a symbolized character: "The Doctor's brother in England . . . shall have an almost irresistible influence over those with whom he holds intercourse. . . ."[7]

But Hawthorne must specify what form this "influence" should take and in his mind such influences were customarily evil. Thereupon he moved into the misty regions of symbolism in order to signify this wandering, yet cold-blooded man. "But if left to himself, or wholly to the society of his contemporaries, the ice gathers about his heart, his hope grows torpid, his love . . . grows cold; he becomes selfish . . . ; so that instead of a beautiful object he is an ugly one, little, mean, and torpid."[8] And just as with the nobleman, Hawthorne plays with the symbolism of the cold heart and seeks for a character who will embody that evil; one of many meditative passages in "G" will illustrate Hawthorne's search:

This old man—what could he possibly be? The inheritor of some peculiarity that has been known heretofore in the history of the family, and the possession of which betrays itself in some of his habits, or in his person. What? I can't make it out. Some physical peculiarity?—'twont do. Some mental or moral peculiarity? How? The art of making gold? A peculiar kind of poison? An acquaintance with wizard lore? Nothing of this. He is an eater of human flesh—a vampire—a ghoul. He finds it necessary to eat a young child, every year, in order to keep himself alive. He shall have some famous jewel, known for ages in the family annals—pah! He shall have undertaken some investigation, which many members of his family have been deluded into undertaking heretofore, and the nature of which is, to change their natures disastrously—'twont do. He shall have been to the Cave of Trophonius. He shall have been to Hell—and I wish the Devil had kept him there. He shall have inherited the Great Carbuncle, and shall be forbidden

6. "G," 7[b].
7. *Idem*, 11[b].
8. *Idem*, 23[b].

to show it to any mortal. 'Twont do. On account of some supposed hidden power of his, the owner of the estate shall seek his aid. What, what, what? How, how, how![9]

The right figure refused to come through all this welter of conjecture and impatient juggling. Then in the same paragraph Hawthorne veered away from the Cave of Trophonius, Hell, and the Great Carbuncle, and began to sketch a less diabolical character, one more in keeping with a helpless old man than the defalcator.

A man aiming, the wrong way, at some good for his race. . . . A panacea for all ills. A friend of Swedenborg? A man with Medea's receipt? There is a latent something lying hereabouts, which, could I grip it, 'twould be the making of the story. A sort of apostle—a devoted, good man, but throwing himself away through some grand mistake! . . . Here, then, is a meek, patient, unpretending, wise old man, who developes peculiarities which draw the attention of profound observers upon him, though others see little that is remarkable in him. This is a better aspect than what I at first thought of. Follow out this clue, stubbornly, stubbornly.[1]

Shortly thereafter the pensioner became symbolized in his conscience: "What shall be his distinguishing trait," Hawthorne asks, "—merely a conscience, and the inveterate habit of acting on it."[2]

Finally resolved that the man's conscience should be the key to his character, Hawthorne went on to project the man more according to the symbol than to the abstract "defalcator." For the wickedness of the old man he could find no emblem, but for his aimlessness and indecision he had the touchstone in "the weakness of too much conscience . . . , the incapacity of action that must result from it, the inability for anything but suffering."

Although there is no hint in Study "F," the model for this character shone in the English notebooks. In 1854 the Hawthornes visited Eaton Hall, in Cheshire, and in their company was George P. Bradford, an old Brook Farmer. That evening after the excursion Hawthorne wrote a penetrating character study of his old acquaintance.

Mr. Bradford has the blood of martyrs in him, through two channels; and I doubt not there is the substance in himself to make a martyr of;—and yet he is a wonderfully small pattern of a man. He has a minute conscientiousness, which is continually stumbling over insignificant matters; and trifles of all kinds seem to be matters of great moment with him. There is a lack of strong will, that makes his conduct, when not determined by principle, miserably weak and wavering. . . . He is always uneasy what to do next; always regretting the last thing he did.[3]

9. *Idem*, 33[a].
1. *Ibid.*
2. *Idem*, 35[b].
3. *English Notebooks*, pp. 75–6.

When the pensioner found his place in the romance, the union of Bradford with the abstract idea of conscience was complete.

As Etherege sat watching the old man in the garden, he could not help being struck by the scrupulous care with which he attended to the plants; it seemed to him that there was a sense of justice—of desiring to do exactly what was right in the matter, not favoring one plant more than another, and doing all he could for each. His progress, in consequence, was so slow, that, in an hour while Etherege was off and on looking at him, he had scarcely [done] anything perceptible. Then he was so minute; and often, when he was on the point of leaving one thing to take up another, some small neglect that he saw or fancied, called him back again, to spend other minutes on the same task. He was so full of scruples. It struck Etherege that this was conscience, morbid, sick, a despot in trifles, looking so closely into life that it permitted nothing to be done. The man might once have been strong and able, but by some unhealthy process of his life he had ceased to be so now.[4]

4

Hawthorne must have put "G" aside with relief, almost with a curse. After all the trouble he had expended on it, there was little to show except a patchwork of narrative fragments alternating with diffuse and extensive meditations. The long strands of fiction had never been woven together and all that remained, as his eyes fell upon the piles of manuscript, were enough suggestions and plans to fill two or three romances.

Yet the central idea of the novel was too good to waste. No one had ever tried to write a fictional criticism of the English, much less to bring the English and American ways of life into startling contact and contrast. Where Hawthorne had failed in "G" was in the portrait of his hero and in the thinness of the satire which, like a steel wire, must be held tautly throughout the tale. The English should receive a neat drubbing for their insularity and snobbery; foolish Americans who aimed at aping their English cousins should be likewise pummeled but the wildness of the events and of the satire must not hang over the precipitous verge of absurdity. There lay the difficulty: the wedding of realism and romance must not be broken by coffers full of golden hair, bloody footsteps, and secret chambers. These mysterious things must be *suggested* but never brought openly or absurdly into the light. Always they should be cast in shadows, in hints and in side glances, just as the Reverend Arthur Dimmesdale always kept the secret of his guilt concealed beneath his clerical garb.

4. "G," 36[a]; *Grimshawe*, p. 239. One minor character, the warden, may have been modeled on Hawthorne's English friend, Francis Bennoch, of whom Hawthorne wrote, "Mr Bennoch is a kindly, jolly, frank, off-hand, very good fellow, and was bounteous in his plans for making my time pass pleasantly." *English Notebooks*, p. 282. See also p. 291.

Perhaps it was with these thoughts in mind that Hawthorne began a revision of his whole narrative, the Draft "H" which was never brought to completion but which stands today as the first half of the published *Doctor Grimshawe's Secret*. Some time late in 1860 or early in 1861 he took up his story anew and wrote one of the finest fragments of these last years. The story from the beginning to the American's arrival at the hospital covers substantially the same incidents as those in the first half of "G" but it is elaborated more than four times the length of the earlier draft. It begins in the old house in Salem, situated beside the Charter Street Cemetery, where live Dr. Grimshawe and his two wards, Ned and Elsie. The Doctor is a rough, pipe-smoking, brandy-tippling old apothecary who scorns his fellow townsmen, but to the children he is both rude and delightfully amiable. An old housekeeper, Crusty Hannah, is the only nurse for the children and they are allowed to roam freely about the spider-infested house and out into the adjoining cemetery where they play amid the old tombstones of Puritan worthies dead and gone. The Doctor himself loves to tell them fabulous stories of his old home in England, of a bloody footprint on a flagstone of a manor house, and of the lost heir who came to America about the time of the colonization of Virginia. The imaginative little boy and girl love to re-create these legends in their play among the tombstones and in the rambling old house.

The Doctor is held in such odium in Salem that one day, during a walk with the children, he is attacked by the superstitious townspeople; he defends himself as best he can with a cudgel stick but, when he is nearly overcome, a wild-appearing stranger intrudes and, by the sheer power of his voice, disperses the angry populace and rescues the Doctor from a terrible beating. This stranger is Seymour, an itinerant New England schoolmaster, whom the Doctor takes into his house and induces to teach the children. The two men do not get on at all well and Seymour leaves the children to pick up any knowledge in any way they can.

The mystery of the Doctor's past life deepens when Mountford, an English lawyer, comes to the house on an investigation of a long-lost heir to an estate in the old country. The Doctor is not able to bring forth any proofs; Mountford even investigates an old gravestone in the cemetery but he finds only the half-obliterated name of the man whom he presumes to have been the heir who died without proper issue. He too leaves and the Doctor in his last days becomes even more hopeful that (by substituting Ned as the claimant) he may get revenge for some past wrong done him in England. Ceaselessly does he fill the boy with notions of a claim to wealth and ancestral holdings; then he dies and Ned and Elsie are left to find their way in the world.

There is a gap and we next discover Edward Redclyffe, grown to man's estate and to a successful career as a lawyer, on a walking tour through the Midland counties of England. He meets with a sudden and almost fatal assault along a bypath he is following but he is rescued by a kind palmer of a local charity nearby. He quickly recovers his strength and is becoming fast acquainted with the personages about him and with the strange folk tales of the place—and the romance comes suddenly to an end. Hawthorne simply dropped his story for the sake of beginning *Septimius Felton,* the romance of immortality.

The narrative in "H" is freer than was "G" of indebtedness to the early studies or even to the notebooks. By the time he was ready to revise his tale, Hawthorne had the romance so well in mind that he could write it off almost without any reference to the sketches which had weighed so heavily on "G." Even the penmanship is quite clear and unblotted in "H" and there are only a few of those marginal notations which had obtruded upon the previous draft. The relationship between the Doctor and the children is exquisitely treated; the portrait of Dr. Grimshawe is drawn with amazingly deft lines. He is sometimes so gruff with the children that he frightens them into tears and yet their terror is short-lived; soon the old man has them both at his knees and is telling them fascinating stories of faraway places in England. Ned is considerably revised. He has a great deal of childish pride which should well suit the later American adventurer in England. And Elsie has taken on those shimmering lights of spriteliness and elfishness in which Hawthorne so well loved to bathe his little girls.

The greatest single revision is in Seymour, the transcendental schoolmaster, who boldly intervenes in the Doctor's behalf during the Salem street brawl. Seymour is none other than pensioner Pearson of Braithwaite Hospital, now in a younger guise. The lawyer Mountford is, of course, the identical man who had come to Salem in "G," but Hawthorne makes him far more vivid than in the earlier draft by having him engage in a long and somewhat acrimonious discussion with the Doctor; the futility of his mission is likewise highlighted by a rather bleakly delightful scene when the Doctor, Mountford, and the children scrape away the gatherings of centuries from the grave of a certain "Thomas Colcord," the lost progenitor of Smithell's Hall, and simultaneously engage in a ghoulish dialogue with a gravedigger standing nearby.

If the narrative in "H" has been extended considerably over the rather brief compass of "G," the characters in Salem underwent no less a change. Perhaps all the wrestlings and plans in the meditative passages of "G" were not altogether wasted, for out of them came a few suggestions which, when once resolved and put in their proper place, gave some body to a group of otherwise rather abstract human beings.

As a child in Dr. Grimshawe's household, Ned is a long-germinating product of several notations in the notebooks. Many years before, Hawthorne had entered the isolated jotting in his journal for 1842:

The history of an Alms-House in a country village, from the eve of its foundation downward—a record of the remarkable occupants of it; and extracts from interesting portions of its annals. . . . There should be occasionally sunshine let into the story; for instance, the good fortune of some nameless infant, educated there, and discovered finally to be the child of wealthy parents.[5]

Just fourteen years later Hawthorne visited the Liverpool West Derby Workhouse, an institution which seemed almost like the direct embodiment of an earlier vision; and there he found a boy very similar to the "nameless infant" of the 1842 jotting: "it was a wretched, pale, half-torpid little thing, with a humor in its eyes, which the Governor said was scurvy."[6] That evening in Southport he busily went to work and drew a sketch of the child in his notebook. From the beginning of his meditations on the early life of his American adventurer Hawthorne clearly intended to draw Ned on the model of the dirty lad in the asylum. Like the boy in the workhouse, Ned is "about six years old"; until he was adopted by the Doctor he had lived in an orphanage in which "there were many wretched infants like himself, as well as helpless people of all ages, widows, decayed drunkards, people of feeble wit, and all kinds of imbecility."[7]

Ned's portrait was made to order before Hawthorne composed his last draft. The notebook entry for 1842 supplied long in advance the idea of a wellborn child hidden in an almshouse; the singular coincidence in 1856 of finding a scurvy-faced boy in the workhouse gave Hawthorne a living prototype; and the meditations throughout "G" established Ned's place in the romance as a potential heir to the manor house of Smithell's. These various and far-separated notations demonstrate how carefully Hawthorne was planning every step; how he kept in mind suggestions in the American journal and how he recalled them when an actual incident in his own life seemed to bring together those "two far-separated points" in time.

The character of Dr. Grimshawe in "H" has been drawn much more clearly and successfully than his predecessor, Dr. Etherege, in

5. *American Notebooks*, p. 100.
6. *English Notebooks*, p. 275.
7. "H," p. 9; *Grimshawe*, p. 24. Compare these descriptive details with Hawthorne's impressions of the West Derby Workhouse, *English Notebooks*, pp. 275–6, and *Our Old Home*, I, 355–6.

"G." For his genesis we might well go back to another entry in the American notebook, this time for 1838.

Singular character of a gentleman . . . living in retirement in Boston,— esteemed a man of nicest honor, and his seclusion attributed to wounded feelings on account of the failure of his firm in business. Yet it was discovered that this man had been the mover of intrigues by which men in business had been ruined . . . ; love-affairs had been broken off, and much other mischief done; and for years he was not in the least suspected.[8]

Dr. Grimshawe is singularly anticipated in this jotting, especially as he came to exercise a mysterious power over Ned and to pull many intricate threads in England. Hawthorne had been fascinated for many years with the idea of one man's directing the destinies of others; this conception, we know very well, he used frequently in his novels.[9]

In the preliminary studies there were no reflections of the Doctor's getting "possession of a human being," but by the time Hawthorne shaped him in "G" these long-standing practices in his workshop gradually, perhaps very consciously, formed the sinister and ugly portrait of the apothecary. Certainly the "moral essence" of Grimshawe's character had ample development in the notebooks and in the meditative passages of "G" but his physical appearance and, in a real sense, the man himself had a quite different origin.

Dr. Grimshawe is none other than Seymour Kirkup, the old English painter, once the friend of Byron, Shelley, Leigh Hunt, and Trelawny. Kirkup was a necromancer of some repute who had almost convinced the Florentine intelligentsia of 1858, especially Mrs. Browning and Miss Isa Blagden, that there might be some validity in spirit rappings and the voices of Roman emperors. He lived with his little daughter Imogene in the old establishment of the Knights Templars on the banks of the Arno. To the penetrating eyes of Hawthorne, however, the most memorable figure in the strange melange of plaster casts and Giotto frescoes was Seymour Kirkup himself:

He is rather low of stature, with a pale, shrivelled face, and hair and beard perfectly white, and the hair of a particularly soft and silken texture. He has a high, thin nose, of the English aristocratic type; his eyes have a queer, rather wild look, and the eyebrows are arched above them so that he seems all the time to be seeing something that strikes him with surprise. I judged him to be a little crack-brained chiefly on the strength of this expression. His whole make is delicate, his hands white and small, and his appearance and manner those of a gentleman, with rather more embroidery of courtesy than belong to an Englishman.[1]

8. *Passages from the American Notebooks*, p. 205.
9. See *American Notebooks*, pp. lxxii–lxxv.
1. *Italian Notebooks*, pp. 386–7. For further information on Hawthorne and Kirkup,

Already in "G" there had been hints that Hawthorne intended to use Kirkup as the prototype for the pseudoscientific apothecary; in "H" he comes forth a startling duplication of the amateur medium of Florence. Grimshawe is "a broad, rather short personage, with a projecting forehead, a red, irregular face, and a squab nose." Although he does not possess Kirkup's appearance of delicacy, he has the painter's strange eyes which are at times "ugly and awful." Hawthorne, it is true, departs from his model in describing the Doctor as having "a rough and careless exterior, and altogether a shaggy kind of aspect." The figure of Kirkup, with its tremulousness and gentlemanly appearance, would not have fitted the uncouth Doctor. The other details— the charlatanism and the eyes with a "wild look"—were perfectly suited to Grimshawe and Hawthorne diligently borrowed them.[2]

The model for Elsie is Imogene, Kirkup's daughter by a late marriage. The parallels are incontestably close: both little girls were born with natural, playful natures and with infectious smiles, and each had a kitten![3]

Seymour, the transcendental schoolmaster, was revised, shifted, retouched, and tossed around more than any other character in "G." He began first as the Doctor's brother and, like the later version of the Doctor himself, had ". . . in him a certain wildness or madness, which, in the last result, is liable to produce ruin."[4] Hawthorne soon found that he could not have two diabolical men who might "produce ruin" and therefore he gradually evolved the pensioner—Pearson in Draft "G," Seymour in "H." But Hawthorne floundered interminably in trying to tie this old man to a semblance of flesh and human bones. In one meditative aside in "G," however, he supplied the key for the character of Seymour: "He might be a Fifth-Heavenly Man; that is to say, obedient to the higher law within himself, and rejecting human law when it interfered. In figure, Mr. Alcott."[5]

If Pearson in "G" was modeled on George P. Bradford, Seymour in "H" is a remarkable portrait of Bronson Alcott. He is not the gray- and thin-haired Alcott of the 'sixties but the transcendental schoolmaster of those early years when he abandoned the birch rod for persuasion and classroom discipline for spiritual influence over his pupils. One might well be astonished at the portrait, for the philosopher whose company was duller than the onerous duties of the Salem Customs House might have been drawn along harsher lines and with

see M. D. Conway, *Life of Nathaniel Hawthorne* (New York, 1890), pp. 200–01; Julian Hawthorne, *Hawthorne and His Circle*, p. 346; *Italian Notebooks*, p. 390; and G. P. Lathrop, "The Hawthorne Manuscripts," *The Atlantic Monthly*, LI (March, 1883), 372.
2. "H," p. 3; *Grimshawe*, p. 8.
3. "H," p. 5, and *Grimshawe*, pp. 13–14, with *Italian Notebooks*, pp. 386, 389.
4. "G," 11ᵇ.
5. "G," 73ᵃ; *Century Notes*, p. 448.

more satire than those which limned Seymour in the last draft of the romance.

[Seymour was] a person of singularly impressive appearance; a thin, mild looking man, with a peculiar look of delicacy and natural refinement about him, . . . plain in dress, and simple in manner, not giving the idea of remarkable intellectual gifts, but with a kind of spiritual aspect,—fair, clear complexion, gentle eyes. . . . He looked middle-aged, and yet there was a kind of childlike, simple expression, which . . . would make you suppose him much younger.[6]

Hawthorne's allusions to Seymour's weak body and lack of manly determination are echoed in Emerson's designation of Alcott as an "Influence . . . and intellectual torso, without hands or feet, without any organ whereby to reproduce his thought in any form whatever."[7] So far Seymour's only success in life had been as a schoolmaster who had laid aside the birch rod because of "moral and religious objections"; and Alcott too had abandoned corporal punishment in favor of enlightening conversations between teacher and student. Yet Boston had regarded Alcott with as little respect as Salem treated Seymour in the romance: both were at last forced to resign the only profession for which they were eminently fitted.

A few minor characters in "H" warrant only slight consideration. Mountford, the English lawyer, is precisely the same man who had appeared in "G." Crusty Hannah, Dr. Grimshawe's housemaid—she was "Sukey" in the earlier draft—a pale reincarnation of Hawthorne's own aunt, Hannah Lord, was drawn straight from Hawthorne's recollections of his youth in Salem.[8] Still another reflection of Hawthorne's boyhood is Dr. John Swinnerton, whose grave, we are told, lay beside that of Dr. Grimshawe. In the early days of Salem he was an actual physician whose tombstone Hawthorne had frequently seen in the Charter Street burial ground; he had already appeared in *The House of the Seven Gables* and would be revived again briefly in *The Dolliver Romance*.[9] The last of these minor figures is the American

6. "H," p. 18; *Grimshawe*, p. 59. See also *Scarlet Letter*, p. 43. For an interesting parallel between Hawthorne's portrait and Carlyle's impressions of Alcott, whom he saw in 1842, see C. E. Norton, ed., *Correspondence of Thomas Carlyle and Ralph Waldo Emerson, 1834–1872* (Boston, 1887), II, 8.

7. J. E. Cabot, *Memoir of Ralph Waldo Emerson* (Boston and New York, 1887), p. 281. Compare Emerson's remark with another note of Hawthorne's: ". . . the children, and especially Ned, were intuitively conscious of a certain want of substance in the instructor, a something of earthly bulk; a too etherealness." "H," p. 20; *Grimshawe*, p. 67.

8. Cf. "G," 42a, *Century Notes*, p. 437, wherein Hawthorne plans for this character of Crusty Hannah. See also G. P. Lathrop, *op. cit.*, 373–4.

9. Julian Hawthorne (*Grimshawe*, p. 129) transcribed the name as "Summerton" but "H" (p. 36) reads "Swinnerton." See also *Passages from the American Notebooks*, p. 118; *Seven Gables*, p. 30, and *Dolliver Romance*, p. 18.

lawyer, Timothy Pickering, who acts as the administrator for Dr. Grimshawe's estate. Pickering had been a Revolutionary patriot, a member of Washington's cabinet and, after his political career was ended, had retired to spend his last years in the town of his birth.[1] He must have been a great and impressive person in the eyes of the youthful Hawthorne; and what would be more natural, to lend verisimilitude to a tale of Salem in the years shortly after the Revolution, than to put the impressive figure of "Old Tim Pickering" into the romance?

5

Doctor Grimshawe's Secret has been forgotten by all but the most diligent and enthusiastic students of Hawthorne. Even in its own new day of 1882 and 1883 it enjoyed only the briefest notoriety, for most critics realized that the romance had been left incomplete and that, in its present form, it should never have been published at all. There were even questions of its authenticity as a genuine work.[2] An examination of the manuscript leaves no doubt, however, that the whole fragmentary tale, curiously wrought and oddly patched, is from Hawthorne's hand; the critics did not have the advantages of photostatic copies nor of helpful libraries where Hawthorniana were deposited. Yet if they had looked carefully at the several pages of manuscript reproduction which Julian Hawthorne inserted after his Preface, they might easily have seen that the editor had exercised considerable license in transcribing the draft. And had they been privileged to view the secrets hidden among the later manuscript pages, their anathemas would have fallen more heavily than a witches' chorus on Julian's head.

At best, the critics admitted, the romance was an interesting fragment, crude as a boy's first effort and lurid as a dime novel. Richard Henry Stoddard, perhaps overwhelmed by the Hawthorne name, trusted faithfully that he had read a nearly complete novel with a beginning, middle, and end and rashly gave it a worthy place on the same shelf with Thackeray's *Denis Duval* and Dickens' *Edwin Drood*.[3] A few reviewers, while not according *Grimshawe* the accolade of a masterpiece, at least thought the Doctor an eminently satisfactory character and pointed out separate passages which were full of "Hawthorne's thought and style."[4] Others halfheartedly praised

1. For Hawthorne's earlier comments on Pickering, see *Sketches*, pp. 102–03, and *Grandfather's Chair*, p. 607.
2. See Appendix.
3. R. H. Stoddard, "Nathaniel Hawthorne," *Lippincott's Monthly Magazine*, XLIII (February, 1889), 256.
4. "Dr. Grimshawe's Secret," *The Saturday Review*, LV (January 6, 1883), 26; see also "Hawthorne's Posthumous Romance," *Literary World*, XIV (13 January 1883), 3.

the "delightful descriptions" and "pathetic touches" and, in the end, commended Hawthorne for staunchly maintaining his American integrity amid the entrancing castles and "border brotherhoods" of the Old World.[5] Even Whittier was moved to conclude his review of the novel, "It is one of his weird, unmistakable creations—a creation not fully rounded, chaotic, peopled with strange shapes, like our planet in its first discovery."[6] Perhaps the wisest remarks of all were made by Holmes immediately after he had read the romance, "I feel as one might have felt who had been admitted into Rembrandt's studio. I have been closeted with a magician and admitted within his mysterious circle."[7]

None of the reviewers of the 'eighties had anything to say about Hawthorne's attitude toward the English. Perhaps the sting had been removed and the venom spent in the essays for *Our Old Home* published in 1863. Twenty years later the literary world, and especially the critical mind of England, had little interest in the maunderings of an old man who concealed his anger with the English in the symbolism of the bloody footprint of Smithell's Hall. There was simply not enough bite in Hawthorne's criticism of his English cousins to make any reader wince. And certainly there was not the strong vein of satire on Americans in search of ancestral wealth to bring any undue discomfort to Hawthorne's countrymen.

The failure of the romance was twofold.

Hawthorne intended at the outset, as the preliminary studies bear eloquent testimony, to bring "the English and American ideas . . . strikingly into contact or contrast," or, as he phrased it again, "The general tenor of the book must illustrate the sympathy and the difference between Americans and Englishmen." Throughout the English notebooks Hawthorne was constantly reiterating his patriotic devotion to the United States; he was, at the same time, frequently harassed at the consulate by his deluded and ridiculous countrymen who were in quest of wealth and honors in England. These foolish Americans he wished to satirize and make idiotic; the English he would sting with his shafts tipped with venom. But to accomplish this double aim he had to make his satire a two-handled sword to cut both ways at once. Very soon he lost his animus against his compatriots, for the vein of satire, never very wide nor deep in Hawthorne's craftsmanship, could not be broadened to include members of two nationalities. The satire on Americans petered out in symbols of blood-soaked

5. *Athenaeum* (London), LXXXI (January 5, 1885), 11; J. H. Morse, "Nathaniel Hawthorne Again," *The Century Magazine*, XXVI (June, 1883), 310; see also "Literature of the Day," *Lippincott's Monthly Magazine*, XXXI (March, 1883), 318–19, and "Editor's Literary Record," *Harper's New Monthly Magazine*, LXVI (March, 1883), 640.
6. Quoted in the *New York Tribune*, XLII (December 23, 1882), 6.
7. *Ibid.*

leaves in the New England forest and, by the time he wrote "G," he had forgotten that he ever intended to blister those American fortune hunters whom he had sketched at the end of *The Ancestral Footstep.*

Yet in 1860 and 1861, when Hawthorne wrote the bulk of the "Grimshawe" drafts, he was angry at the British—just as angry as when he published *Our Old Home* two years later. Not only had he endured the bluff snobberies of Englishmen during his tenure of the consulate but his blood had been stirred time and again by English tourists who had come to this country, had earned fat lecture fees and then, like Dickens in his *American Notes* and *Martin Chuzzlewit,* had laughed at the Americans. Year after year had seen this steady tide of English tourists who, like Mrs. Fanny Trollope in her report on the crude Americans who spat tobacco juice in their theaters and had no culture, must have made Hawthorne's gorge rise. Undoubtedly the "patriotic motive" in the English notebooks and in the Romance of England stemmed from his righteous anger over the drubbing his countrymen received at the hands of English literary tourists.

Therefore, in the romance, Hawthorne would turn up the other face of the coin. He would be a tourist; he would be a satirical traveler, whether in the guise of Middleton, Etherege, or Redclyffe, and he would demonstrate that the land of tobacco-spitters could likewise produce a man of culture and social presence far superior to the decayed English gentry.

Unfortunately, Hawthorne failed to produce a "Domestic Manners of the English" or a *Martin Chuzzlewit* in reverse; he even failed in a milder satire on his own countrymen, maddened by dreams of estates with moated castles. Thus the failure was complete and the two-edged sword dropped from his hand, not with a crash but a clatter.

It was the symbol of the bloody footstep which marks the trail of his collapse. He could not give it any force nor render it any way intelligible. Mrs. Ainsworth on that day in 1855 unwittingly did Hawthorne an irreparable harm in asking him to write a romance about her house. From that time he was seduced into believing that he could make the footprint assume any form he wished. It might be the trail of a younger brother expelled from Smithell's Hall in the seventeenth century; the track of a Catholic martyr who begged sanctuary in America; the mark of a "bloody religionist" who beheaded King Charles I; the trail of old ancestral crimes which must someday be expiated. Hawthorne could never decide what was the symbolism of the footprint and, dependent as he was on the tautness which a consistently drawn symbol would give a romance, he spent his strength in conjectures and futile analysis. For all the preliminary studies and the meditative asides in "G," he had at the end no more idea of what his tale would be than he had when he started. He was completely beyond his depth when he tried to write a romance of England. The most pitiable example of his failure comes after Dr. Grimshawe's death in "H." At that point Hawthorne paused to gird himself and gather his forces for writing the English portions of his novel. Despite all the material in the notebooks and despite the endless experiments and rearrangements of scenes in "G," he felt so unsure of himself that he hastily jotted down a memorandum, another index to the English journals[8] very similar to study "F," with which he might guide his scratching pen and bring close an essentially foreign land.

The truth is that Hawthorne's artistic range was so neatly confined to the New England he knew that, when he stepped beyond the certain reaches of his native place, he was lost.

Therefore, in the spring of 1861, he abandoned the English romance forever.

8. This curious memorandum ("H," p. 36) Julian Hawthorne reproduced in *Grimshawe*, Appendix, p. 354.

IV

"Septimius Felton"

1

IN 1852 Hawthorne purchased Bronson Alcott's house "The Hill-side," which stood on the main road running from Concord to Lexington, and in June of that year he moved his family from West Newton. He did not live there very long, for his old Bowdoin friend, Franklin Pierce, was in that year elected President and Haw-thorne was rewarded for writing a campaign biography with the appointment to the Liverpool consulate in 1853.

But during his brief residence in Concord Hawthorne renewed his friendship with Henry Thoreau. One day Henry told him an extraor-dinary story about the house: many years ago there lived in the Wayside a man who thought he would never die.[1] That was the sub-stance of Henry's tale; what was the strange man's name or appear-ance no one knew, but for Hawthorne's purposes the mystery was more interesting than any facts with which Thoreau might have em-broidered the legend.

Throughout the intervening years in Liverpool and Italy, Haw-thorne was haunted by that spectral figure and, as he confessed, the tale gave him a special interest in his home. When he returned in 1860, the ghostly and deluded man hung about the rooms and de-manded that a romance be written about him. But in 1860 the ro-mance of England was pressing and not until the following year, when he put aside the tale of a young American who went to Eng-land, did Hawthorne finally return to the mysterious inhabitant of the Wayside who seemed still to haunt the chambers and make spec-tral moans at night.

Septimius Felton, the third of Hawthorne's last and unfinished novels, was a product not only of Thoreau's legend of the deathless man but also of a lifetime's meditation on the theme of immortality.[2] Quite early in his career Hawthorne may have been attracted to the subject by reading William Godwin's *St. Leon,* the story of a man who would reform the world by living forever. In Godwin's account, the results of earthly immortality would be beneficial to mankind, but as early as 1836 Hawthorne had taken a different view of the

1. See Study "A."
2. *American Notebooks,* pp. lxxxii–lxxxiii.

matter: an indefinite extension of life might be detrimental to society.[3] Again, in 1840, he reiterated his conviction that men should terminate their lives on this earth at the customary term of threescore and ten.[4] Thus twenty years before he began his longest romance of immortality, Hawthorne was working on the conventional assumption that the abolition of death would produce no improvement in human character and that it might shatter the whole human fabric by which mankind was kept in order.

Yet, strangely, in 1843 a different point of view occurred to Hawthorne and in a notebook entry he began to play with the idea that the annihilation of death might be man's greatest triumph. "The advantages of a longer life than is allotted to mortals—the many things that might then be accomplished;—to which one life-time is inadequate, and for which the time spent is therefore lost; a successor being unable to take up the task when we drop it."[5] In "The Artist of the Beautiful" (1844) Owen Warland "was incited to toil the more diligently by an anxiety lest death should surprise him in the midst of his labors."[6] Thus an indefinite extension of mortal life, Hawthorne maintained throughout the 'forties and 'fifties, would be indispensable to the improvement of human society. His final statement of that conviction was made in the notebook for January, 1855, seven months before he heard the fascinating legend of Smithell's Hall. "God himself cannot compensate us for being born, in any period short of eternity. All the misery we endure here constitutes a claim for another life;—and, still more, all the happiness, because all true happiness involves something more than the earth owns, and something more than a mortal capacity for the enjoyment of it."[7]

For more than twenty years Hawthorne had therefore planted the germinal seeds in the notebooks and had given them a brief life in the short stories. In 1861, when he returned to the theme once more, he had apparently reached the conclusion that man is cut off untimely before he really begins to live. Hawthorne had, throughout these extensive meditations, long prepared himself for a novel on the subject of a man who lived forever; now he needed only an idea which would start him on his way; and he came back to the haunting figure of the deathless man who had once lived in the Wayside and had walked those very pathways.

3. *Idem*, p. lxxxiii; *Passages from the American Notebooks*, p. 36.
4. *Idem*, p. 212.
5. *American Notebooks*, p. 100.
6. *Mosses*, pp. 525–6.
7. *English Notebooks*, p. 101.

2

After he had finally abandoned the fragments later to be known as *Doctor Grimshawe's Secret*, Hawthorne returned to this tantalizing theme. The romance of immortality would be his crowning achievement on this subject and in the early months of 1861 he revealed his plan to James T. Fields, the publisher, while the two men were walking on the hill behind the Wayside. "An enchanting memory," Fields later wrote, "is left of that morning when he laid out the whole story before me as he intended to write it. The plot was a grand one, and I tried to tell him how much I was impressed by it."[8]

In the autumn of 1861 Hawthorne began to compose the first experimental studies for his tale. The outbreak of hostilities between the North and South in April had given him a new impetus to get on with the work and to use the stormy days of 1775 as a setting for his romance. On the very grounds of his home had been enacted one of the minor skirmishes during the British retreat; and the days of '75 had a peculiar significance when, just eighty-six years later, the boys marched through Concord to entrain for the war in the South. To plan his story, he need only look out the window of his tower and see the ridge along which the British had retreated; or he might walk up the hill itself, part of his own property, and touch the trees which were saplings in those memorable days. He would take Thoreau's legend of the deathless man, thrust it back into those storied times, and draw the parallel and the moral for his own days of 1861.

In October he was at last working on his novel, for he told his friend, Horatio Bridge, "I find myself sitting down at my desk and blotting successive sheets of paper as of yore."[9] Hoping that he might complete the romance by the middle of 1862, he led Fields to believe that the *Atlantic Monthly* might have a serialized novel from his hand within a few months and in November Fields answered optimistically, "I think you had better allow me to put your story into my prospectus for 1862."[1]

Throughout this brief exchange of letters with Fields, Hawthorne was by no means so far along with his tale as he led the editor of the *Atlantic* to believe. The "blotting successive sheets of paper" which he mentioned to Bridge referred not to the writing of a final draft but to the jotting of a series of preliminary studies. The first hesitant steps in the romance can be quite accurately dated: one of the sketches is written over the encouraging letter from Fields on putting

8. *Yesterdays*, p. 96. Fields mistakenly believed that this plan referred to *The Dolliver Romance*, which was not begun until two and a half years later.
9. *Septimius Felton*, pp. 223–4; G. P. Lathrop, *A Study of Hawthorne* (Boston, 1876), p. 271.
1. This letter is in the Morgan Library.

the story into the "prospectus for 1862." Although he may have been goaded by his friend's stimulating words, Hawthorne was in no wise coming to grips with the final composition of his tale and it is therefore little wonder that the *Atlantic* would have to wait.

Shortly after the opening of 1862 Hawthorne began to put his story on paper in a partially complete and straightforward manner. Yet he was continually forced to lay the manuscript aside while he journeyed to Washington in March and April of that year and wrote his impressions of the civil strife in "Chiefly about War Matters," or contributed the "Our Old Home" essays to the *Atlantic*. Perhaps by the middle of 1862 he had hurried his story to an unsatisfactory conclusion and then undertook a revision of the whole romance. He labored over his second draft throughout the latter half of 1862 and perhaps into the early months of 1863. He never finished this revision and when he put it aside he was done with the young man of the Wayside who thought that he might live forever. He had written nearly one hundred and fifty thousand words and he had nothing but the accumulated piles of sketches, studies, and unfinished drafts to show for his effort. Later in the year he would try again but with a different central character.

3

There are eleven manuscript items which pertain to *Septimius Felton*. Of these, eight are preliminary studies which Hawthorne jotted on any loose paper which was at hand. They are reproduced below, "A" through "H," not necessarily in the order in which they were written (since actual dates of composition are impossible to determine), but in the sequence which may closely approximate their chronology and in the order which best illustrates Hawthorne's craftsmanship from the first hesitant steps to the final writing. Following these eight studies is the one completed manuscript, labeled Draft "I," which Hawthorne composed some time in 1862. Then, dissatisfied with his tale as he had written it, Hawthorne retraced his steps in a scenario "J," a thorough summary of his narrative in fifteen clearly outlined scenes, with supplementary notes and memoranda at the end. The last item is another draft, "K," on which Hawthorne labored valiantly from the latter part of 1862 until the early months of 1863 and which he then abandoned in its unfinished state.

These studies and drafts were found among Hawthorne's papers some time after his death. In 1868, Mrs. Hawthorne took them to Germany and began a transcription of Draft "I" for a subsequent publication.[2] The difficult handwriting of the manuscript—far more difficult than the chirography of the notebooks which she had already

2. *Hawthorne and His Wife*, II, 372; *Septimius Felton*, p. 221.

submitted to the press—prevented her from finishing the transcription before her death in 1871. In that year Una Hawthorne undertook the task and, with the assistance of Robert Browning, completed her edition of *Septimius Felton*, which was issued serially in the *Atlantic Monthly* from January through August, 1872, and published in book form in July of that same year.[3]

Miss Hawthorne was wise in her choice of drafts for publication. Of the two, "I" was complete and brought the tale of Septimius to a conclusion; the handwriting was easier to decipher than that of "K"; there were fewer excisions, marginal notes, and hasty improvisations with the plot. Una Hawthorne was also a conscientious editor: the draft she elected to publish she edited with taste and, for the most part, exactness.[4]

These eight preliminary studies may, for the purpose of watching Hawthorne generate his story, be divided into three groups. Group One includes Studies "A" and "B" in which Hawthorne first projects his chief character, a young man living about the time of the American Revolution who thought he might be able to discover the secret of living forever. Temporarily assigning the name "Septimius Flint" to this dabbler in occult science, Hawthorne then gathers about him a few representatives of the conventional attitude toward death; first, there is a brother "Jarius," whom Hawthorne soon abondons in favor of a New England farmer and a minister of Concord; then he briefly sketches a pretty girl, temporarily called "Alice," who may effect a struggle in Septimius' mind over his desire to live eternally; and finally he introduces some neighbors, Cyrus Maine and his wife, who will likewise typify the differences between the life of Septimius and that of ordinary men and women.

STUDY A

[1] It is strange how these familiar places are haunted. We think that it is only by old memories, but my belief is that it is by ghosts of those who once dwelt here, and whose spirits took such hold of the spots, the dwellings, that they cannot easily be disjoined with them, when they would fain be so. I could almost swear, for instance, that there is such a haunting spirit gliding about, sitting at my fireside, peeping through the twilight windows, shrinking into dusky corners

3. The first English edition was published on July 1 (*Publishers' Circular*, July 1, 1872, p. 421), the first American edition on July 25 (*The Publishers' Weekly*, II, July 25, 1872, p. 86).

4. I say that Miss Hawthorne edited the draft with some degree of "exactness." She did omit some of the intercalary notes, a few of which I cite in this chapter, and she did some amount of improving of her father's style. In the Berg Collection of the New York Public Library is Browning's brief reply to Una Hawthorne in which he disclaims any great share in the editing of *Septimius Felton*.

of the house where I have taken up my abode. If a man ever lingered about the house of his earthly abode, this man might be expected to do so, from the strong hold which he took of this house, this hill side, during his life-time.

Thoreau first told me about this predecessor of mine; though, I think he knew nothing of his character and history, nor anything but this singular fact, that here in this simple old house, at the foot of the hill, and so close to the Lexington road that I call it the Wayside, (partly for that, and partly because I never feel as if I were more permanently located than the traveller who sits down to rest by the road which he is plodding along) here dwelt, in some long past time, this man who was resolved never to die. He, at all events, did not mean to make of his earthly abode a mere wayside seat, where he would sit while the sun threw his shadow a little further on the soil; he would sit here while roses grew up and decayed; he would always be here.

This was all that Thoreau communicated; and that was many years ago, when I first came to live at the old cottage, which Alcott had relinquished, after terracing the hillside, and building fragile summer houses, and giving it beauty, as if his genius had a recipe to change common scenes into rare ones.[5] I staid here but a little while;[6] but often times, afar off, this singular idea occurred to me, in foreign lands, when my thoughts returned to this place which seemed to be the point by which I was attached to my native land. It gave me a strange interest in this spot; and according to my custom, I mused and meditated, and thought within myself, and tried to make out what manner of man this might be, that deemed it within his power to subvert the usual conditions of humanity. How did he mean to do it? Had he discovered, as he might suppose, the great secret which philosophers used to seek for? Did he think himself born with a frame unlike that of other mortals?

[2] Much time has now passed; and the contemporaries of Septimius were beginning to show a little the wear of life. Shrunken, dried, they were becoming, after the manner of New England men, when they begin to grow old—as if they had lain out drying through a succession of hot summer sunshines, as if they had stood up facing easterly winds and gales, beating right into their faces for years and

5. G. W. Curtis described Alcott's improvements of the "Hillside": "When Alcott came into possession in 1845 it was a miserable little house of two peaked gables; but his tasteful fingers touched it with picturesque grace. It lies at the foot of a wooded hill, a neat house of a rusty olive hue, with a porch in front, and a central peak; a piazza at each end. Upon the hill behind he built terraces and arbors, and pavilions, of boughs and rough stems of trees. Fine locust trees shade them, and ornament the hill with perennial beauty." F. B. Sanborn, *Bronson Alcott* (Cedar Rapids, Iowa, 1908), p. 78.
6. The Hawthornes lived in the Wayside from June, 1852, until July, 1853.

years together. Anxious, struggling, the struggle had wrought itself into their manner of being. They were accustomed to look at Septimius, and tell him, "You wear well; you have not grown older these ten years!"—and so, indeed, it seemed. Seemed, on a casual notice; but if you looked closer at Septimius, you began to doubt whether he was really younger than his contemporaries. There was a singular wrinkle, or fold, that had established itself between his eyebrows, strong, stern, and it gave him the expression as if he were holding on with a fierce grip, and as if, should he let go his hold, his very life might be the sacrifice. This look, when you once observed it, went far towards counteracting all the effect of his youthful appearance. It was as if age lurked in those stern folds, and if he should once allow his brow to unfold itself, forthwith age would spread itself over his features. But, it never happened; there was this mark, through toil, through pleasure, through sleep itself; there was good evidence; for once, Septimius had fallen asleep in the house, beside his field, and there was this stern restraint upon his brow, unrelaxed just as if he were already awake. There it was, too, on the day of rest, when he sat in his pew at the meeting-house, looking up into the pastor's face, scowling back upon him the kindly or awful words that he addressed to the congregation, with a cold indifference, as if they were nothing to him. It was probably much in consequence of this air of indifference, that a rumor got abroad that Septimius Flint was an infidel.

It might have been so; but more probably not. He had merely taken himself out of the category of the rest of the human race. He might not question that the Bible, its promises, its threats, were true for the rest of mankind; with him they had nothing to do. His lot was not with theirs. It was with the rich, beautiful earth where they all dwelt, in which they would lie, but never he.

[3] "Septimius, Septimius, where are you going from us? What is taking you away from us? Is it true, then, that we have never belonged to one another?" and Septimius shook his head, as not knowing whether it were true or no. For, certainly, something there was, that daily and continuously separated him more and more from his kind, from father, from mother, from minister, from men, from women, from Alice, from all—flinging him back upon himself; so that he lugged himself along with weary shoulders; whereas always there had been a hitherto unestimated portion of himself borne on the kindly shoulders of his fellow-men. Oh, this weary weight! was it never to be got rid of? "Perhaps not," quoth Septimius somewhat hopefully, "But I shall get used to it,—there will be time enough." And at that thought, he laughed in the kitchen where he was sitting alone—and went out laughing, laughing still as he climbed the hill. So here now were these two brothers, living in their little inheritance,

and agreeing so ill, and loving so well:—one content to share with his fellow men whatever came to them—the other aiming at something removed from them, unexampled; and yet pretending to seek it in no remote way, but only to take this birthright which any other might have as well, if the force were in him to claim it and make it good. Jarius was his only confident [*sic*], the free, joyous fellow, the love of men and maidens. "Oh, Septimius," said he, "don't you see how you are losing all this youthful time of life, by your projects for prolonging it[?] This is not worth while, at all events; for life stretches out ever so far, youth cannot come back again. You will have but one youth— not renewable. Take hold now and enjoy it. Don't you see you are giving up the good of life[?] You are turning it into a thing of stone, without the price of growth; for all that is dependent upon change, the coming of decay, which is sweet to its place." "There is something in what you say," quoth Septimius. "Then will not you give up this mad notion?" said Jarius. "Not a bit," coolly returned his brother. "I tell you I have made my choice so firmly that it is impossible for me to change it. My will is petrified, and is no longer in my own power." "Then, Septimius," quoth his brother, "you are a mad man, and should be confined.["]

[4] Septimius, as he felt that he was forcing himself from all other ties—taking a lonely lot—yet clung the closer to this brother who so much differed from him; he could not bear to leave him behind. Therefore, though this pull of their different dispositions had removed them to a little greater distance from one another, still the cord was not broken. Septimius felt it the more sensibly for the tug, the strain, the painful pull, because their mutual life lived so vividly along that cord. He felt as if, should that be broken, there would be nothing to keep him human; he should go off into unknown infinite space, that moment. Oh, why would Jarius persist in keeping himself down to that horrid death, that cold, heavy, leaden, solid phantom! But sometimes, on the other hand, Septimius had a perception that it was death, after all, that gave the warmth to life—that kept the sap running, which would otherwise petrify; kept things green and vegetable, which else were stone; it was what made sentiment high and holy; the dark shadow that brought into high relief the beautiful things of this life; this promise of better; without it, how hard and prosaic. Such were the representations which the young clergyman made to his brother; and their earnestness showed how much the stern emphasis and faith in himself of Septimius had done towards convincing him that his brother had really this power of self-continuance which he claimed. In fact, whenever they talked together on this subject, Jarius usually did believe it; he argued against his brother's determination in the full belief that unless his

argument were potent and prevailed, the unfortunate Septimius would really make his awful choice to be earthly immortal; and the choice once made, every succeeding hour would produce such baleful changes, that there would be continually less and less chance of his being redeemed. I think the brothers never loved each other so much, as at that time of direst difference between them.

Jarius, however, had something to keep his thoughts from dwelling too continually upon his brother. In the next house to the Wayside, as I have said, a little further along towards the village, between the hill and the Lexington road, dwelt Cyrus Maine, his wife, and one young daughter, a pretty, rustic belle, with the somewhat petite appearing frame that our women were already getting; but which, often is capable of exertion and endurance greater than those who have more flesh to bear.

STUDY B

[1] Begin with a reference to a certain room in my house, which I hint to be haunted; or to be remarkable or interesting to me for certain occult reasons.—Leave the matter thus, for the present, and diverge to a description of the hill and ground generally, the distant village where the clock is heard to strike, the Academy bell to ring, &c.—give an idea of the quiet of the place—mention Alcott, &c & Mr. Bull with his grapes; refer to the battle long ago, how the feet of soldiers trod over the hill.

Then come to the annals of the house, and introduce Thoreau's legend of the man who would not die. Make the impressions about the room, or chamber, more striking, and begin to connect this legend with this particular locality of the house. In the process of making repairs and additions to the old house, I may fable that a manuscript was found, containing records of this man, and allusions to his purpose to live forever. It might be a journal, extending over a long series of years. This would help me out, as regards Thoreau's legend, and also seem to account, or further parabal [sic], for some of the strange phenomena of the east-room. Terribly stained and almost illegible shall this old record be, only decypherable here and there. I shall also have stories about him from old people, some of whom may have personally known him, and recognized certain queernesses. [2] The records introduce him as longing for an immortality on earth, and as convinced that he is to have it. He shall perhaps have strong affinities for earth, a love of the soil, of this particular spot, of the house which he himself has built on it; of eatables and drinkables—taking strongly hold of earth. He gets into a delusion—which shall likewise be communicated to the reader—that he can and will live forever. It shall appear as if he had given up all his spiritual life for this eternity of earth. He shall be a very narrow man, but of great strength of purpose; he shall keep himself young and vigorous by the force of his will, his determination, his faith that he can resist death. So his hair shall be dark, his limbs vigorous, longer than usual; but a settled frown of a determined purpose shall gather on his brow. He shall grow apart from the world, hard, selfish, isolated, estranged from his nearest and dearest. Perhaps he shall lose the first love of his youth for this passion; the woman for whom he built his house—the building of which shall be described, and how he thought it would be but like a hut of boughs, so transitory as compared with his long duration. All these anticipations shall be mixed up with the trivial details of a husbandman's daily life. He shall discover that any engagement of the affections draws off his mind from its intentness, and makes him grow progressively older; so he gives up all that, for he is determined to live.

4

The second group, consisting of Studies "C" and "D," forms a closely knit unit in that it shows Hawthorne preparing for some action in his story. Hitherto, he has been concerned only with the cast of characters and with their symbolic meanings. Now he steps from the shadows, throws out the wrinkles and folds in the forehead, and fashions a few narrative incidents which will make his tale move. Study "C," written on both sides of a small leaf of notepaper, introduces the duel which Septimius will have with the British officer, the death of that young man, and the mysterious papers which Septimius will find in his pocket. Study "D," likewise written on both sides of a single sheet of notepaper, makes a tentative outline of the story to the end of the second chapter. With these two sketches, Hawthorne has moved into the real business of getting his narrative on its way from the first alarms of April, 1775, to the unhappy effect which the grave of the young Englishman will have on Septimius' life.

STUDY C

[1] Septimius has a share of some kind in the fight of Lexington; he shoots a man, and brings him into his house, and views the corpse, and is affected with strange remorse at it. It seems not fair for him, a deathless one, thus to give death to another. His horror of death must be expressed over this corpse, and all the shuddering and shrinking of his nature therefrom. He brings him into the room and lays the body down. Some few words pass between him and the corpse,

who perhaps shall be a young British officer, and shall say something mysterious and soul-stirring before he dies. In truth, perhaps the story might open here; and Septimius first conceives his notion of earthly immortality on this occasion. But I think not. At any rate, this interview with the dying soldier, whom he has shot, has an influence on all this story; and often his grave is referred to, for probably Septimius buries him on his own ground, claiming the corpse for his own, and saying nothing to anybody. A root springs out of this grave, as it were. Perhaps the young stranger gives him his own secret of immortality; which of course is good against natural death, by disease or old age, only. It cannot turn aside a bullet or ward off a sword. Perhaps the secret is contained in a written paper which Septimius finds on his body, or which the dying [2] man confesses to him. Septimius has been deeply thinking on this subject of death, already. The paper might be a recipe for immortality, which an uncle of the dying man, a recluse student and natural philosopher, had given him, but which the young man had despised, never believed it, or desired to profit by, from generous motives of sympathy, and English love of fair play. It falls in so with Septimius's previous state of mind, that it gets full possession of him. "You have given me death, I give you life!" Certain conditions are required by this recipe, the general tendency of which is, to contract a man within himself, estrange him from his fellows and all the earnest struggle of humanity, cut off the foliage of his affections &c. Perhaps the recipe shall be given in a letter to the young man from his uncle, written in a quaint style, with moral precepts, indicating egotism under the guise of a philosophy of restrained passions. The old gentleman himself had made some attempts towards immortalizing himself, but had failed partly by a love of wine and cheer. Septimius buries the body on his hill side, and with it all the property he finds on him, his purse, his silver-hilted sword, &c. all in his regimentals he buries him, and plants a tree over his grave; and keeps back nothing but the paper. After this epoch, a change is perceptible in Septimius's life, conduct, character; so great a one, that his position in society is changed by it. The minister [hopes] to see him worst it; having been his [sincere?] friend heretofore.

STUDY D

[1] Express strongly the idea that the shortness &c of life shows that human action is a humbug.[7]

The story opens, discovering Septimius a young man of some education—possibly a student of theology with the clergyman. A young girl, living next door, must also be brought soon into sight. Septimius

7. This sentence is written as a marginal note at the top of the page.

muses much on life and death, and is dissatisfied with death, on noble grounds, because it so breaks off and brings to naught all human effort; so as [to] make a man a laughing stock to whoever created him. Thus his sense of life and love of life must be strongly expressed in this first part of the story; the beautiful, young, vivacious girl being the medium of bringing out this characteristic. He, I suppose, is of a melancholic temperament, and therefore the fonder of life—the more horrified at death. He conceives the idea, from an instinctive sense, that he may possibly live forever. In this first chapter, the house, the hill, the village, must all be sketched more or less distinctly, and the time, at the commencement of the Revolution. There must be a conversation between the clergyman & Septimius; perhaps the story might open with one.

Next chapter; begins with the tumult of the April morning when the British marched to Concord. Everybody is astir, except Septimius, whose brooding spirit does not heartily share in any action; besides he is a theological student. As the troops pass by, there is a little scene between a young British officer and the girl; he steals or forces a kiss from her and Septimius interferes fiercely; but the order to march is given, and so they are separated for the time. Septimius remains at the house, [2] or on the hill, listening to the sounds and signs of the morning—the reports of musketry &c. By and by, come the troops in retreat; and Septimius again meets the gay young officer; a rencounter ensues, and Septimius shoots him;—the troops and the Americans meanwhile passing on, leaving Septimius, who supports the dying officer into his cottage. A scene ensues, in which the young man and he become friends, though of such different characters. The Briton dies, after giving Septimius the letter of the old philosopher, his uncle. Septimius, for some reason, to be sufficiently specified, buries the body on his hill; perhaps the young man desires it;—on the spot where he was shot. Possibly, too, the clergyman happens to come, and performs services over his grave, and has another talk with Septimius, who does not mention the secret of immortality. Here Septimius's state of mind on the idea that he has the means of living forever. The composition of the recipe; it is partly moral, partly material.

His figure must not stand alone in the story; perhaps his beloved may be still alive; a woman of very decrepit age; or, at least, something living to link the imagination more closely with him, after all these strange attributes shall have been imparted to the reader's idea of him. She may have been a child when he lived; but still there might be some testimony she would give that would add to the weirdness of this.[8]

8. This paragraph was written upside down at the bottom of p. 2 of the study.

5

The third group of sketches, "E," "F," "G," and "H," all written on loose sheets of notepaper, add no new action nor do they project any fresh scenes into the tale. The characters begin to assume a little more form than they had in the preceding studies. Septimius' Aunt Keziah (although she is several times named "Aunt Nashoba") begins to acquire that witch-like aspect which marks her way through the final drafts; Dr. Portsoaken, the evil eye of the story, finds his place, and Sybil Dacy, the strange English girl who takes Septimius' affections away from Rose, enters the story as the mistress of the young English officer. But Hawthorne is careless of names and relationships and these characters have a way of fading from view when the reader is just beginning to see them formed.

STUDY E

[1] The clergyman is the more terribly earnest in his religion, because he is conscious of the devil in his blood.

Traditions of the temptation—the Divine used to have to go into the Forest and meet the Devil, and his wizard ancestor, and how his whole life was a struggle thereby, and his death troubled.

The secret of the elixir of immortality is said to be in the family, in a fragmentary way; but there is something missing, & persons have since tried to put it together, but in vain.

[2] The person, who had contrived this crime, was in love with the girl, and also heir presumptive of the estate; and so he was acting through jealousy, and also from cupidity, and meant to be the death of them both. The alchymist bids her drink first, which she does; but when he lifts it to his own lips, he grows pale, finding that by the smell that the poisonous flower has been distilled into it, instead of the other. Perhaps, the heir is his dearest friend, and assists him in his process.

The younger member of the family succeeds to the estate; but his descendants die after a generation or two; and thus there is a disputed succession. Some important documents are missing, that should prove the claim, and also entitle the representative of the name to an ancient baronial title long in abeyance. The estate goes into chancery, where it is at the present day, waiting for the true heir to come.

Sybil's story must not refer to the alchymist having migrated to America; this the reader is to infer from Aunt K[eziah]'s story. Perhaps Septimius may make that inference, and follow it out in his thoughts, but without speaking of it to Sybil.

Aunt K has some strange story about a bloody footstep's being seen round the door of the wigwam. The sufferer must have been his brother.

The drink is fabled always to bring fatal and accursed consequences with it; however fine the motives of those who manufacture it.

There has always been a tradition in England, that the missing heir went to America, and that the family is still extant there; or that, at least, the documents necessary to prove the claim to the estate and title are there, or may be there. So Doctor Portsoaken, a quackish adventurer, has been sent over by the claimant, to possess himself if he can of the papers in the possession of the young officer;—that might be the main purpose. He discovers this American claim, to his own surprise, and seeks to get hold of the iron box, and is at least willing that Septimius should poison himself. When he at first comes to Concord, it is with the purpose of getting hold of the papers left by the young officer, he having no suspicion of any others; but what he hears from Aunt K. & Septimius, convinces him that these are the true heirs. Sybil had been used by him to get the papers from the young officer, but she fell in love with him and was seduced.

Of course, the Doctor contributes all he can to the mystification of Septimius.

Aunt Nashoba mixes some strong, intoxicating herb with the tobacco she smokes.

[3] As regards the inheritance:—The ancestor of Septimius had left England, on account of some dark domestic tragedy, before the Pilgrims came; perhaps ten or twenty years before. He throws off civilized uses, and betakes himself to the wilderness, where he becomes chief of a tribe of Indians, a great medicine man, or prophet and priest; and when the Puritans come, they find him in this position, and consider him a wizard. Possibly they slay him. He leaves a son, whom they adopt and bring up in the Christian faith, though many think his father was the Devil himself. The son lives and dies among the Puritans, a respectable person enough, though with some wild traits; he transmits to his posterity some heirlooms, singularly preserved among them, the goblet, and the iron-bound box; and also traditions of his father's home in England, of the bloody footstep, of the family being entitled to rank and wealth; and these come down, mingled with wilder legends. In the next generation, the grandson of the old wizard is a clergyman, eloquent, dark, mighty, a son of thunder; with something of the devil in him still. He marries a beautiful and tender maiden, who softens the race a little. Then there are two generations of husbandmen, in whom the the [sic] talent of the race, and their dark characteristics seem dormant; to awake again in Sep-

timius. His mother, after his father's death, had married a second time, and had a daughter Rose, who was free from the morbid taint of all the rest.

The place where Septimius now lives was that where his ancestor, the wizard, had his wigwam; and there, perhaps, he finds a spear or arrow-head, which may have been his. It was on that hill-top, over-looking the wide scene of meadow land; and his ghost might be some-times fancied as meeting Septimius there. Bloody footstep.

The Puritan Divine has great share in Septimius's speculative turn, his gloomy, soberly enthusiastic characteristics; all his ancestry is represented in him.

Aunt Keziah's story embodies these traditions made as wild as pos-sible. The bloody footstep is seen on the fresh leaves.

In England, it was an old family, long occupying an ancient Hall, on the model of Smithells. In the reign of Elizabeth or James (leave it uncertain which) there was an ancestor who partook in the great intellectual movement of the time, and became a philosopher, as Bacon did. Many alchemists lived in those days, and searchers for immortality; he was thought to have discovered secrets beyond hu-man nature. He is jealous of his wife, or his mistress, and tries some magic out upon her, or poisons her. It is said that he possessed the secret of immortality and of poison; and that once a mistress of his drank of one by mistake for the other, wishing to share his immortal-ity, and so died; or perhaps he tried the experiment on her, and killed her, having mistaken one kind of flower for another. A brother of his, who likewise loved the girl, had caused this catastrophe by wilfully changing the flowers; the wizard slays him on the threshold, and takes flight, stepping in his blood. Thus comes the bloody footstep, by which he was tracked everywhere, and even to the last verge of Eng-lish ground. She is admired for her golden hair; and long afterwards, an ancient chest being opened, it was found full of golden hair, to which this maiden had turned.

STUDY F

[1] The old man and Septimius discourse about the recipe and other matters; & Septimius asks him whether he has ever drunk it himself?—and why not?—to which the old man makes some mys-terious response. Septimius, at this latest stage, falls into a vein of reflection (and perhaps addresses it to the old man) on the benign influence of the usual course of time, in its action on the human be-ing, on age, on death. The greatness of old age, how it softens hard and weary manhood, making it our nature and happiness to be af-fectionately helped, taking down our pride; the sweet prospect of

rest before us; the doing away of all that is hard and bad; the putting all action on a higher plane. So a sweeter, lovelier flower springs out of our death and decay, than we can nowise produce from our richness and vigor. The dreariness of the prospect of living forever amid these small and mean necessities of life—feeding, getting up, going to bed, dressing ourselves in an interminable series;—seeing this wretched old skin live forever; especially when, as in Septimius's case, the highest and tenderest interests would be sublimated from it. Were he to marry, [2] his wife would be but a concubine, because she would soon be divorced from him forever by death; his children mere playthings of a moment. And then he begins to feel that his own choice has confined him eternally in a wretched prison house, dark, so that you cannot see whither you are going, sordid, grimy, when, on the other side of the low door, is bright sunshine, and all sweet and noble things. He remembered the sweet and triumphant expression that he had seen on the countenance of the young officer after his death; it was his joy at seeing the glories of the other world, through the open door—opened for his admittance. From all, the cold, bright liquid, which he has been so long brewing, and preparing himself to drink, is to debar him.

The old man sits by, and watches this struggle. But how is it to terminate; that is to be left to further development.

By and by, the toil of preparation for availing one's self of this recipe, besides the concoction of the recipe itself, is such that not one in a million would undergo it. It may be, too, that Septimius had quite broken down his constitution by study, vigil, poisonous fumes, &c &c &c; so [3] that, so far from seeming likely to live forever, he would appear to need instant medical advice to enable him to last even a little while longer. His deathly appearance, in the eyes of outward observers, to be contrasted with his prospects of illimitable life, in his own idea.

Perhaps the curtain shall drop on this conflict within himself, and rise the next morning. The friend and his wife shall come into the cottage, sent there by the old man, and shall discover Septimius dead in his chair; the fragments of a broken vase; a strange perfume in the room.

The old man shall have disclosed himself in the last scene; and boast of his revenge for his slaughtered nephew, whether Septimius shall choose to live or die. In one case, only lengthened misery; in the other, untimely death, without having lived, or done anything good in the world.

Septimius felt that the drinking of this potion would sever him from the whole human race—would make him cease to be a man, in fact.

It may be, that Septimius becomes curious to use up some other human being in the process of preparing himself for earthly immortality. He at first fixes on the girl of his first love, but afterwards takes [4] another female, who turns out to have been the paramour or beloved of the young officer; she must be introduced very impressively. She might have dwelt either in Boston or in old England.

The diamonds, emeralds, rubies &c. seen on the surface of the snow, in the early morning sunshine.

Warwick—Redfern—Old Curiosity Shop.[9]

STUDY G

[1] Perhaps the young man had some personal defect that made him earnestly desirous that he should be buried without being undressed; and therefore he makes this request of Septimius. And perhaps afterwards, in the story, it comes out what this defect was.

Septimius has a wild genealogy, being descended from an old witch on one side, who was said to have had connections with the devil; on the other from an Indian prophet and powwow. This mixture of bloods had given him a strange and exceptional nature; and he had brooded upon the legends that clung around his line, following his ancestry, not only to the English universities, but into the wild forest, and into hell itself. The mixed race had probably made him morbid, in reality, besides giving his dark imagination this unwonted scope & lawlessness. [2] His mind and character had a savage and fiendish strain, intermixed with its Puritan characteristics; so that he was particularly liable to unbridled thoughts.

By shooting this young man, Septimius has influenced the fortunes of an old family in England.

When he goes to see the old Doctor, he recognizes something that he buried with the young man.

Rose is a schoolmistress of a district school, and so may have a decent degree of cultivation.

It shall be observed that the requisitions of the scheme for prolonging life deprive a man of the glow and gush of life, of generous impulses, of youth, and all that makes life desirable.

Septimius thinks that he shall live to see the glory and the final event of the American Republic, which his contemporaries, perishing people, are fighting to establish.

STUDY H

[1] These preliminary incidents having taken place, Septimius remains with his recipe for immortality. It is a very abstruse matter,

9. These few words were written upside down at the bottom of p. 4 of the study.

requiring great study to comprehend it, and after all appearing to be partly incomprehensible. There are various ingredients of a recipe, some of which can be found, others are unknown to Septimius; these lead him to chemical and botannical studies, in which he abstrusely employs himself; he finally becomes sure of all the ingredients except one, which he takes to be rarest on earth. The conditions of the recipe require, too, a great moral circumspectness, and government of the passions, a restraint, a suppression over the food; all of which Septimius endeavors to practice, and so gets his whole way of life within rule. The effect is perceptible to everybody who comes in contact with him. Through it all, however, there is nothing spiritual, nothing affectionate. He is thus gradually estranged from the girl, between whom and him, there has never been any declared love, but only the possibility of such development; he now sometimes gazes at her as from another sphere, sadly, perhaps wishing that he could get into her, but feeling the impossibility. She possibly falls in love with another man, yet not without a sighing instinct that she might have better loved Septimius.—These things, on his side and hers, may perhaps be developed in an interview. The clergyman has also an interview, and [2] is astonished at the improvements, the deterioration, the changes, that he finds in Septimius; now whatever was best in him seems blighted, at the same time that his intellect has acquired wonderful force and expression. The old man is not revealed till the end.[1]

Years pass; the war is over; and Septimius is still pursuing his studies, which by this time have led him to a profound depth, though, at the same time, so estranging him from the world that nobody is aware [to] what eminence he has attained. One day, there comes along a coach, or it might be a man on horseback, or else on foot, a stranger, an old man, inquiring for Septimius, and finding his way to his door, where he enters with a certain freedom and establishes himself in the house and study. He is a coarse, unprepossessing old man, but with a certain grandeur about him, and state; a roughness, which yet is anything but boorishness. He looks at Septimius with a scarcely concealed hatred, yet engages in discussion with him. For the first time in his life, Septimius feels that he has met a man who understands his object; he is terrified at the idea, but still will not let go of the man. He receives him as a guest; they converse together. The old man shows his knowledge of Septimius's recipe, and points out the wanting ingredient, growing abundantly on his own ground. The conversation sometimes [2] turns on the war, and the old man seems

1. This last sentence was written as an interlinear note.
2. Hawthorne wrote "some" over "often" and failed to decide which one he would use.

interested in the sword and watch of the slain officer, which Sep-[timius] [3] has hanging up in his study. At last, it turns out that the old man is the very Uncle who gave the young officer the receipt of immortality. He has come for vengeance, doubtless, but this Septimius does not know; nor does he, till the old man's purposes are accomplished, suspect who he is. Neither should the reader more than suspect him.

The old man, having then instructed Septimius, goes away. Septimius remains, pursuing his studies, concentrating himself more and more within himself, acquiring a mighty force, but at the expense of whatever makes life beautiful, benevolent, holy; giving up the great aims for which he had desired earthly immortality, despising mankind, relinquishing love, friendship, brewing his secret which still requires great research and elaboration. There should be a friend introduced very early, who sticks by him long—a natural man, loving, hating, shunning none of the ties that connect him with his kind. He shall have had an early and secret affection for the girl, which he stifles and represses, because he saw that Septimius was inclined to fall in love with her. But, at last, seeing how Septimius has allowed this impulse to wither, he indulges it, and perhaps gives him notice that he shall press his suit. Sep-[timius] [4] is at first shocked at this, and has a glimpse of how lonely he has made himself—the fearful strait that he has arrived; but, at last, he gives her up, and becomes still more egotistic. His friend should have fought through the Revolution, and come back an officer; and the story must be relieved with his character and that of the girl throughout. His suit to her is successful, although she has some reminiscence of her early, virginal, tender feeling towards Septimius.

Thus things go on. The reader is made to see how all that is highest and holiest in this life depend on death and the expectation of it; how it immortalizes the love that, at first sight, it seems to blight and make a dream; how, without, man would be but an intellectual brute. At last, Septimius's recipe is fully concocted, ripened by the years that are necessary for that purpose; a beautiful, clear, golden liquid, with a strange perfume; but with an unearthly coldness; and he is prepared to drink it one evening. His friend, meanwhile, is married to the girl, and they are living at one of the neighboring houses. Perhaps he makes a festival, as the christening of his little son; or for thanksgiving; or some such thing; and invites Septimius, who (feeling that the drinking of his draught will separate him forever and finally from mankind) accepts the invitation, by way of taking leave of humanity. The old man, too, reappears on this occasion. Septimius has a reflux of the natural feelings of humanity, but returns to his house, bringing the old man with him.

6

Before we can trace Hawthorne's craftsmanship in this romance of immortality, we should pause to see how these jumbled notations and abortive plans were finally resolved into the narrative. For the purpose of facilitating the subsequent discussion, a summary of the plot of Draft "I" may well be in order at this time.

Septimius Felton, a young man who has completed his studies for the ministry at Harvard, lives with his old Aunt Keziah on the main road between Concord and Lexington. Not far away are Rose Garfield, a pretty schoolteacher with whom Septimius is in love, and Robert Hagburn, a lifelong friend who is Septimius' rival for Rose's hand.

One day in April, 1775, the three friends are discussing the advantages and difficulties of an indefinitely prolonged existence; Septimius expresses his conviction that one life is too short for the realization of any great achievement, while Rose and Robert uphold the normal view that death is the logical conclusion to any mortal life.

On the following morning a disheveled and wild-crying horseman rides through Concord to warn the villagers of the approach of the redcoats, who are marching from Boston to Concord to seize the military stores in the possession of the colonists. Shortly afterward a detachment of British cavalry enters the town and its commander, a handsome young officer, asks Rose for a drink of water and, in payment for her gracious favor, laughingly steals a kiss. Septimius is so angered by this affront that, abandoning his customary indifference to affairs outside his studious life, he rushes into his house, seizes an old flintlock which belonged to his ancestors, and climbs to the top of the hill behind his home to wait in ambush for the return of the invaders.

Soon the cavalry troop passes by his hiding place. The young officer, bringing up the rear, discovers Septimius and challenges him to stand and fight. Before Septimius is aware of what he is doing, he raises his gun at the proper signal, fires, and mortally wounds the officer, without suffering more than a scratch from his enemy's bullet. He rushes forward to receive from the dying Englishman, whose name is Cyril Norton, a mysterious packet and to hear that the slain man wishes to be buried where he fell. Septimius digs a grave for Norton on the hilltop and there he walks so regularly throughout the succeeding months that he wears a bare footpath along the crest.

Meanwhile, the Revolutionary War is going on. Robert Hagburn has enlisted and joined Arnold's campaign against Quebec; and Rose, in "the disturbed state of the country," accedes to Septimius' proposal of marriage and becomes engaged to him. In the second year of the war a strange English girl, Sybil Dacy,[3] comes from Boston to find a haven in Concord and to puzzle Septimius with her mysterious interest in the mound which marks young Norton's grave. She speaks weirdly of her kinship with the hillock and especially with a purple flower, the *sanguinea sanguinissima,* which appears overnight on the top of the grave. She further deepens the mystery by relating a long legend of the bloody footprint at Smithell's Hall and of a lost English heir who disappeared into the wilderness of New England before the arrival of the Puritans. Aunt Keziah seems to add a sequel to Sybil's tale by telling the tradition about Septimius' forefather, an Indian sagamore, who may have come from England and brought with him a magic potion for prolonging life. Shortly thereafter Sybil's uncle, an ugly physician named Dr. Portsoaken, visits Concord in order to ferret out some secrets in the young student's family and informs Septimius that he may be the heir of a noble English estate.

Then, quite without warning, Hawthorne suddenly revised his tale. Rose became the half sister of Septimius and Sybil took her place as the hero's sweetheart. Thereafter the plot moves to a swift conclusion. Septimius tries desperately to brew a magic elixir according to some mysterious instructions found among Norton's papers, but when he administers some of the potion to poor Aunt Keziah she dies in agony. Still convinced that he can perfect his elixir by distilling the purple flower on the officer's grave, he induces Sybil to drink and share immortality with him. On the night of Rose's marriage to Robert Hagburn, they chart their way through centuries of life on this earth and envision their plans for the betterment of society. Sybil's wild and whirling words do not, however, disturb Septimius, until the girl seizes the glass, swallows a large draught, and falls dying at Septimius' feet. The elixir which she drank gladly to save her lover is a fatal poison. Her passing is followed on the next day by the death of the wily Dr. Portsoaken, the evil genius behind all of these designs on Septimius; he is discovered with the hollow shell of his companion, a large spider, beside him. At the close of the novel Septimius is presumed to go to England and there claim an estate which had once been in the possession of his earliest ancestors.

7

It is obvious from the very first study that Thoreau's legend of the deathless man was to be the mainspring for the romance. Yet a backward glance into Hawthorne's earlier work often reveals how dependent he was on old ideas which, because of his ill success in treating

3. Throughout her edition Una Hawthorne spelled the girl's name as "Sibyl Dacy" but I have followed the spelling of the MS.

them, seemed to dare him to try his hand again; furthermore, we have seen how long he had pondered through a lifetime of meditation on the theme of the elixir of life. Thus a clue may be established which links *Septimius Felton* with the English romance of Dr. Grimshawe; in one of the last sections of Grimshawe "G," Etherege, having been drugged by Mr. Braithwaite and cast into an underground chamber, awakes to find a haggard and ghostly old man who had been long imprisoned there. In his stupor of semiconsciousness he tries to remember the numerous legends which he had heard about the house and especially "whether there might not be something of fact in the legend of the undying man."[4] There had been no preparation for this tradition in the English romance; the allusion is just one of many notations and asides which Hawthorne intended to expand in a revised draft. This deathless man never saw any more light than the dusky glimmers which filtered into his subterranean chamber, but when Hawthorne abandoned that draft he kept the reference in mind for the romance of immortality. Thus it would be perfectly natural that, sitting at his writing table facing the hill over which the British had retreated in 1775, he should transfer the whole imaginative fabric of the bloody footprint of Smithell's Hall, the hidden chest full of golden hair, and the silver key to his own land behind the Wayside.

And yet, despite this rather close bond between the two romances, the tale of Septimius Felton is, in one sense, a better story than that of the young American's search for ancestral wealth in England. The main reason is that for once Hawthorne freed himself of the heavy thralldom to the English notebooks. Page after page of the English journals found their way into *Doctor Grimshawe's Secret;* yet *Septimius Felton* both in Draft "I" and in Draft "K," is remarkably free of this reliance on actual scenes which Hawthorne had seen and on persons he had known. He may have realized that the romance of England had collapsed under the very weight of these borrowings and that he could never blend his own experiences, as he had partially succeeded in accomplishing in *The Marble Faun,* with the actions of characters in a romance.

Another notable deduction which we may draw by peering into Hawthorne's workshop is his failure to make any real use of his preparatory studies. The fact might well be argued that such a failure suggests a lack of practice in sketching. The studies had served him just as badly in the English romance; and the studies for *Septimius Felton* supplied him only with a cast of characters which he continually revised as he proceeded with his tale. The rest he must spin from his imagination.

4. "G," 65b; *Grimshawe*, p. 330. See also Anton Schönbach, "Beitrage sur Charakteristik Nathaniel Hawthorne's," *Englische Studien*, VII (1884), 267.

Hawthorne depended on the first scene, the first piece of narrative action, to get him well under way. The preliminary studies bear witness to his concern over that initial start. Not until he began Study "C" did he finally hit upon that central action which was so necessary to bring the secret springs of his imagination to the surface of his mind. In that sketch is the first intimation that Hawthorne intended to use the Revolutionary War as a background for his romance: "Septimius has a share of some kind in the fight of Lexington; he shoots a man." This notation called up several old memories which were woven into the narrative. The first was a story which Lowell told him and he had thought so well of it that he inserted it into the introductory chapter of *Mosses from an Old Manse:*

A youth . . . happened to be chopping wood, that April morning [in 1775], at the back door of the Manse, and when the noise of battle rang from side to side of the bridge he hastened across the intervening field to see what might be going forward. . . . The British had by this time retreated, the Americans were in pursuit; and the late scene of strife was thus deserted by both parties. Two soldiers lay on the ground—one was a corpse; but, as the young New Englander drew nigh, the other Briton raised himself painfully upon his hands and knees and gave a ghastly stare into his face. The boy . . . uplifted his axe and dealt the wounded soldier a fierce and fatal blow on the head.[5]

In planning his new romance in 1861, Hawthorne recalled this story and then began to wonder what had impelled the boy to commit such an act of barbarism; more especially did he ponder the "ghastly stare" on the British soldier's face. That "stare" sent Hawthorne's recollections back to a day in 1857 when an old Kentucky soldier, named Philip Richardson, called at the consulate to obtain passage back to the United States. Richardson was a garrulous old fellow and during one of his several visits to the consulate he related to Hawthorne an incident which had occurred in the Battle of New Orleans. During one of the British attacks against the American lines, Richardson shot an English officer and then, after the redcoats had retreated, he ran forward to collect a few trophies from the dead man's uniform. To Hawthorne the most important item was Richardson's description of the dead man's face. "The officer was a man about thirty-eight, tall and fine looking; his eyes were wide open, clear and bright, and were fixed full on Richardson, with a somewhat stern glance; but there was the sweetest and happiest smile over his face that could be conceived."[6] This entry in the English journal seems almost a fulfillment of a jotting in the American notebook for 1837. Two United States naval officers had a duel and when one was shot his countenance

5. *Mosses,* p. 18.
6. *English Notebooks,* p. 438.

". . . looked as if he were already in the infernal regions; but afterwards it assumed an angelic calmness and repose."[7] The link which joined the notebook entry for 1837 and Richardson's tale is found in Study "C" wherein Hawthorne is plotting the outcome of the duel between Septimius and the British officer: "Septimius . . . views the corpse, and is affected with strange remorse at it. . . . His horror of death must be expressed over this corpse, and all the shuddering and shrinking of his nature therefrom." The effect which young Norton's death has on Septimius goes directly to Richardson's narrative and to the American notebook of many years before.

What a change had come over it since, only a few moments ago, he [Septimius] looked at that death-contorted face. Now there was a high and sweet expression upon it, of great joy and surprise, and yet a quietude diffused throughout. . . . It was [as] if the youth were just at the gate of Heaven, which, swinging softly open, let the inconceivable glory of the blessed city shine upon his face, and kindle it up with gentle, undisturbing astonishment and pure joy.[8]

For this one scene Hawthorne used material which he had gathered over twenty years of his life. Lowell's story supplied the locale; the notebook entry of 1837 sowed the germinal seed; Richardson's recollection gave Hawthorne the touch he needed, the "stare" which seemed to reveal the blisses of the next world and the happy consummation of this one; and the brief memorandum in "C" became the intermediate link which brought these far-separated points together.

The legend of the bloody footprint was Hawthorne's chief levy on his own previous work. Despite its track through the various unfinished drafts of the English romance and despite Hawthorne's evident dissatisfaction with his numerous and tortured treatments of Mrs. Ainsworth's tale, he seems never to have given up hope that he might even imbed it in the romance of immortality. Sybil Dacy's story is almost identical with the accounts in *The Ancestral Footstep* and in Grimshawe "G." Long ago a crime had been committed at Smithell's Hall and an indelible bloody mark forever stained a flagstone at the old manor house.[9] The only variation is in the person of the criminal, Sir Forrester, who tried to brew an elixir of life according to some rules set forth by Friar Bacon and to accomplish this end he sacrificed the life of his beautiful young ward. In Aunt Keziah's sequel to this legend, Sir Forrester (if it were really he; Hawthorne intentionally leaves the identity "romantically" vague) fled to America and

7. *Passages from the American Notebooks*, p. 108. Cf. T. W. Higginson, "Hawthorne's Last Bequest," *Scribners Monthly*, v (November, 1872), 101.
8. "I," p. 18; *Septimius Felton*, p. 261.
9. "I," p. 53; *Septimius Felton*, p. 331.

established a new home among the Indians whom he eventually ruled so wisely and so eternally that the medicine men induced him to vanish into the wilderness.[1] Thus the two branches of the family, represented in 1775 by Cyril Norton and Septimius, had stemmed from the same progenitor long ago at Smithell's Hall; the formula for the elixir, like the mystery of the iron-bound box in Grimshawe "G," had been preserved both in England and in America. Were Septimius successful in bringing the two halves of the secret together after Norton's death he would be able not only to distill the magic potion of immortality but also to return to England and claim the estate.

The only addition to this old and tattered legend is the formula for the elixir. To thrust the tradition of Smithell's Hall into Septimius "I" required no leafing through the studies and drafts for Grimshawe. By the time of his latest writing, Hawthorne had so well practiced his hand that he could set down the familiar legend without glancing at his notes.

Another jotting in Study "C," later given some treatment in "E," is the purple everlasting flower which bloomed overnight on Norton's grave. Already the symbolism of flowers had been a favorite device with Hawthorne; in passing, one might mention that in The House of the Seven Gables Phoebe Pyncheon had cultivated "crimson-spotted flowers" in Aunt Hepzibah's garden.[2] And other flowers had frequently made their appearance, for adornment or for the revelation of the latest stage in the atonement of Hester Prynne in The Scarlet Letter.[3] Therefore, without necessarily foreseeing how important such a symbolism might become, Hawthorne noted in Study "C," "A root springs out of this grave . . . ;" later in "E" he moved the image of the flower back to the days of Elizabeth and James I and to the brewing of an elixir by Sir Forrester. An early hint of this idea had already appeared in the American notebook.

A girl's lover to be slain and buried in her flower-garden, and the earth levelled over him. That particular spot, which she happens to plant with some peculiar variety of flowers, produces them of admirable splendor, beauty, and perfume; and she delights, with an indescribable impulse, to wear them in her bosom, and scent her chamber with them. Thus the classic fantasy would be realised, of dead people transformed to flowers.[4]

Yet not until 1862 did this entry have any real bearing on Hawthorne's work; the memorandum in "C" and its slight development in "E" look back to a memorable experience in England.

While on an excursion to Eaton Hall in Cheshire, the Hawthornes

1. "I," p. 47; Septimius Felton, p. 318.
2. Seven Gables, p. 338.
3. Scarlet Letter, p. 122–3.
4. Passages from the American Notebooks, p. 39.

and George Bradford were wandering through the extensive green-houses on the estate. Suddenly, for no more apparent reason than a certain Old-World courtesy, a gardener presented Mrs. Hawthorne with "a purple everlasting-flower."[5] Like other undramatic incidents in Hawthorne's life, this visit to Eaton Hall had two important conse-quences: George Bradford, in the notebook entry for that day, be-came the prototype for the old pensioner in that romance of Eng-land;[6] and the strangely colored flower was transplanted from Chesh-ire to the hilltop behind the Wayside. Here was the symbol of endless life implicit in the very name of the flower: the everlasting flower (or *sanguinea sanguinissima*, as Hawthorne subsequently labeled it) would burst with a springtime dawn from Norton's hillock. Not only would it supply the missing—and poisonous—ingredient for Septim-ius' drink, but it would also strengthen the tenuous link between Concord and an old barony in England where identical flowers were presumed to grow. The fact that Hawthorne failed to make any con-vincing use of this second of two symbols only demonstrates his in-ability to unify his romance with these master symbols he had woven into his novels of another day.

The third symbol, the spider which typifies Dr. Portsoaken's evil designs, was taken directly from *Grimshawe*, where, in turn, it had been borrowed from the British Museum.[7] Dr. Portsoaken, like his predecessor, propounded the medicinal value of spiders' webs. " 'Every thread of a spider's web is worth more than a thread of gold, and, before twenty years are passed, a housemaid will be beaten to death with her own broomstick, if she disturbs one of these sacred animals.' "[8] Dr. Etherege ". . . was but a great fly which the spider had subtly entangled in his web."[9] Similarly, Dr. Portsoaken's spider looks ". . . like the symbol of a conjurer or crafty politician in the midst of the complexity of his scheme. . . . And could it be," Haw-thorne asks rhetorically with the remembrance of Dr. Etherege's trickeries in mind, "that poor Septimius was typified by the poor, fas-cinated fly, doomed to be entangled in the web?"[1] But unfortunately the symbolism was as stale in Septimius "I" as it had been in Grim-shawe "G," for in both drafts Hawthorne left only the hollow shell of the enormous spider to mark the end of both quackish adventurers.

Yet this is about as far as source hunting can go in the romance of immortality. From the preliminary studies, wherein he had sketched his main characters, the British march to Concord, the death of young

5. *English Notebooks*, p. 75.
6. *Idem*, pp. 75–6. See above, p. 49.
7. See above, p. 000.
8. "I," p. 40; *Septimius Felton*, p. 303.
9. "H," p. 4; *Grimshawe*, p. 10.
1. "I," p. 69; *Septimius Felton*, p. 365.

Norton, and the basic outlines of Septimius' pursuit of endless life, Hawthorne spun his whole tale through ninety-four pages of Draft "I." For the first few pages the narrative moves along quite well and then rises to an excellent scene, Septimius' duel with the British officer, which may stand favorable comparison with other incidents in his greater fiction. But from that moment Hawthorne's imagination lost its edge and his inventive powers, never very wide nor deep, began to be confused in a morass of symbols and unhappy improvisations with the plot.

8

Among the many glimpses into Hawthorne's workshop revealed in Draft "I," some of the most significant are the marginal notations, which point clearly to Hawthorne's ambitions to plant symbols in the romance. At the top of the first manuscript page is this jotting, "Septimius must have a weird, half supernatural genealogy, in which the devil is mixed up."[2] Again, when the troop of British cavalry is in retreat along the hilltop and just when Norton discovers Septimius in the pine trees, Hawthorne writes another terse reminder, "Septimius's fierce Indian blood stirs in him, and gives him bloody excitement."[3] The first note is partially fulfilled in Aunt Keziah's narrative on the Feltons' Indian ancestry[4] but otherwise the symbols of genealogy and blood are in no wise satisfactorily resolved. And unfortunate as it is for the story, Septimius feels no "bloody excitement" after he has shot the young officer; in fact, he displays a quite notable calm as he walks down the hill to his house, gets a shovel, and deliberately scoops a grave beneath the pines.

If the symbols of genealogy are not successfully developed, neither are the simple, day-to-day actions of Septimius himself. Hawthorne must so plant the properties in the wings of his drama that Septimius may walk casually into the Wayside and, like an actor in rehearsal, find the requisite "props" for his next walk-on. Again the first page of the draft shows the puppeteer's hand behind the curtain, "Septimius has a gun in the house," Hawthorne notes.[5] Thus, after Norton has unceremoniously kissed Rose, Septimius may rush into his home and find the old flintlock standing ready for him.

Throughout the draft there are further evidences of Hawthorne's reluctance to face certain rudiments of plotting. Such a notation as

2. "I," p. 1.
3. *Idem*, p. 14. Una Hawthorne revised this note and included it as a part of the text. *Septimius Felton*, p. 254.
4. "I," pp. 46–8; *Septimius Felton*, pp. 317–20.
5. "I," p. 1.

"He [Septimius] makes an arrangement to meet Rose the next day"[6] would suggest that the writer were back in the days of sketching his first novel, *Fanshawe;* although five pages later in Draft "I" Rose and her lover do have a meeting, it appears to have come about more by chance than by artistic design.[7] Two pages following this jotting occurs another notation which shows Hawthorne's hand tinkering with a minor detail of his story. He was trying to describe Aunt Keziah's last illness and he had so far written:

It so happened, about this time, that poor Aunt Keziah . . . was in a very bad state of health. She looked all of an unpleasant yellow, with bloodshot eyes; she complained terribly of her bowels, or inwards. She had an ugly rheumatic hitch in her motion from place to place, and was heard to mutter many wishes that she had a broomstick to fly about upon; she used to bind up her head with a dishclout, or what looked to be such, and would sit by her kitchen fire, even in the warm days, bent over it, crouching as if she wanted to take the whole fire into her poor cold heart or gizzard; groaning spitefully whenever she had to move, or sometimes regularly with each breath, a spiteful and resentful groan, as if she fought womanfully with her infirmities. . . .[8]

Hawthorne was not satisfied that he had fully detailed the appearance of the sick old woman; perhaps the description was lacking in the minute particulars of her clothing; whatever were the missing essentials, the passage must be so revised and sharpened that Aunt Keziah's death will have a profound effect on Septimius, for it is he who will cause her death by giving her a drink of his lethal elixir. Having written so far or a little farther, Hawthorne stopped and reread his paragraph. It was not right and he went back to the first available space in the margin to pen a memorandum, "Describe the old woman's dress and appearance minutely, as affected by illness."[9] In order to heighten still further her groans and complaints, he entered an interlinear note in the description at the point where he is detailing Aunt Keziah's "rheumatic hitch," "She blamed the cat, the old rheumatic cat, sleeping in the chimney-corner, or on its cushion."[1] A third jotting comes at the end of that same paragraph; Hawthorne does not know in what part of the house he will locate Aunt Keziah's last hours on earth and he anticipates his next step with "She gets up to breakfast, but goes to bed again."[2]

6. *Idem,* p. 28; *Septimius Felton,* p. 279.
7. "I," p. 33; *Septimius Felton,* p. 287.
8. "I," p. 59; *Septimius Felton,* p. 346.
9. "I," p. 59. This note would be in *Septimius Felton,* p. 346.
1. *Ibid.*
2. "I," p. 59. This note would be in *Septimius Felton,* p. 347. Rose Hawthorne Lathrop suggested that Aunt Keziah was modeled on Mrs. Peters, a Negro servant of the Hawthornes in Lenox. *Memories of Hawthorne,* p. 161. Cf. *American Notebooks,* pp. 214, 328.

Throughout the last ten pages of the draft these marginal jottings become more profuse as Hawthorne let Septimius and Sybil spin airy dreams of their eternal life together. None of these memoranda, to take a few examples, was resolved or developed in the final pages, but they demonstrate that Hawthorne was struggling to thicken the texture of his romance and point up the futility of seeking endless life: "He [Septimius] would see, in one age, the column raised in memory of some great deed of his, in a former one."[3] "The rampant unrestraint, which is the joy of wickedness."[4] "He would write a poem, or other great work, inappreciable at first, and live to see it famous—himself among his own posterity."[5] Not wishing to spend time over the wedding of two minor characters, Rose and Robert, Hawthorne cut rapidly across lots and briefly summarized a quite functional part of his narrative, "Rose asks Sybil to be her bridesmaid."[6] On the next page he realized that one sentence might not be a sufficient reminder, even for an extended treatment of the marriage in a revision. He then paused to expand the jotting and to add a short colloquy between the two girls:

It is to be observed that Rose had requested of her friend, Sybil Dacy, to act as one of her bridesmaids, of whom she had only the modest number of two; and the strange girl declined, saying that her intermeddling would bring ill-fortune to the marriage.

"Why do you talk such nonsense, Sybil?" asked Rose. "You love me, I am sure, and wish me well, and your smile, such as it is, will be the promise of prosperity; and I wish for it on my wedding."

"I am an ill-fate, a sinister demon, Rose; a thing that has sprung out of a grave; and you had better not entreat me to twine my poison tendrils round your destinies. You will repent it."

"Oh, hush, hush!" said Rose, putting her hand over her friend's mouth. "Naughty one, you can bless me, if you will; only you are wayward!"

"Bless you, then, dearest Rose; and all happiness on your marriage!"[7]

This passage Hawthorne placed in large parentheses to indicate, as was his custom, that he wished to expand it and give it a better place in the narrative. Once having foreshortened this section of plotting in a mere aside, he might then move rapidly forward to the climax of his story—the fatal drinking of the magic potion.

If these marginal jottings reveal Hawthorne's struggles to keep his

3. "I," p. 86; *Septimius Felton*, p. 409.
4. "I," p. 86; *Septimius Felton*, p. 409.
5. "I," p. 87; *Septimius Felton*, p. 412.
6. "I," p. 88. This note would be in *Septimius Felton*, p. 413.
7. "I," p. 89; *Septimius Felton*, pp. 416–17. This whole passage, part of which Una Hawthorne printed as narrative, is in the MS. actually a meditative aside and a brief working out of the plot.

narrative in line, there are still other notes which show how he constructed his characters as he moved through a fairly complete draft. From the first preliminary studies, both for *Grimshawe* and *Septimius,* he was quite indifferent to the names of his characters. In these sketches the first reference to a character is the generalized "young American," the "New England girl," "the defalcator of the Nicholas Biddle stamp," or the "quackish adventurer." The shape of a man's head, the particular gait of an old person, the fine gestures of a young woman, or an "old woman's dress and appearance"—all these were unimportant to Hawthorne; they would take care of themselves and, if they failed to shine forth in bright hues and memorable shapes, then all the better for a romance where shadows and light played behind veils of mist; the business of the romancer was to draw aside one misty cloak after another and let the reader see for himself.

In the romance of immortality the hands of the magician had lost their smooth touch and the winds of imagination blew the mists, not away, but into curious whirls and designs. Perhaps the initial fumblings were just as crude in *The Scarlet Letter* but we shall never know what names or forms Hester Prynne may have borne. From the one complete Draft "I," however, we may infer that Hawthorne was not so much enfeebled as he was following long and well-established customs in his workshop.

Septimius Felton, to take the most obvious example, suffered fewer transformations than did the other characters and yet from the outset he is the victim of his creator's bewildering indecision. Throughout the studies he consistently bears the name "Septimius," although he has the surname "Flint" for several pages of "A"; he is more consistent as a noble young man who is doomed in his search for an elixir of life. It must be presumed that Hawthorne had the name of this youth well in mind throughout Draft "I": the name "Septimius Felton" remains fairly regular. But toward the end of the draft Hawthorne anticipated that, as he planned to have Septimius go to England and inherit a noble estate, there must be more symbolic connections between the Old and the New Worlds than some suspicious documents locked in an iron-bound box. Therefore, shortly before the end of the draft, he tentatively assigned the name "Norton" to the youthful experimenter, the same name which the British officer had borne.[8] Yet such a shift brought him into immediate difficulties and the story showed decided signs of falling apart at the end. The ancestry of the Feltons had been too deeply fused into the tale; Hawthorne would be forced either to retrace his steps and rewrite the fanciful legends about Septimius' ancestor, the sagamore, or drop that significant identity of names on

8. "I," p. 82. In the published text this change occurs on p. 399.

both sides of the Atlantic. At the end of the story he chose the latter course and the young man is "Septimius Felton" at the final debacle of his hopes.[9]

Although Hawthorne sketched Septimius as a young idealist in the first studies, he grew tired of the absurd youth and began to heap satire on the poor fellow's head. In the writer's own mind a tension was created and Hawthorne was torn between a favorable and a ridiculous portrait. This tension brought the tale tumbling about his head.

The first hint of this collapse lies in a curious parallel between Septimius and Miss Delia Bacon—a parallel which Una Hawthorne chose to delete from her edition. There might be no better way to heap ridicule on Septimius than to compare him with the lady who had likewise played with ciphers and had published her delusion in six hundred pages of *The Philosophy of Shakespeare's Plays Solved*. When Septimius finally penetrated the secret in the papers he had stolen from Norton, "he thought an instant, and was convinced this was the full expression and outwriting of that crabbed little mystery; and that here was part of that secret writing for which, as my poor friend Miss Bacon discovered to her loss, the Age of Elizabeth was so famous and so dexterous."[1] In short, Septimius became a fool and justifiably suffered for his folly. And so likewise did Hawthorne suffer for his inability to square his main character with the story as he had originally intended it. In a revision that folly would be fully prepared for and eventually resolved, if that revision were ever written.

Rose Garfield underwent even more shifts than did her half brother. According to Hawthorne's general method of making a character first abstract and then specific, she is, in Study "A," merely "a pretty rustic belle." In "D" she assumes slightly more distinction as the "beautiful, young, vivacious girl" who lives next door to Septimius; in "E" she becomes Septimius' half sister Rose, because Hawthorne is beginning to fashion Sybil Dacy, who will fall in love with Septimius. In Draft "I" she might just as well have been called Phoebe Pyncheon of *The House of the Seven Gables*, for both girls are extremely competent in household duties and mistresses of local schools. In appearance they are nearly identical, down to the last freckle on their charming noses.[2]

It was not Rose's appearance but her place in the novel which Hawthorne had not adequately planned in the studies. Despite the sketch in "E" and her kinship to Septimius, the first page of the draft finds her "Rose Garfield" for whose favors both Septimius and Robert are rivals. But midway through the writing Hawthorne discovered to his amazement that Rose must be Septimius' sister in order to fit Sybil

9. "I," pp. 92–3. See *Septimius Felton*, pp. 424–8.
1. "I," p. 81; *Septimius Felton*, p. 397.
2. *Seven Gables*, pp. 99, 100, 103, and *Septimius Felton*, pp. 355, 231–2.

Dacy into the narrative. Yet he did not retrace his steps and make any preparation for this change; he merely let the name stand as "Garfield" and ignored the discrepancies which would be quite evident in the last part of the story. Thus, having once introduced Sybil, he proceeded to let Septimius fall in love with her and, like many another novelist who wishes at the end to dispose of unnecessary baggage, he married Rose off to Robert, just as Dickens might send a wedded couple to Australia. An additional reason was at hand for this rather hasty wedding: Rose and Robert offered not only an easy way through the dilemma but also a moral conclusion at the climax of the romance. While Septimius and Sybil drank off the potion of eternal life, the more commonplace Rose and Robert would be initiating their life together on a far more mundane, though certainly happier plane.

A subordinate person like Robert offers additional and amusing glimpses into Hawthorne's craft. Whether the first name "Robert Hagburn" was unsatisfactory or whether it was obviously ugly, we cannot say, but the young soldier of Arnold's forces shifted back and forth from "Hagburn" to "Garfield" to "Hagburn" again;[3] once he is even called "Roger Hagburn."[4] Little can be said of him beyond the fact that he stands as the typical man of action in contrast with Septimius, the man of study.

Hawthorne did not have the faintest idea what Sybil would be called. She begins as "Sybil," it is true, in Study "E" and we learn in "F" that she had been seduced by Norton. When Hawthorne began to write the final draft, either he had forgotten those few notes he had made, or he did not consult his studies to see how she was supposed to fit into the story. He had vaguely in mind a girl like Priscilla in *The Blithedale Romance*, a maiden wearing poor but attractive dresses whose sickly graces are enhanced by a pallid complexion and dark, melancholy eyes; or, like Zenobia in *Blithedale* and Hester in *The Scarlet Letter*, she has sinned in her love for a man and must suffer accordingly.[5]

Before she is introduced in "I," the story is nearly half told, the studies are far away in time, and Hawthorne pauses momentarily to sketch her over again, "Perhaps there might sometimes be something fantastically gay in the language & behavior of the girl."[6] So completely has Hawthorne lost his bearings that, when she is first named, she is hastily called "Alice Ford."[7] Next she is "Edith"[8] and on the

---

3. "I," pp. 2, 26, 49, 90. These shifts may be noted in *Septimius Felton*, pp. 232, 274, 322, 420.
4. "I," p. 78. See *Septimius Felton*, p. 389.
5. *Septimius Felton*, pp. 290–2, with *Blithedale*, pp. 350–1.
6. "I," p. 34; *Septimius Felton*, p. 290.
7. "I," p. 39; *Septimius Felton*, p. 302.
8. "I," p. 45; *Septimius Felton*, p. 314.

third occasion "Sybil Dacy,"[9] the name which Hawthorne may finally have remembered from the study. Yet he is still not satisfied with the girl herself nor with her name and she momentarily becomes "Sybil Dark,"[1] a ticket name to her murky history and to her mysterious hold over Septimius. At her death she is at last "Sybil Dacy."

Two final characters may be passed over briefly. Dr. Portsoaken is Drs. Etherege and Grimshawe brought back to feeble life. Cyril Norton, the boy soldier killed on the hilltop behind the Wayside, has no name throughout his ten-page traffic in the novel but, when his uncle Portsoaken comes to Concord, he suddenly acquires the ridiculous name of "Willie Rogers."[2] Several pages later in the draft Hawthorne was impelled to assign him a name commensurate with his heirdom in England; thereupon he becomes a member of the "D'Aubigne" family.[3] Not until the close of the romance did Hawthorne draw a few of his raveled threads together in a summary of his plot and call him "Cyril Norton."[4]

Not only was Hawthorne indifferent to his creatures of fancy and casual about their names, but he had them so dimly in mind when he began a novel that he improvised as he went along, revised their relationships one to another, and experimented with names to make them fit into a romance. No doubt, as it is for most novelists, a character's name made a great difference to Hawthorne. Once he struck a good name, he could see the man or woman, but if he could not hit off a satisfactory name, he went on with his writing and waited for chance to supply him with one. Dickens considered names so important that he always kept a notebook in his pocket to jot down a strange, amusing, or immediately revealing ticket name. In other words, he began with particulars, with the person reduced to small dimensions. But that was not Hawthorne's way; he peered through the other end of the binoculars to see the character first in the large and then gradually brought his view down close, until he could see the figure assuming dress, mannerisms, and distinction. He may have followed this method throughout his whole career: begin with a generalized character-type, group around him a few subsidiary figures, sketch a loose plan for the narrative, and then start writing and see what would come forth. If the first draft did not come off well, he would "try back again"—as he did in "K."

9. "I," p. 49; *Septimius Felton*, p. 322.
1. "I," p. 50; *Septimius Felton*, p. 324.
2. "I," p. 41; *Septimius Felton*, p. 306.
3. "I," p. 43; *Septimius Felton*, p. 310.
4. "I," p. 94; *Septimius Felton*, p. 429.

9

Before he began this second and revised draft, Hawthorne paused to write a Scenario "J" in fifteen clearly outlined scenes. He worked hard on this summary. The handwriting is evidence of thoughtful workmanship, not hasty improvisation; he was diligently charting his way in order to bring logic into the tale. When Hawthorne knew where he was going in the last years, his penmanship was concise and the sentences moved smoothly. When affairs were going badly, as they were in "I," he showed all the signs of uncomely craftsmanship by drawing lines through sentences and whole paragraphs, by entering curious hieroglyphic signs to mark shifts of whole passages, and by the thickening of marginal notes.

Yet this scenario was not a revision of the narrative. It introduced no new characters nor did it create any fresh incidents; it merely allowed Hawthorne to see what parts of his previous draft had not matched the design and to decide what was important and should be expanded. The only real change was in the final acknowledgment that Rose Garfield was Septimius' half sister, not his fiancée. Aunt Keziah became Aunt Nashoba toward the latter half of the scenario; perhaps the new name had more overtones of Indian and witch legends than had the previous one.

This four-page outline was written on the same linen bond paper which Hawthorne was using for his long drafts. Jottings and marginal notations are starred.

SCENARIO K[5]

[1] *(It was whispered that Aunt Nashoba brewed herself in the jug, to make her drink; so much did it look like her.) *(Dwell upon Aunt Nashoba's Indian love of the woods.)

First Scene:—Three young people sitting on the hill side on a cheerful & bright April morning. Their characters must be slightly developed. No; I think that Septimius must first be shown in a conversation with the minister, the afternoon previous; in which is developed this peculiar trait in Septimius, in desiring to live always on earth; his hereditary traits must be hinted at, or slightly sketched, to be brought out more strongly hereafter. Their talk is about Septimius's studying

5. My reasons for placing this scenario after Draft "I" are as follows: (1) Hawthorne resolved the relationship between Rose and Septimius and in this study made them half brother and half sister; it seems unlikely that, with this scenario behind him, he would have confused that relationship in "I"; (2) the handwriting of "I," while rather small for Hawthorne, is fairly legible; the handwriting of the last Draft "K" is very small and cramped. The scenario stands almost midway between the two manners of penmanship and, if anything, resembles "K" more than it does "I."

for the ministry, which has been an understood thing hitherto; but latterly he has relented, and has seemed more inclined for physics; he clings strongly to the earthly and material, yet in an intellectual way. The minister is somewhat dissatisfied, and alarmed at the state in which he finds him. This conversation takes place on the hill-top, and there is a glimpse of Robert Hagburn & Rose Garfield; a peaceful, Arcadian spectacle of two rural lovers. Allusions to the troubled state of public affairs. Aunt Keziah is seen.

Second Scene:—the next morning, after a night troubled by the preliminaries of Lexington battle, horses are galloping; muskets discharged, dreams troubled &c &c. Septimius, his sister, and Robert meet on the roadside, and talk together, and Aunt Keziah bursts forth upon them in a savage characteristic way. While they talk, a horseman, at full speed, ghastly with terror and excitement, dashes by. There must have been previous, half-jesting allusions to an ancestor of Septimius, a wizard, and another among the Indians; all predisposing him to wild speculative ideas. On the passage of the ghastly horseman, Robert rushes into his house, and snatches an old gun of his father's, used in the old French War, and goes to the village. Septimius, partly because he is studying for the ministry, and partly that he is merely speculative, remains behind; yet in a strange state of cold, quiet excitement. He hears the town bells, he sees the march of the British troops, and witnesses the treatment of Rose by the young British officer. Then he listens to the sounds from the village, the beat of drum, rattle of musketry &c. Finally, overcome by the warlike impulses of the moment, he takes an old gun, said to have belonged to his great-grandfather, and to have been bewitched, and goes up on the hill-top. I think here will be an opportunity to introduce more of Septimius's characteristic modes of thoughts, and wild aims, founded on the superstitious legends about his ancestors. Something, too, should [be] very early said, and decidedly, about the claims of the family to rank and wealth in England; this might come from the minister, in the first scene.

Third Scene:—Septimius meets and slays the young officer on the hill-top. The officer was a collateral relative of Septimius, and perhaps was a claimant of the estate of England; it being now in possession of a man not rightfully entitled to it. He is poor, having little except his commission in a cavalry regiment. He wishes to have the papers buried with him; so that they should not fall into this man's hands; also, perhaps, because he wishes this receipt for a deadly poison to be hid from men. He has been much persecuted and wronged by this man, and feels that he escapes a struggle in dying, which has lasted in his family for two or three generations. Perhaps he learns that his name is the same as that of his slayer, and therefore warns him of mischief, if he does not bury him & all that belongs to him—at least the papers. Aunt Keziah comes, & shows the strangeness of her nature, mixed with Christian characteristics; also, the minister, and they three are the funeral;—probably Rose, but I think not. He finds a silver key &c.

Fourth Scene:—Robert Hagburn, having fought through the day, is going to Cambridge to enlist, and there is a parting scene between him, Rose, and Septimius, who also feels some motives towards going, but gives up the idea, under pretense of his studies. After the parting, he shuts himself up in his study, and examines the papers. Here must be introduced, more fully, the ancestral traditions of the family, about wizard and powwow, and certain heirlooms must be alluded to; for instance the splendid old goblet used in certain sacraments; also an iron-bound box, once set with precious stones, now fallen out, that had not been seen for a great many years. The legend about the long-lived Indian must be dimly alluded to, to be brought out more fully by Aunt Keziah; also, Aunt Keziah's herb-drink, said to have been of witch brewage. All these things considered and long lamented, the reader will see the propriety in Septimius's giving a sort of credence to the idea of an immortal drink; also, the English alliance must be covertly insisted upon. Thus, he is prepared to be greatly bewitched by the young officer's old papers; and broods over them continually and unavailingly. Meanwhile, he has written to Boston to give an account of the event, as the young officer requested; and his request was made with some allusion to the circumstances of his claim to the estate, mysteriously couched.

Fifth Scene:—One day, during Septimius's much walking on the hill-top, he sees a pale young woman there, who seems attracted by the grave; indeed, she appears so suddenly, that he could almost have thought she springs up out of it. She looks at him, he thinks, in a care-less sort of way; but they enter into conversation, and her talk strangely chimes in with the tenor of his thoughts. On descending afterwards to the house, he learns [2] [from] Rose that this girl is living with Robert Hagburn's mother and grandmother; Robert, who is now with the army, having been commissioned by a high officer to find her a boarding-place; she being out of health and needing coun-try air. She is understood to be an English girl, whose protector has fallen in the war. She remains so long, that at last she becomes an ac-customed thing. Sometimes, in her conversation with Septimius, it shall appear as if she wanted to find out something about the dead man, or what was buried with him; for, probably, she is an agent of the person in England, and was employed as a spy upon the young officer, but fell in love with him and was seduced by him. Her rela-tive is Doctor Portsoaken, who has used her for various purposes of his; he being a quack, adventurer, humbug, astrologist, &c &c &c. Thus the winter passes, Septimius puzzling over his papers, and talking with the girl, who prepares the way for the appearance of Doctor Portsoaken by frequent allusions to him, his scientific knowledge &. so that Septimius almost expects to see a picturesque ancient magician.

Sixth Scene:[6]—After the seige of Boston is over, the Doctor appears in person, the queer moody old fellow already described. He is wicked, a humbug, yet partly believing in his humbuggery. He shows a desire to find out what was discovered in the grave, but Septimius, being of a secret nature, is careful not to declare it to him; yet from his covert inquiries, the Doctor suspects that he has found something. He chimes in with Septimius's thought, and half-believingly, talks of the possibility of deriving the secret of endless life, and how, hand in hand with this secret, are said to run that of deadly poison so that the ingredients of each are almost identically the same. The herb-drink of Aunt Keziah gives occasion and illustration to much of this talk. During his stay, or after it, Septimius is visited by a transitory idea that the grave has been opened; and this recurs to him afterwards, when he sees something, that was buried with the young officer, in the Doctor's study. The Doctor, during his visit, may discover that there is a new, and the rightful, claimant to the estate in the person of Septimius; and so, he is ready to see him concoct a poison, instead of the immortal drink, and forwards this mistake as much as he well can. He professes himself a believer in the virtues of the spider's web, and so prepares the reader to see his laboratory, by and by. He goes away, after private colloquies with Sybil, and inviting Septimius to come to Boston to see him. There must be a mixture of love and science with his villainy. The estate is in chancery; and the Doctor is to have half its value if he gets it for the claimant. Perhaps he writes a letter to the claimant in England, after he returns to Boston. *The ancestors of the family were greatly interested about death, as well as life, & sought easy modes of it.

Seventh Scene:—Septimius digs away at his manuscript, and begins to see glimmerings of light; he also holds colloquies with the girl, and gets into a sort of intimacy with her, fitful on her part; she being influenced by a remorseful feeling on her part, by Doctor Portsoaken's instigations likewise, to subtly impell him onward to concoct the deadly poison and drink it instead of the draught of immortality; and on the other hand, her own woman's nature is moved with pity for him, and perhaps she has a struggle not to love him; so that there may be very queer and picturesque phenomena in her behaviour towards him. His sister Rose instinctively shrinks from Sybil, and warns Sep-

6. With the "Sixth Scene" Hawthorne began to underline his headings.

timius against her. In this conversation, they may come to [a] discussion of the question of endless earthly life, Rose taking a tender woman's view of it. All through the book, Rose must peep, with sisterly sweetness. *Iron box, Aunt K keeps the secret so long that she dies, it untold.

Eighth Scene:—The flower grows out of the grave. This flower had figured in a legend told by Sybil, and also in one told by Aunt Keziah; and likewise Septimius found a reference to it in the recipe which he has puzzled out of the manuscript, but could not make out what earthly flower it was. It must be described with great elaboration. On some slight disorder of Aunt Keziah, he puts it into her herb-drink, and she dies in great torment. Sybil seems a good deal interested in this event, and behaves and talks so that Septimius is struck, but not made suspicious.

Ninth Scene:—By this time, Septimius has been much acted on, morally and intellectually, by his strange pursuit. A description given of him. He is estranged from everything but himself, his studies, and Sybil. Bethinking himself at some crisis, of Doctor Portsoaken's assertions, he makes a journey to Boston, and spends a day and night with him. Again the Doctor endeavors to ascertain what papers he possesses, either of his own or of the young officer's; he talks of his English ancestors, and hears that there [3] was formerly an iron-bound and ornamented box, one of the family heirlooms; there is a lock of golden hair, bright as ever, in this strong box; of which, perhaps, the secret has died with Aunt Keziah. Indeed, Aunt Keziah has treasured this up, and meant to tell the place of deposit at the last moment to Septimius; but defers it until she is unable to speak. The Doctor, on scientific grounds, as he pretends, expresses a great wish to have the contents of this box. Septimius determines to find it, not to give up the contents to the Doctor, but to use them himself. He finds the box, which is to be described as made with a great deal of antique art, and opens it with the silver key found in the young man's bosom. *Before this, & after his return from Boston, he makes renewed efforts to distill the drink & fails.

Tenth Scene:—The opening of the iron-bound box. Its contents are some ancient documents, on parchment and paper. Some of them appear to be certified proofs of descent, being papers which have long been sought for in England, to prove claims to a title and estate; for lack of which the title has long lain dormant, and the estate has been many years in chancery. All these, Septimius looks at carelessly, and with disappointment, although he knows that they give him an undeniable claim to the estate; he connecting them with stories that he has always heard, and with Aunt K's traditions. But, while throwing these aside, indignant with Providence for offering him such a paltry boon, instead of earthly eternity, an old wasted writing falls out from among them. This he snatches up, & finds that it supplies vacancies in former papers, makes out the receipt, and gives an interpretation to whatever he was in darkness about before.

Eleventh Scene:—The distillation of the drink; and description of the process, and how aetherial the liquid looks; then, he sets it in the sun by day & the moon by night, for a certain time; and all the beautiful changes that take place in it; and in one stage of the process he seems to see past features in the crystal goblet, among others the face of the old progenitor, in his scholar's garb, and his Indian one, and perhaps the dead young soldier's face, &c. &c. the old English hall, too, with its quiet ancient beauty, contrasted with an Indian wigwam. At another stage, he sees future personages and events. All these may be accounted for by his watchings, and fastings, his perturbations of mind and disturbed fancy. At last, it settles down into a pure, cold, bright crystal fluid, cold, cold, as death; whereas, in its previous changes, there has been a good deal of color elicited, indicating chemical action. No images whatever can be seen in the fluid now.

Twelfth Scene:—An interview between Septimius & Sybil on the hill-top. His heart is flowing out with success, and he feels a love and pity for the world. In this new warmth, too, a latent passion for Sybil, which he has long been cherishing unconsciously, bursts forth, and hurries him into a declaration, and a solicitation to her to share his endless life. She treats his proposal with a kind of scorn, and ridicule, but with coquetry, or somehow does not yield, nor yet discourage him; they have a playful, half-earnest discussion of what they would do with their earthly immortality. In this scene, Sybil should struggle with her enmity; perhaps she finds, and is surprised to find, that it is converted into love; for, after all, in Septimius's dark and wild nature, there is something that suits her own better than that of the young soldier. All through the book, there should be tokens of pity, remorse, and finally love, contending with her evil purpose. Finally, Sybil gives a kind of consent to drink the liquid with him, on the eve of his sister's wedding.

Thirteenth Scene:—The wedding of Rose Garfield and Robert Hagburn, who has come back with military rank (a major perhaps) and distinguished honor. A good deal of rustic pomp and magnificence to be displayed. Septimius throws off a good deal of his reserve and astonishes people by his gaiety, which has a tincture of extravagance. Sybil, too, appears to be under a similar influence, and between them they make the company wildly merry. The talk of old women and men, about the family, to be told. Towards the last, a strain of pathos comes over Septimius, because he feels that he is taking leave of his sister Rose, and indeed of all mankind, and is stepping forth into a dim future, shelterless and lonely. He disappears quietly from the company and so does Sybil, and soon after Doctor P. makes his appearance, and sociably sits down among the company. He makes himself appear gay; yet symptoms of disquietude might be seen by a keen eye; for he has been informed, perhaps by letter from Septimius, that he has succeeded in concocting the drink, and means to quaff it.

Fourteenth Scene:—Septimius and Sybil in the study with the vase of immortality before them. They talk; and by and by Septimius pours out the liquid into the antique goblet. Sybil is in a strange, fitful mood; she seems to love him, and yet hate breaks through. Covert allusion is made to her having been seduced by the young soldier; perhaps she says so herself. Septimius wishes to kiss her; she resists decidedly. At last, she gives him a hint of the trick that she has played on him, drinks off the liquor herself, and throws down the goblet with the remainder on the hearth. The sensations of this sort of dying are delightful intoxication, in which she becomes sweet, amiable, delightful, most fascinating, and Septimius cannot believe that she is dying. It is the peculiarity of this poison to give an enthusiasm. [4] Perhaps she acknowledges her affection here; maybe lets him kiss her lips, because she knows she is dying. At last she tells him, "Septimius, it was poison;" and dies.

Fifteenth Scene:—Sybil Dacy is discovered dead in Septimius's study; on the hearth, the fragments of the crystal goblet, with gilding on them. Also, cinders of burnt old papers. Also, a shattered apparatus for chemistry, &c. The iron box is there, empty. Septimius has vanished. Doctor Portsoaken comes, and gives vague hints. He returns to Boston, and is found dead, with his great spider hanging over him, who is supposed to be a devil who has got his soul. On examining the spider, it is found to be only the cast off skin of one. Nothing is certainly known about Septimius subsequently; but there are rumors that he went to England, proved his claim to the estate and title, and got them, and my own English reminiscences are here brought in. It might have happened, while for so many years, the intercourse with England was broken off, during the Revolution.

[The scenario concludes with a series of random notes.]

In the last interview, Sybil sports with Septimius, laughing at his rage under the influence of the intoxication of the draught; at first drinking it, its cold made her shudder; then it deliciously intoxicates; and he thinks this is the natural effect of the elixir. She seems to look forward to a heavenly prospect of life on earth. She is tender, bewitching, this girl heretofore so elusive and unattainable; she lets him kiss her lips; then asks him, "Do you know why I wiped my lips? No? The draught was poison."

Here explain that there were two flowers, which made all the difference in the liquor;—one (which was an extinct flower now) producing immortality, and probably a painful one; the other, death.

Septimius must be endowed with grand and heroic qualities; and must desire long life, not meanly, but for noble ends. No mean dread of death, but an abhorrence of it, as being cloddish, inactive, unsuitable. Make his nobility of character grow upon the reader, in spite of all his defects. It shall be on this occasion, too, that Sybil finally loves him, and spares him, and sacrifices herself instead; punishing herself with death for having plotted his.

Sybil must be introduced with very little display of beauty; a girl merely colorless in her first appearances, as to character. She is very young. Perhaps Septimius at first is inclined to treat her almost as a child, so simple and helpless she seems; but gradually she comes out with stronger traits.

One of Septimius's grand objects is to reform the world, which he thinks he can do; if he can only live long to study and understand the nature of man, and get at the proper methods of acting on them. The reason why the world has remained dark, ignorant, and miserable is, because the benefactors of the race have been cut off before they more than partially understood their task and the methods of it. This must be broached in his first conversation with the minister; perhaps in reference to the troubles of the country, and the war, then about to begin. When he shall have completed the reformation of the world, seen war, intemperance, slavery, all manner of crime brought to an end; then he will die. His love for Sybil shall be a falling off from his high aims; and, in truth, he naturally grows more selfish as he goes on. Some satire on men's philanthropic aims might be introduced by this view of Septimius; their short sighted aims, their absurd hope of success in a single lifetime, the fragmentary way in which the strife against evil is necessarily carried on.

Septimius, if he might otherwise have felt any remorse for Aunt K's death, shall console himself with the thought that she dies for a good end. So does the young soldier; their graves are the footmarks, in which he plants his giant steps, on the way to a mighty and magnificent result.

Perhaps, the moral will turn out to be, the folly of man thinking that he can ever be of any importance to the welfare of the world; or that any settled plan of his, to be carried on through a length of time, could be successful. God wants short lives, because such carry on his purpose inevitably and involuntarily; while longer ones would thwart and interfere with his purpose, by carrying on their own.

Medea's cauldron, in reference to Aunt Nashoba's brewing people. There may be a young man about to die, whom she is supposed to have saved, and recreated from an old one; so like he is to his grandfather. And he has that queer flavor and aspect of old age, which we sometimes see in youth.

All through, represent Septimius as visited by frequent fits of despondency as to the pursuit he is engaged in, perceptions of its utter folly and impracti[ca]bility; but after an interval, without any apparent reason why, he finds himself in full faith again—just as in writing a poem or romance.

10

With this scenario occasionally on the table for easy consultation, but more often put aside and forgotten, Hawthorne began the second Draft "K" of his romance of immortality. It was written in a small hand on thirty-six loose sheets of bond paper, numbered regularly in Hawthorne's hand on the rectos and versos from "1" to "72." The handwriting is so cramped and difficult to read that Una Hawthorne wisely spared herself the trouble of editing it. Julian Hawthorne later transcribed a few passages which he published, along with a running summary of the plot, as "A Look into Hawthorne's Workshop" in *Lippincott's Magazine* for 1890.[7]

The narrative in "K" is incomplete. Following the main outlines of "I," with a few reflections of suggested revisions in the Scenario "J," it carries the story of Septimius' search for an elixir of life only through the "Seventh Scene" of the scenario. Yet it is such an expansion of "I" that, though covering only about half of the narrative, it is even longer than "I." It is substantially the earlier draft elaborated to an incredible degree; while no new scenes and no fresh characters are added, it rewrites and overwrites the same incidents until the reader wonders if Hawthorne will ever be able to move from one scene to another.

On every page is evidence of Hawthorne's dissatisfaction. Notes are scribbled singly and in clusters at the end of paragraphs; jottings run up the margins and almost disappear off the end of the paper; short memoranda dot the tops of leaves and even burst from between parentheses in the middle of sentences; cryptic signs and markings appear frequently to suggest shifts of paragraphs and whole pages. Even the handwriting, for all its closely packed, minutely written style, is the penmanship of an old man whose fingers cannot shape his words without a tremor. Since he was substantially following the narrative in "I," with a few side glances at the scenario, the conclusion of the tale would doubtless have been the same as in the first draft;

7. *Lippincott's Monthly Magazine,* xlv (January–April, 1890), 66–76, 224–35, 412–25, 548–61. Julian Hawthorne published only a few paragraphs from this draft. Since I am quoting unpublished material, I shall not clutter the text with footnote references which no reader can find until the whole draft is someday printed.

but we shall never know. The story breaks off abruptly. In the late spring of 1863 he was tired of the young man who thought he might live forever.

If, as we have seen, the figure of Septimius nearly wrecked the first draft, the same young man made a shambles of the revision. In "I" he had at least borne a consistent name. For two-thirds of "K" he is called "Septimius Norton," a surname identical with that of the slain British officer and a symbol to bring the American and English branches of the same family into "stronger contrast and contact." Then suddenly his name is changed, for no discernible reason, to "Hilliard Vance" and the nickname "Hilly," which his aunt bestows on him, leads Hawthorne into a feeble pun on the young man's favorite walking place behind the Wayside. Likewise the aunt is now "Aunt Nashoba," the name she was assigned at the conclusion of the scenario. Fortunately, as one improvement in the narrative, the kinship between Rose and Septimius is that of half sister and brother so that the introduction of Sybil Dacy is amply prepared for and will not cause a violent rift in the tale.

Yet this revised draft, despite all its wordiness, provides new glimpses into Hawthorne's workshop. In the marginal notations we can see the artist's hand touching his canvas with small flakes of pigment and gentle swirls of color.

Revealed in these brush strokes are strong hints that Hawthorne found great trouble in moving his story forward. Once he had set a scene and placed his characters in proper order on the stage, he could easily put words into their mouths or give them gestures for their hands. Perhaps he still remembered too well the lessons of his short-story writing: a "tale" required considerable compression and throughout his novel writing days he never got far away from his craft of telling a long story by means of a sequence of clearly defined scenes.[8] In Draft "K" his peculiar technique of shifting from one scene to another is amply illustrated in the marginal notes.

At one point early in the narrative he was not happy that he had properly made a transition and he turned back his page and wrote a reminder, "Septimius goes from the hill-top to his study, instead of being summoned to split wood by Aunt Nashoba." To spend a paragraph or two describing Septimius at the chopping block would retard the story; the young experimenter must be kept always before the reader as a student, indifferent to outside events. A few pages later Hawthorne is not certain what will be the next element to introduce and he asks himself the question, what must Septimius then do? Although he does not carry out his own suggestion, he notes in

8. I owe this very perceptive idea to F. O. Matthiessen, *American Renaissance* (London and New York, 1941), p. 203.

the margin, "Septimius goes out and looks up to the sky, being much disturbed." One very succinct jotting illustrates how clumsily Hawthorne sometimes moved his men and women, "Rose better go somewhere" and she does—into the house, for the stage must be cleared for the walk-on of another character.

A second group of notations demonstrates how much Hawthorne disliked a long narrative in the first person. It is true that in Draft "K" he expanded Sybil's legend of Smithell's Hall over three times its length in the earlier version and he spent hundreds of words to make mysterious and ghostly the legend of the deathless sagamore which Aunt Nashoba recounted. But he meant to cut them or cast them into a different form; he found more to his liking the aloof, third-person narrator's position which he had usually assumed in his novels. Thus he added toward the end of Sybil's long narrative, "Telling the story with the voice, you can run off into any wildness that comes into the head, whereas the pen petrifies all such flights." After Aunt Nashoba's interminable tale of the sachem who could not be killed, he confided to his manuscript, "Italianize Aunt Nashoba's language a little; for except as Lowell uses it, I hate the Yankee dialect for literary purposes."

Although conversation did not give Hawthorne any trouble, he was, however, plagued constantly with the problem which Henry James faced, namely, the exposition not only of what a character said but what he did not say.[9] There must be shadows hovering over the dialogue, little shafts of light playing in and out, and queer overtones which the words of the artist must intimate while, at the same time, they conveyed exact, literal meanings. Early in the book there takes place a conversation between a minister of Concord and Septimius, in which Hawthorne tries to set clearly before the reader the strange delusion in Septimius' mind that he can live forever. The dialogue is, at best, blunt; the overtones—the words the two men did not say—never come through and Hawthorne almost immediately recognized his failure with a marginal note, "The talk of the two men is not exactly in earnest, but rather, in part, a playful exercise of the wits." If he could not cast the talk in just the way he wanted, he might be able sometime to return and bring forth that magic which makes a successful novelist's conversation so meaningful. For the present he must be content with a brief note of what he had intended, not what he had accomplished.

Yet conversation must be not only so shaded that it reveals more than the words themselves or the sharp lights of characters but so well planned that from it spring the motives and actions of characters.

9. Again I am indebted to Matthiessen; see *Henry James: The Major Phase* (London and New York, 1944), p. 169.

Hawthorne well comprehended this necessity of subtly planting the motivation of action still to come. After he had composed the long colloquy between Dr. Portsoaken and Septimius on the possibilities of distilling an elixir, he noted, "Before the Dr. goes away, he must say one thing that dwells on Septimius's mind, and makes him follow him to Boston."

Hawthorne is not concerned with the skeleton of his story. That he has satisfactorily committed to paper, both in the preparatory studies, in the complete Draft "I" and in the scenario. He is now concerned with those tiny spots which he will lay on the canvas and make it glow with life. A romance, especially a romance of immortality, needs all the bright hues of everyday life—the hour of the day, the slope of a hill, the quick step of a young woman, the flowers which bloom over a grave. But it is not Hawthorne's way to think of them automatically, to picture them first in his mind or see the next view just around the curve. He must get the whole thing down on paper as swiftly as he can and then go back and stipple with his paintbrush those delicate tints which will make the difference between a dull and a brilliantly glowing novel.

Yet he cannot trust his imagination to see around the bend. In the flux of impressions which pour into his mind as he writes, he is never certain that he will choose the right one or, if he has made the choice, remember it when the time comes to fit it into the pattern. A few of these jottings will suffice to show his concern with these small items.

Describe the mildness, sweetness, balminess of the April morning. . . . Rose's school to be alluded to. . . . Pale-faced women huddling together with shawls over their heads. . . . Some remarks on these women. . . . The ponderous old gun might once [have] had a match-lock. . . . The chirp of birds & squirrels, the hum of insects, & other sounds. . . . His [Robert's] arm is in a sling, but he carried it with a sort of grace. . . . Intersperse ludicrous things [in the story of Smithell's Hall]. . . . [Aunt Nashoba] binds her head with a dish-cloth, or what looks like it.

Even though most of these marginal suggestions went unused, they show that Hawthorne's mind was forever concerned with weaving in the small details and with building and ever more building his tale in size by multiplying the minutiae.

Yet despite his long practice with blending these strange colors and overtones into his tales, Hawthorne found that some of his greatest difficulties arose when he tried to give substance to the dim, crepuscular light of analogies and parallels which would reveal deep human truths for all men. He illustrates his curious reliance on what he had already composed in one of his favorite figures: the grass or shrubbery withers when it is touched by a man of evil powers. In Draft "I" he had written:

But many a year thereafter he continued to tread that path till it was worn deep with his footsteps, and trodden down hard; and it was believed by some of his superstitious neighbors that the grass and little shrubs shrank away from his path, and made it wider on that account; because there was something in the broodings that urged him to and fro along the path, alien to nature and its productions. There was another opinion, too, that an invisible fiend, one of his relatives by blood, walked side by side with him, and so made the pathway wider than his single footsteps could have made it.[1]

This passage was made wordier and more fantastic in the revision, Draft "K."

In course of time it came to be said and half believed by some of his superstitious neighbors that the grass and little tender shrubs shrank away from this path of Septimius's, in a way not to be accounted for by his mere tread; and some thought it was on account of [an] unnaturalness that seized upon himself, or was caused by the nature of his meditations, having for their gist to change a law of nature, and so all forms of nature shrank from him, and the herbage withered, and the branches turned their tender twigs away, and even the pitch-pine branches looked brown on that side. Others whispered that the sooty shape of that strange, old legendary Sagamore, him of doubtful race, walked there with his descendant, and taught him secrets that had better never have been known, and that Francis Norton got up out of his grave, and demanded back the papers which, he said, had been fraudulently kept above ground.

Instances of this kind of habitual verbal expansion can be multiplied four or fivefold. Only two more examples of Hawthorne's reliance on the first writing to give him the effect he wanted can be retailed here.

In one of the best scenes in the published version of *Septimius Felton,* Hawthorne went quite into detail to describe the dirty, sweaty horseman who lashed his horse through Concord that April morning of 1775 to warn the colonists that the British were coming. In that earlier draft he finished the picture with the sentence, "And trailing this sound far wavering behind him like a pennon, the eager horseman dashed onward to the village."[2] The comparison with a "pennon," or battle standard, Hawthorne thought a vivid one. But when he came to the same scene in his revision, he forgot the simile. He had already written the description of the rider; then he leafed through his earlier draft and found that sentence, boldly staring at him from a paragraph. Thereupon he hastily inserted the marginal note in Draft "K": "Trailing the sound behind him like a pennon." He intends to work that brilliant image into a still later draft when he returns for

1. "I," p. 26; *Septimius Felton,* pp. 274–5.
2. "I," p. 10; *Septimius Felton,* p. 247.

a final polishing of his story and for a laying in of the details which he must insert to give the incredible tale some semblance of life. But in the end that was as far as he got.

One final example of Hawthorne's heavy reliance on his own work will suffice. Early in his meditations on the romance he had been forcibly struck by the effects of war on the women, both young and old, who were left behind when the men went off to the battle fronts. When he came to write Draft "I," he made Septimius speak his own private thoughts in a conversation with Rose:

"Those young men, many of them, at least, will sicken and die in camp, or be shot down or struck through with bayonets on battlefields, and turn to dust and bones; while the girls, that would have loved them, and made happy firesides for them, will pine and wither, and tread among many sour and discontented years, and at last go out of life without knowing what life is. So, you see, Rose, every shot that takes effect kills two, at least, or kills one, and worse than kills the other."[3]

So struck by this pensée that he must make certain he will not forget it, Hawthorne, early in Draft "K," wrote a memorandum in the middle of a page, "remarks on the fate of young virgins in war-time." When he arrived at the proper situation to introduce this idea, he had already made sure that he would not omit that necessary touch. Therefore, later in the romance he came to the identical situation which he had drafted in the first writing and he turned back to his early version and virtually wrote the same words:

But these poor fellows—how many of them will sicken and die in camp, or be shot down with bullets, shattered by cannon-balls, pierced through with bayonets, and turn to dark and dry bones on the spot where they fell. The girls, meanwhile, that could have loved them for the asking, and made happy firesides for them, will pine vaguely, and . . . wither and grow yellow, not knowing what has blighted them, and loiter along many sour and disconten[te]d years, and at last go out of life without ever tasting the reality of a definite disappointment and grief. These poor girls are the real martyrs of the war; more so than are the wives and mothers of slain men.

These are Hawthorne's repetitions, his borrowings from himself. Certainly the rewriting in the romance of immortality is not always good. Time and again he initiates paragraph after paragraph of his revision with the exact wording of the same paragraph in the first version; then he begins to expand and elaborate by adding qualifying phrases and clauses until the sentences become burdened with a weight they are unable to bear.[4] Seldom is anything new added: the

3. "I," p. 28; *Septimius Felton*, p. 278.
4. A comparison of two passages will illustrate this tendency. In Draft "I" Hawthorne wrote: "In short, it was such a moment as I suppose all men feel (at least, I

story exactly parallels the original writing; only the welter of detail and fanciful legends—the legends of Smithell's Hall and of the deathless sagamore—make the same tale grow into two or three times its original size. This method of inflating a romance of merely short-story dimensions brought its toll of troubles in the last years. Without the imaginative freshness and audacity to erect a whole new structure when the old one had failed, Hawthorne went on with his romance throughout 1862 and into 1863 until he laid it aside with the same despair that came to him with the romance of England.

11

When Una Hawthorne published her version of the novel in 1872, most of the critics wished that Hawthorne had abandoned it earlier than he had, or that Una Hawthorne had never revealed her father's incompetence to the world. The reviewer in *Harper's New Monthly Magazine* confessed that "not even the pen of Hawthorne can give a semblance of reality to so weird and ghostly a story; everything is, as it were, a shadow; the very characters are impalpable spectres."[5] To the critic in the *Southern Magazine* the men and women were "psyche-moths" that had failed to extricate themselves "from the constricted cocoon."[6] Yet even these adverse reviewers were forced to admit that the fragment was interesting as a revelation of the author's method of work. The reviewer in *Harper's* concluded that ". . . the book will achieve its reputation rather as a literary curiosity than as a popular romance."[7] The *British Quarterly Review* likewise stated that "Septimius is a 'study' for brother artists, but hardly more."[8]

Most of the favorable critics were disturbed that Hawthorne should

---

can answer for one), when the real scene and picture of life swims, jars, shakes, seems about to be broken up and dispersed, like the picture in a smooth pond, when we disturb its tranquil mirror by throwing in a stone; and though the scene soon settles itself, and looks as real as before, a haunting doubt keeps close at hand, as long as we live, asking, 'Is it stable? Am I sure of it? Am I certainly not dreaming? See; it trembles again, ready to dissolve.' " "I," p. 55; *Septimius Felton*, p. 336. In "K" he wrote: "It was, in short, a moment with Septimius such as many men have experienced, when something that they have deemed true and permanent, appearing suddenly questionable, the whole scenery of life shakes, jars, grows tremulous, almost disappears in a mangled and confused mass, as when a stone is thrown into the smooth mirror of Walden Lake, and seems to put in jeopardy the surrounding hills, woods, and sky itself. True; the scene soon settles itself again, and looks as substantial as before; but a haunting doubt is apt to keep close at hand, persecuting us forever with that troublesome query—'Is it real? Am I sure of it? Did I not once behold it on the point of dissolving?' "

5. "Editor's Literary Record," *Harper's New Monthly Magazine*, XLV (October, 1872), 784.

6. *Southern Magazine*, XL (September, 1872), 378.

7. *Harper's New Monthly Magazine*, loc. cit.

8. "Contemporary Literature," *The British Quarterly Review*, LVI (October, 1872), 540.

have written such a wild story, but to the reviewer in the London *Times* that "sensation in super-abundance" lifted the tale "altogether above the commonplaces of crime and horror."[9] The *Annual Register* went even farther, "Extravagant as any fairy tale in its conception and details, it is cast in a mould as sombre as anything Edgar Poe ever wrote."[1] Even though T. W. Higginson made an elaborate comparison of *Septimius* to Goethe's *Faust*,[2] the favorable reviews contained very little sensible criticism. They concentrated chiefly on the right of the book to exist in print; the imperfections in the narrative might be overlooked in a document which stood as an index to Hawthorne's mind.[3]

These reviews of 1872 established the critical opinion of *Septimius* which has been maintained to this day. Like the other fragmentary romances of the last phase, it has been almost completely ignored by the biographers and critics of the novelist. It is a literary curiosity and simply as a curiosity it is invaluable, both because it reveals Hawthorne's method of work and because it summarizes his last meditations on the theme of immortality.

Nevertheless, half of Hawthorne's intentions had been sound. He wanted to write a novel on a vital contemporary theme and, in accordance with his usual custom, he would "throw the story back" eighty odd years to the American Revolution. Such a method might serve him in two ways: he would be able to mirror vivid events of his own day—civil strife in Concord, the effects of battle casualties, the slow creeping despair of those who stayed at home; and secondly, he could find, in the days of the Revolution, an effective setting for that long-deferred study of immortality which was haunting him for a full treatment.

Perhaps Hawthorne did not go back far enough. Even from the long-ago days of the Revolution he heard too many echoes sounding into the present to let him feel that he was on safe ground. By investigating the local history and the contemporary accounts of the British march to Concord, he could make his tale as accurate as any study in the Massachusetts Historical Collections but he could not find those strange, dusky elements of romance which had given such strength to *The Scarlet Letter* and to *The House of the Seven Gables*. For Hawthorne, a novel must be either timeless or, at most, vaguely topical. *The Blithedale Romance* was certainly topical when he wrote it, but

9. "Hawthorne's Last Romance," *The Times,* London, October 11, 1872, p. 5.
1. "Septimius: A Romance of Immortality," *The Annual Register* (1872), p. 356.
2. "Hawthorne's Last Bequest," *Scribner's Monthly*, v (November, 1872), 104.
3. See "Literature of the Day," *Lippincott's Monthly Magazine*, x (September, 1872), 367; "Notices of New Books," *The New Englander*, xxxi (October, 1872), 785–6; "Literary Notices," *The London Quarterly Review*, xxxix (October, 1872), 262; and "Belles Lettres," *The Westminster Review,* xxxix (October, 1872), 262.

he lifted the novel out of place and time by making it a great study in human error. The romance of immortality wavered between a fantastic idea and a real scene. Yet the scene itself, like the strange subject, might just as well have been his ruin. To Hawthorne, his own house and the hill which rose to the rear looked just the same in 1862 and 1863 as it had in 1775; Boston in *The Scarlet Letter*, on the other hand, was bathed in the storied lives of Governor Winthrop and the Apostle Eliot. With these few grains of historical truth he could build a whole romance. But in *Septimius* he created neither the exciting stir of war nor the slow withering of a young man's soul.

No doubt the seeds of his failure lay far back in the years of success. He had at his disposal only a very limited number of plots and an even more limited number of scenes than we have ever suspected. In the short stories and in the earlier novels he had quite thoroughly exhausted his restricted budget. In the romances of England he had tried to break loose from those tight moorings by voyaging across the ocean and writing of what was really a foreign country. And in the last version of that romance he had turned sadly home to Salem. He would not make the same mistake again; he would stay in his own back yard and *Septimius Felton* is the result.

The man was old in 1863, miserably old. Not only does his handwriting bear witness to his senility but the repetitions of his own ideas and characters and the borrowings which increase with the number of pages he wrote tell a story of tragic exhaustion. He could not even remember what he had written in the preceding draft; he must be forever planting guideposts along his way, not only to plot the main development of his tale but also to remind himself of the minute colors and touches which he must add to every page.

Yet he forced himself to go onward and turned again to another version of the romance of immortality.

V

"The Dolliver Romance"

1

WHEN Hawthorne could not bring his first romance of immortality to an end, he turned to the essays on England which, for nearly three years, he had been submitting regularly to the *Atlantic Monthly*. "Civic Banquets," the last of this series, he sent to Fields in the middle of June, 1863.[1] Then he took up again the writing of some studies which, later that year, developed into three chapters of *The Dolliver Romance*.

But Hawthorne was rapidly growing old. Every day he could feel age creeping more deeply into his bones. Throughout the fall and early winter of 1863 he could barely summon enough strength to climb his favorite hill behind the Wayside and for days on end he sat shivering beside the fire until night came. His hair was turning white; his hands shook with a kind of palsy that made it difficult for him to hold a pen; and, as if the very blood in his body had no more work to do, he was annoyed by frequent nosebleedings.

Fortunately, his friends were still kind and encouraging. They continued to send him good letters and well-meant compliments on the books he had written long ago. Once in while a stranger would send him a note and ask for his autograph. In order not to disappoint these many well-wishers and to get his old pen at work again, he thought he might make another attempt at a romance, just one last effort which would close his life in a blaze of fire rather than in a puddle of mud and frustration. These friendly letters gathered on his desk throughout the summer of 1863; they taunted him to try again.

In the blank spaces and on the backs of these letters he got his "poor blunted pen to work again" on the first studies for his second and final romance of immortality.[2] He contracted with Ticknor and Fields to issue the romance serially in the *Atlantic Monthly*, but by the first of December he had completed only the first chapter which he left with Fields in Boston while he journeyed to Concord, New Hampshire, for the funeral of Mrs. Franklin Pierce.[3] On his way home two days later he spent a night with his friend who gave "him

1. See *Letters to Ticknor*, II, 123.
2. *Idem*, p. 124.
3. See *Hawthorne and His Wife*, II, 323; *Dolliver*, p. 9, and *Yesterdays*, p. 112.

better heart to go on with it."[4] The publisher's encouragement was to no avail, for, when the proof sheets of that first installment were sent to Hawthorne on the fifteenth, he did not have enough strength to look at them. Then with an almost paralytic slowness he pushed forward and wrote two more chapters; at last early in 1864 came his final admission of defeat:

I cannot finish it unless a great change comes over me; and if I make too great an effort to do so, it will be my death; not that I should care much for that, if I could fight the battle through and win it, thus ending a life of much smoulder and scanty fire in a blaze of glory. But I should smother myself in mud of my own making.[5]

The manuscript of the first chapter lay on Hawthorne's coffin during the funeral services in Concord. Not long after the burial, Fields persuaded Mrs. Hawthorne to allow him to publish that single fragment. Oliver Wendell Holmes agreed to write an introductory essay and the long-delayed first chapter appeared in the *Atlantic* for July, 1864.[6] Thereafter the second installment was issued in the same magazine for January, 1865, and the final chapter was not revealed until the collected edition of Hawthorne's works was published in 1876.[7]

2

Between June and September, 1863, Hawthorne drew up his plans in eight studies; five of these were written over letters from friends and business associates who were trying to encourage him in any way they could. One after another he placed these letters on his writing desk and scribbled in his large and ill-formed handwriting on the backs, in the margins, between the lines, and even directly over the words of his correspondents. It is therefore little wonder that the studies do not tell a continuing and evolving story.

Hawthorne at first had in mind an old man, warm with a love for his fellows and intelligent enough to realize that the boon of immortality might not be the answer to the world's problems. Thus in the first studies the old man's aim is a high one: he wishes to live and see "the new order of things" in the world. As the meditations moved forward, however, Hawthorne reversed his point of view and began to fashion his old man as a ruthless seeker of immortality.

All that Hawthorne actually resolved in these eight studies was a

4. M. A. DeWolfe Howe, ed., *Memories of a Hostess*, p. 58.
5. *Yesterdays*, p. 116.
6. *The Atlantic Monthly*, xiv (July, 1864), 101–09. See *Dolliver*, p. 12.
7. *The Atlantic Monthly*, xv (January, 1865), 1–7; *The Dolliver Romance and Other Pieces* (Boston, 1876). Cf. Nina E. Browne, *A Bibliography of Nathaniel Hawthorne* (Boston and New York, 1905), p. 32.

scene and a few characters. Again he would use Dr. Peabody's home beside the Charter Street Cemetery. Plundering further from the *Grimshawe* drafts of two years before, he revived a little girl and decided to make her the one vivid tie the old man has with the everyday life of men who must someday die. Lastly, there should be a conflict between the genial apothecary in Charter Street and a rich colonel of Salem who would die as a result of drinking an undiluted elixir of life.

Studies "A" and "B" form a unit and take as their starting point Thoreau's legend of the deathless man who had once resided in the Wayside. This strange fellow insisted on being portrayed in a romance and Hawthorne was not one to abandon a project because of one or two failures. This man, however, must be quite in contrast to the selfish and hardhearted Septimius Felton; now Hawthorne would portray an amiable character who might bring to his book that "sunshiny quality" so long absent from the fiction of the last years. This new seeker of immortality would have the hazy twilight of age about his head and genial wisdom in his heart.

Study "A" covers both sides of a single sheet of notepaper; Study "B" was written over a letter, dated June 16, 1863, from Ticknor and Fields enclosing a payment of one hundred fifty dollars for the article "Civic Banquets."

STUDY A

[1] A husband & wife in their old age, after a long and happy wedded life.

The husband has been addicted to occult studies with reference to the principle of physical life, and, by natural means, has attained to a secret of finding that principle, so that, at last, not only has he become able to keep decay from going farther, but can make life go back upon its steps. He communicates to his wife that he possesses this power, and proposes that, hand in hand, they shall go back, and gradually be young again. But the wife is submissive to the common law; she has had children, and lost them long ago; she has religion; she shrinks from the thought of going back, she has an instinctive sense of what would be best for them both; she prefers to live out her life, and die. Perhaps the agi[ta]tion of his proposal (for, with her reliance on his intellect and power, she little doubts that he can make good what he says) contributes to hasten her end. She dies and leaves him alone.

He lives on, and gradually it begins to be noticed that he does not decay—that he seems to grow younger—but this is attributed to such things as a wig, false teeth &c.; so that it is long [2] before it strikes his acquaintances that it is marvellous; he is considered a well-preserved old man, aping a younger age than his real one. And this might last till his contemporaries have passed on and been buried. He becomes more and more a wonder, growing younger, year by year, but, being alone and a recluse, it very gradually grows miraculous. This effect may be given in a grotesque way, which should be the tone of the whole narrative.

There should be some particular reason for which he wishes to live back—for instance, in order to discover some secret, left unravelled in his previous youth—to study out some particular secret, of an earthly nature,—to effect something that shall give a substance to all his life. What? Something which, once effected, he feels as if he could die willingly, and with a sense of completeness. The gist of the thing lies in this idea. There must be some clear connection with human sympathies in the particular object of his desire. He shall seem just to have missed something in his onward course, which he never goes back to finish and perfect.

STUDY B

[1] He lives for the sake of an infant boy, not his own descendant, but that of a friend, who sacrificed his own life for him. There should also be some other motive: perhaps to study the new order of things that seems to be opening on the world. That would open too wide a vein. Well then, leave his motives to be determined after the incidents have been settled. He leaves his wife, and immediately begins to grow young. He has been heretofore a weary and sympathizing old gentleman; and everybody is sorry for him & comes to condole with him on the loss of his wife. But there makes itself apparent, by and by, a certain briskness which rather shocks them: they think perhaps that he revives himself with strong liquors to make his troubles the more tolerable. And so there is a great deal of wonderment. An old contemporary comes to see him, and they have a long talk, in which the other expresses a vague suspicion, perhaps, and a wish that he might share this advantage. What if he should see the bottle, and secretly put it to his lips and drink a great gulp, and go home and be found dead the next morning[?] Yes. The scene to be described with grotesque horror: he dances, he sings, he falls dead. This old person should, if possible, be somehow connected with the course of the story. After this event there are some sinister rumors as if it were the chemist's fault that his old friend had died; at least, something vague survives from it, and thus the rumors spread, and curiosity is awakened by his youthful aspect, and he becomes a marked man vulgarly thought to deal with the devil. He lives in an old house, alone, with only this child (a girl whom he has taken to bring up) and in her he satisfies himself for solitude. So pass ten years till Alice comes to a

young maid (perhaps 15 or more) and she does not see that anything is amiss with his age; because one old man looks as old as another to the young &c &c. But outside the scandal waxes great, and at last the [2] people raise a riot, intending to take him out of his house and hang him.

He flees with Alice and a few valuables, and his bottle of medicine, away into the country, afar, and finds shelter with an Indian Doctress, an herb woman who herself pretends to know some secrets of herbs. The figure and character of this wicked old thing to be detailed picturesquely. She shall be the representative of the New England witches, being hereditarily descended from them. The herb woman and the doctor carry on trade together; she having some wily and evil purpose or other, which the Doctor foils, whereupon she poisons herself. In the meanwhile, Alice has fallen in love with a young man of the neighborhood, and the Doctor finding it out, promotes the marriage, though feeling in terrible despair and solitude, and goes away; indeed, Alice has begun to wonder at his continued and increasing youth; and it is time for him to do so. The young man may be a college graduate, just beginning the study of law—perhaps a minister.

He sets forth again on his quest (?)[8] which has been somewhat remitted during these events; and he has now gone back to about his 55th year. He finds it impossible to remain two or three years in a place without attracting much attention to his youthful tendency. Sometimes he meets a man who[m] he had known when he was about the age he now pretends to be. His true contemporaries are by this time dead.

Being put into this singular position with regard to mankind, he contracts a most intense scorn of all human pursuits and things, which must be developed; at the same time, his failing belief in spiritual things, in high objects. It must be so handled as to show the necessity of Death in order to keep us tender and loving. His tendency is to make matter of observation of everything, and sport of many things, he finds himself growing to be a devil by force of solitude and long life. It should have been a benevolent object for which he desired to live, and when the time comes for accomplishing it, he has ceased to desire it, or thinks it not worth the price he would have to pay. This happens when he is 35 years old. But not doing it, it becomes a curse to him thenceforward.

[3] The difficulty is to know what he wants to live for; it should appear to be a great object when he adopts it, but should gradually lose its importance in his view. Can it be that he wants to find some particular person, or is it something that affects a great landed prop-

8. This question mark is in Hawthorne's hand.

erty; or does [he], being a very conscientious man, wish to live in order to discharge a heavy debt, which, if removed, would be the dowry of little Alice[?] He may have discovered this medicine accidentally, seeking merely to concoct a restorative; and so he is himself taken by surprise at his effects, and only slowly comes to the idea that he has discovered the elixir of life. The receipt should be ancient, a mouldy old document which existed among the papers of an ancient man of science. He might be a simple minded kind of person himself. Thus he is rather betrayed into living, than designs it, though he finally becomes attached to it. A simple old chemist or apothecary, of some skill, but no widely extended reputation. He comes slowly to the idea of his gradual youthfulness. The old woman shall have been a brother [*sic*] of the person who found out the secret. It shall have been a physician's recipe, left with him long ago for concoction; but which was never called for; and he shall not know the reason till he meets with the old herb woman, who by and by, confides [in] him about its having been left with her family. Her brother perished by some accident. When he knows he has this power, a thousand reasons immediately impel him to exercise it; but there must be one particular reason, in order to give interest and animation to the story. Perhaps I had better look to the end to suggest the beginning.

The most interesting fact about this old apothecary sketched in these two studies is that the chemist very much resembled Hawthorne himself; perhaps he too looked at his own stooped figure in the mirror or watched the gray lines of worry in his wife's face and thought to himself what a great boon it would be if he and she could retrace their steps through their happy wedded life. Hawthorne was doubtless too hardheaded and critical to allow this idea a moment's serious thought; it might be a pleasant whimsy, a fanciful bit of nonsense with which he toyed casually as he sat before his writing desk but it could be nothing more. Nevertheless, there are interesting autobiographical reflections in these first studies. Like the husband in "A," Hawthorne had "been addicted to occult studies with reference to the principle of physical life."[9] Although he had never attempted to brew an elixir for the extension of his own life, he had a haunting fear of closing his own term of years before he could complete one last work. This curious similarity between the old apothecary and Hawthorne himself lends considerable interest to the growth of *The Dolliver Romance*.
Yet the mood of personal reminiscence soon passed. Study "B"

9. This statement is based on Hawthorne's lifelong preoccupation with the theme of immortality, particularly as that interest was reflected in *Septimius Felton* and *The Dolliver Romance*. There is no suggestion in the biographies that he was actually "addicted to occult studies" in the last years, in so far as he may have read books or consulted investigators concerning the "principle of physical life."

projected a little boy who had been left in the apothecary's charge but suddenly Hawthorne changed his plan and substituted a small girl who may bear certain resemblances to Elsie in Grimshawe "H." Again, the picture of the aged man living "in an old house, alone, with only this child" is a clear plundering of the opening scene of the Grimshawe drafts; and finally the apothecary, as a result of his occult studies, arouses the suspicions of his neighbors and, like Dr. Grimshawe, is "vulgarly thought to deal with the devil." Such plans as these demonstrate that Hawthorne was beginning once again to recast material which had proved unsatisfactory in the romance of England.

Now with these two studies and with the tentative sketching of the old man behind him, Hawthorne turned to the central incident and to the plotting of some narrative which may help him to group some other characters around this main design. Study "C" was written over a letter from an admirer who requested Hawthorne's autograph. In this four-page sketch, as well as in the two pages of "D," Hawthorne began to develop a few characters—the little girl, Alice, and the old friend of the apothecary's who drinks a magic potion and falls dead on the floor.

STUDY C

[1] *Begin here*

First, the old chemist to be introduced in his shop, in the very act, in the very first sentence, of taking a single drop of liquid in a tumbler of water; and in this first sentence, too, must be introduced the little girl, reaching up, attracted by the old bottle, to get hold of it. He seems doubtful and fearful what it may [do] to him; regretful, hopeful, but seems a little moved by it. Possibly he drops it into a glass of wine—which is made to foam by it?—no, yes, doubtful.

Then comes a description of the chemist, his present aspect, his origin, his fortunes &c, all [2] in a grotesque way, yet with a certain earnestness. All this time, the child is playing about, interesting the reader, and amusing suggestions as [to] the old man's character and purposes. Refer to some mysterious way in which he has got possession of the receipt.

Then a few years pass, and the old man continues to take his drop a day, and it produces its effect as a powerful cordial; and it must be described in its inevitable evidences, in various physical ways. People begin to wonder about him, but think it is only false teeth and perhaps false hair. He, by his drops &c, makes himself look as young as he can. Besides, being an emigrant, nobody knows exactly how old he is. The women say, the old man is looking out for another wife &c &c. Nevertheless, a certain rumor and wonderment spread abroad concerning him.

Then comes in another old man—perhaps an old gentleman of eminence in this place, who had never condescended to notice the chemist before, being entirely above him. Powdered, finely dressed, but old, old—aristocratic, puffed up, but wanting something very particular of the chemist. He talks about his age, and about the chemist's, and the two old men discuss old age together—the chemist being the freest in talking about infirmities, though in his case they get lighter every day. But he wants to conceal that fact. At last it appears that his visitor has, in some mysterious way, a knowledge of the recipe and even of the way in which it came into the chemist's possession. A great mystery should be made on this point. And he demands that the bottle be given up to him—then that he at least share in it. To this the chemist [3] strenuously objects, being now in love with life, and determined not to give up a drop of it. Finally, the chemist being called hastily into his outer shop, the old gentleman rummages for the bottle, and drinks a wine glass full of it, which operates in some strange way, to be hereafter understood—ending in his death.

This old gentleman may be of the same family as that of the Smithell's Hall, and a brother or a nephew of the man who brought it there, and whom he may have murdered, or played foully with, in order to get possession of the secret.

[4] His whole life is a quest for the means of living longer—utterly neglectful of all the high opportunities which long life and indestructible organs would seem to offer him. He has no scruple in violating any law for the purpose of attaining his object; and at last fate seems to point out that the thing which he has sought all over the world, is really in the keeping of his own granddaughter and her family. So he comes back thither.

The utter, utter loneliness of the poor monster must be brought out. I think that this should be exemplified by a love affair after he has grown to be a young man again.

Long ago, a stranger came, and got him to make up this recipe, leaving it behind him for that purpose. The ingredients were chiefly poisonous, some of them rare, others common herbs enough; there was one thing left blank or written in indecipherable characters, and this the stranger supplied by giving it to the chemist in a small lump, to be put in with the rest. While the preparation is concocting, he goes away, promising to be back at such & such a time, but never returns. Or possibly, he dies on the spot, or in the chemist's presence, in some mysterious way, so as to suggest the idea that there is something fearful and awful about the matter. The process of preparation demands very rare skill, which none but an expert chemist could possess.

The recoverable days could only be [5] recalled one by one; if you tried to do it faster, you perished. If more slowly, you might slip back along down the whole height which you had regained.

STUDY D

[1] *Points thus far.* The hero an old apothecary. Years before, a prescription for an invigorating medicine had been left with him to make up, by a strange old man; he had made it up, some of the ingredients having been left by the old man, but it was never called for; and he has a suspicion that the old man had come to a violent death. But ever since, the medicine has remained in his possession, 50 years perhaps; he had sometimes looked at it, and seen a strange brightness in it gleaming forth from it. Ten drops at a draught. In this last stage of life, apparently, having something to do which he deems of greatest moment, he deems it well to take a dose of this medicine; it seems to produce an invigorating effect, and he follows it up till he begins to suspect that he is growing young again.

Then follows the death of his old acquaintance; which brings some discredit and suspicion on him. Thus the popular odium settles upon him as dealing with the black art; and he takes flight and comes across the old herb-woman. After he & Alice have dwelt there some time, it turns out this was an old family recipe. A great deal of wild Indian traditions shall be introduced here and told by the old herb-woman.

Alice falls in love with the young lawyer, and besides the youthful briskness of the old man is again attracting attention from her and others, and perhaps the old woman tries to poison him, & so he sets forth again.

There is need of some great central event.

He is to seek for the evidences of a great estate coming to Alice?

After leaving Alice he returns at intervals of years, being veiled from her by his youthful aspect, and remains round her, for longer or shorter spells; and then goes away again on his quest. She shall always appear to have some dim recognition, perhaps to be on the point of knowing him. The approaches of age which [are] to be described; and they affect him very sadly indeed. The central thought; the central thought.

[2] The title to an estate in England? To find whether a child were alive that he had lost long ago? He has been long regretting some error in middle life, or earlier, which, he thinks, has caused a long ill success through subsequent years; he wishes now to return and retrieve that error, in the hope of living to some purpose thereafter? It need not have been a very high motive, but perhaps ridiculously

homely in consonance with the simplicity of the man's character. To recover an antique gold coin, belonging to a friend, which he had lost, and thus a discredit had fallen on his character? To get an ancient sarcophagus to be buried in? Something not startlingly strange, but homely and familiar, I think, should be the motive; and he might gradually get drawn into living on, forgetful of the first motive, until, at some unexpected moment (for instance, when he is a little boy playing in the street) he shall find the ring, or whatever it was, which first inclined him to live. Might it be some crime, committed long ago, which he felt himself bound to live to bring down justice upon? The ring, or ornament, or coin, should be the material symbol of some spiritual matter. Old Dr. Harris of Dorchester, whose ghost I saw.[1] This thing that he is in search of should guide him into all sorts of trouble, change, and devilish turnings of circumstances. Something connected with the witchcraft of New England. It might seem to be some light and trivial thing that he is in quest of; but by and by he finds that fishing at random he has got hold of something so impossible to pull up as the bottom of the sea. Alas! What a bother!

The rough skeleton of Hawthorne's craftsmanship is laid bare in Study "E"; the bones pierce the skin and the joints creak with every motion. The need for "one particular reason" why the apothecary should want to live forever was lacking in the four preceding studies. The little boy or girl whom the old man had adopted would not supply the dramatic force for a man's wish to live forever; neither would the righteous aim of regenerating the world. "Perhaps," Hawthorne had noted at the end of "B," "I had better look to the end to suggest the beginning."

On two small sheets of notepaper he moved the whole story forward a number of years, took his narrative to England, and revived the romantic manor house of Smithell's Hall. The last surviving representative of the ancestral estate would die and the apothecary must feel bound to go abroad and assert his claims. With this visit of the American to England, Hawthorne hoped to levy considerably on the piles of manuscript for the English romance.

But nothing in the end came of the old man's visit to England and Study "E" was a shift in the wrong direction; Hawthorne was afterwards, in the succeeding studies, content to restrict his narrative to the confines of Salem. Yet the study is a fascinating document in the

1. Hawthorne saw the ghost of Dr. Harris during his residence in Boston (1839–40), when he frequented the reading room of the Boston Athenaeum. He wrote the story, entitled "The Ghost of Doctor Harris," in 1857 and dedicated it to Mrs. John T. Heywood, the wife of his English friend. It was first published in *The Living Age*, Ser. 7, vi (February 10, 1900), 345–9.

Hawthorne canon; it demonstrates how disappointed he must have been to the very end of his life that he could shape no fictional material from his own English adventures.

STUDY E

[1] The Englishman shall be a quiet and respectable old English squire, who talks to him with English ideas and prejudices; and has himself an objection to living too long, because he feels that he is bound to leave his estate in due time to his son, and not to contravene the laws and conventionalities of old establishments. Nevertheless, he throws himself upon his rights, and demands that the stranger shall surrender to him his hereditary secret. There is a struggle, perhaps; or somehow the old Englishman dies, but the Young Old's foot treads in the Bloody Footstep and smears it. There should be something which he hopes to find at Smithells hall;—perhaps the original receipt, in order to help him to concoct another bottle-full of the medicine when the first shall be exhausted, which he sees prophetically, because the time seems comparatively so short to him now.

At first, the simple old man thinks that he will only live till a certain tree bears fruit; then, his ideas growing larger, he thinks he will live to see and to help in certain great affairs, political changes, public prosperities, all, however, of an earthly realm, because he is so conservative; then, the risks that he runs of using the secret, and his new measurement of time, lead him to care for nothing but getting the power of recovering his life to any extent, so that he is wholly absorbed in this one pursuit, wasting life to get the means of living, and growing, through the years, more and more hard, cruel, selfish, ready to commit any crime to gain his ends.

[2] At the last advice, the old herb-woman has come to her death; it seems as if he bought his own prolonged life at the expense of periodically sacrificing another. After this, he finds it necessary to leave the place, Alice having perhaps evinced a kind of suspicion of him; and so he determines to go to Europe; and there, too, he finds somebody in quest of his secret, the descendant of the original family whose ancestor had discovered it; so that it seems to him as if the whole world were in league against him. He comes upon the traces of the Bloody Footstep. Everywhere, if he stays awhile, somebody starts up, who seems to know his secret, and is sure to to [sic] be in close relation with him. Perhaps there is some mark by which the initiated know him: a peculiar expression of the eye, it might be, a look of age, or possibly a gray lock of hair, or a withered hand with the prominent veins of age—some one little mark, which, once seen, gives the lie to all the appearance of youthfulness, and throws the aspect of

age over his entire person. This keeps him continually uneasy. It often makes people turn to look after him in the street. It throws a mystery, terror, and hatefulness around him, which spreads far wider than the knowledge of its cause. People of insight see it; people of innocence and delicacy. Children see it. The insight, however, should not be frequent.

After writing these five studies, Hawthorne saw that he still needed a "central event." The riot in the streets or the apothecary's visit to England was not strong enough to move the book forward through more than a few chapters. Furthermore, he had not yet fully decided on the character of the old man; if he made the chemist a "monster" like Septimius Felton, he would alienate the sympathies of the reader and destroy that mellow sunshine which he wished to pour into his romance. Then, he asked, what might be the reason for the apothecary's desire to extend his life?—and he answered, something commonplace, even trivial, which would reveal a large human truth.

In the final group of studies, all written over letters from July to September, 1863, Hawthorne chose a new approach in order to enlist the sympathies of his readers and, at the same time, to increase the old man's stature in the book. He was still infatuated with the idea that the apothecary should live interminably for the sake of an infant boy or girl. The waif in the West Derby Workhouse remained vivid in his memory and, after the abandonment of *Grimshawe*, appeared to be stretching out his rickety hands in supplication; or again, a defenceless little girl, portrayed with all possible tenderness, might supply the perfect motive for the old man's desire to live forever.

STUDY F

[1] He must have been a man of high purposes, which he hates to leave unaccomplished. The nostrum to bring back his youth is a thing to which he otherwise attaches no importance. He knows that it is inconsistent with the plan of the world, and, if generally adopted, would throw everything into confusion; he therefore considers it justifiable only in his exceptional case. It is but a side-thing, in which he takes no pride nor considers it of much importance; indeed, being rather ashamed of it than otherwise.

It might be a metaphysical discovery that he wishes to complete. Perhaps physical. He might have imagined a way to clear disease out of the world; some great beneficence, at all events. Perhaps the object for which he wants renewed youth may appear to [2] the reader ridiculously trifling compared with the means used, as for example, to find out the solution of an algebraic sum. No; better to confer a material benefit on the world, how to get rid of poverty, or slavery, or war —and, the gist of the story might be, that while he was trying to accomplish this by so much toil and disturbance of the order of nature, the real tendency and progress of mankind accomplishes it without any agency of his; whereas his method would have destroyed the whole economy of the world.

[3] As he returns down the road of life, he meets all mankind full in the face coming towards him. A most earnest desire to finish a poem; to ascertain some historical facts; to find out the whereabouts of a lost daughter, or a son, who was left, uncertain whether dead or alive, for many years past. Well; he is reluctant to leave a baby, entrusted to him, friendless in the world, and therefore avails himself of this secret, which he had discovered in the course of his researches, but would not, on his own account, have thought of using it. No; there must be some mystery, which perhaps, missing it all through maturity, he discovers when he is a little boy again; and as the story ends, you shall see it in his childish eyes. The cordial might be taken [4] at intervals of five years.

STUDY G

[1] He tries to make out the missing ingredient by engaging in scientific studies, in which he spends precious years of manhood, making discoveries which he flings aside as useless, because they do not tend to lengthen his life. Delusive theories spring up, suggestions, dreams, which lead him to-and-fro, and everywhere he seems on the point of gratifying his desires—but always comes the disappointment.

All through the book, the prettiness, sauciness, cheerfulness of Alice, & her humour, expressions—as child, girl, woman, grandmother, may redeem the gloom, selfishness, morbidness, unwholesomeness of the rest.

Perhaps the old man, who dies, may have evinced a certain knowledge about this thing, which may cause the chemist afterwards to regret his death. It may have been a flower, which was to be put in at a certain stage of the concoction; or some rare natural production. But the English & American branches of the family have retained some incomplete tradition of the secret. The first old man, who brings the receipt to be made up, has a rustic ap-[2]pearance, like a country schoolmaster, or minister, dark, keen, disagreeable, acute, intelligent, but homely & unrefined. He shall be the elder brother of the old herb-woman.

The drug which is wanting—what is it? A mysterious and rare flower that grows out of a grave—a jewel—a mystery—a powder—a distillation of various rich ingredients—a charm—some herb known to the old woman, and transmitted down to her from her witch ancestors. Gracious, mercy me!

The little bright-eyed old man—perhaps his eyes should not be so bright at the beginning of the story, but should have a mild look, gentle, slumbrous, aged; but they grow brighter and brighter through life, with the intensity of his search. He grows into an intensity of selfishness from all the bad and unnatural influences acting on him.

Begin with the old man first taking the cordial because he does not wish to leave this little girl; and because he wants to see a tree grow up which he had just planted &c &c. Have him seem tender, grotesque, natural. His wife shall have died long ago, his daughter more recently; the child has no guardian but himself. The moral ruin of this character must be exemplified in the book. Great affection, at first, between the old man and the child. The decline of this to be distinctly marked. Make him in the first place a picture of happy old age. Let the means by which he has the elixir be a secret until revealed, I think, when he meets the old herb-woman. She knows what he lacks of the secret, and he what she lacks.

STUDY H

[1] The Apothecary and the Colonel must be specimens of two different modes of growing old; the former [i.e., the latter] fossilized, harshly defined, narrow, hard, selfish, with the humanity petrified out of him, his communications with mankind getting dammed and stored up, the good humor, which belonged to him in health and well being, yielding to the fierceness that characterizes an old brute—so selfish that he would eat child broth, and have a daily child slaughtered to make it with, if he thought it would do him any good &c &c &c; the Doctor mild, gentle, getting worn away and defined by age, readily melting into tears, fading out, cackling into mild laughter &c &c &c &c.

The Colonel is famous in the town, for desiring to continue young, and there are strange and absurd stories about his contrivances to keep so, such as his kissing children, his counterfeiting a love for them in order to inhale their breath &c &c.

When he goes back to young manhood, he shows a remnant of fidelity by falling in love with a young woman who reminds him of his long dead wife. She seems to have her excellent traits, but perceives something wrong in him, and so avoids him. Perhaps she has a glimpse of his age.

[2] He questions with himself whether he would share his beloved

liquid with the girl with whom he falls in love; but finds himself incapable of that sacrifice. She tries to convert him, speaking just as his wife would.

After the old Colonel dies, there is a look of youthfulness in his face —perhaps it is quite the face of a wild, passionate, excited young man; but as the old Doctor stands gazing at him, it suddenly withers, wrinkles, and changes into the face of an old man again.

Love which he feels for the above girl, brings him back his real youth, and makes him feel what a dry, dusty, miserable, mockery he has been in. All the hopes, the generosity, the magnanimity, the hope in the world's behalf, are re-awakened for a time.

3

The narrative of *The Dolliver Romance* is in such a fragmentary state that the three chapters which were transcribed from Drafts "I," "J," and "K" form individual scenes wherein only the main characters are constant.

The first chapter opens in Salem where resides an old apothecary who has lived so long by means of a secret potion that he can remember the first settlers in New England. His house adjoins an ancient graveyard where are buried his wife, his children, and even some of his grandchildren. The only member of his family who remains is a small great-granddaughter, Pansie. She was the child of Dr. Dolliver's grandson, Edward, who died after experimentally drinking an elixir. It is this potion, afterward perfected by the old Doctor, which has granted the great boon of immortal life.

Not until the second chapter does the action really get under way. One afternoon Dr. Dolliver is weeding the flowers in his garden. Pansie assists him in her elfin fashion and unwittingly uproots a mystic plant from which, we are led to believe, Edward Dolliver had brewed the fatal poison. The old apothecary is much troubled by her childish prank and, pursuing the child, pleads with her to drop the plant until she finally lets it fall into an open grave.

The third chapter begins at quite another point. Dr. Dolliver has for years been drinking his magic cordial and has thereby grown younger and younger until he has become the wonder of the town. At last Colonel Dabney, a disagreeable aristocrat, learns of the potion and demands a share of it so that he too may prevent old age from overtaking him. Before the frightened Doctor has had a chance to add the necessary dilution to the powerful elixir, Colonel Dabney seizes the bottle, hastily drinks two or three large draughts, and almost immediately falls dead. At this climax the manuscript suddenly breaks off without a hint of what is yet to come from Hawthorne's pen.

Whether Hawthorne himself or Mrs. Hawthorne, who edited *The Dolliver Romance,* left the manuscript in its present mangled state, no one can determine. What remains today is even more fragmentary than the loose sheets which Hawthorne abandoned at his death. The first chapter (Draft "I"), which lay on Hawthorne's coffin during the funeral, is now deposited in the Concord Free Public Library, Concord, Massachusetts. But the two remaining drafts, "J" and "K," now in the Pierpont Morgan Library, have been seriously abused. Any reader who moves from the end of the second chapter of the published version into the beginning of the third realizes that there has been a considerable cut. The manuscript as it exists today gives no hint of the intermediate action. Someone has lifted out and destroyed a number of pages, not only from the beginning of the second chapter but from the opening of the third chapter as well.

From the evidence of the pagination, any literary sleuth can see that, when the second chapter (Draft "J") is numbered in Hawthorne's hand from "1" through "18" and the third from "11" through "25," someone has manhandled the drafts. And having seen Hawthorne's unwillingness to destroy any portion of his other manuscripts of the last phase, we may tentatively make the assumption that it was Mrs. Hawthorne who, as literary executor of these drafts, threw out the pages for reasons which only she knew. Perhaps the lost sections were from her point of view unworthy of serial publication in the *Atlantic Monthly;* perhaps her husband had been drawing his characters too close to living models in the Wayside or in Concord. We shall never know.

In the late months of 1863 when Hawthorne finally pushed himself into actual composition, he was in no way prepared to write his tale as a straightforward account. Apparently he was working with what Henry James called "compositional blocks" of narrative; each of the projected chapters would deal with quite isolated incidents in the apothecary's life and each new chapter would have its separate pagination. After he had written a number of these segments, he obviously intended to patch them together, either by throwing away those sections which did not fit into his scheme or by weaving them into a continuous strand which would bring the disparate fragments into some kind of unity.

What remains is a strangely disorganized tale, with a very modest and leisurely beginning, then a dramatic moment when Colonel Dabney dies, and finally a breaking off. The action proceeds in a series of jerks; characters change names without warning. Pansie, after a few leaves, is "Posie"; sometime between chapters two and three, Dr. Dolliver has become "Doctor Dorsey"; and, most indicative that Hawthorne was writing a semiautobiographical romance, the apothecary's wife becomes for a short time "Phoebe," Hawthorne's own pet name for Mrs. Hawthorne,[2] and then at the last "Alice." Mrs. Hawthorne, in preparing her transcription, made occasional improvements in her husband's grammar, changed many words, deleted a few of the long qualifying clauses and phrases which she seems to have felt plagued her husband's style, and modernized some of his old-fashioned spelling. Lastly, she omitted from her text the marginal jottings which are occasionally spattered on the manuscript.

4

I have mentioned that the first chapter of *The Dolliver Romance* is a semiautobiographical fragment. In fact, the only interest of this section is its picture of Hawthorne in those last months of his life. Dr. Dolliver is Hawthorne himself; the long-dead wife, by the very mention of "Phoebe" in the manuscript, is Sophia Hawthorne; and Pansie or "Posie" is Una as she was in 1849 when her father was writing *The Scarlet Letter*.

This very real picture of an old man's suffering from the New England winter and his nosebleedings during the last months of 1863 is lifted from the Wayside in Concord and set bodily in Salem beside the Charter Street Cemetery where Dr. Grimshawe had once lived with his two wards.[3] Dr. Dolliver wears a many-colored dressing gown; no doubt the same robe which Grimshawe had worn in the tale of 1862 or the very gown Mrs. Hawthorne had sewed for her husband in the early years of their marriage.[4] On coming down stairs in the morning, Dr. Dolliver is afflicted with a faintness which nearly makes him lose his balance; similar dizzy spells were a common occurrence in Hawthorne's own last days.[5]

These mirrorings of Hawthorne's own life stopped at the end of the first chapter. Thereafter he went back to his old habit of borrowing from his previously written romances. Dr. Dolliver's "mystic plants," which have a long tradition in the Old World, are the purple everlasting flowers of Eaton Hall and of *Septimius Felton;* the Norton papers, with their cryptic writing in Latin and English, find their way into Grandsir Dolliver's recipe; and in the third chapter the bloody footprint, forecast by the abortive plans in Study "E," breaks through Colonel Dabney's cry, " 'And I told you there was a Bloody Footstep bearing its track down through my race.'"[6]

2. This pet name for his wife appeared as early as 1844. *American Notebooks*, p. 328; see also *idem*, p. 214 ff. and *Love Letters of Nathaniel Hawthorne*, II, 113.
3. Cf. G. P. Lathrop, "The Hawthorne Manuscripts," p. 372.
4. *Hawthorne and His Wife*, I, 307; *Dolliver*, p. 20.
5. *Dolliver*, cf. p. 21, and *Hawthorne and His Wife*, II, 332.
6. *Dolliver*, pp. 60–1.

The characters are likewise duplications of well-known figures in the last phase. Dr. Dolliver, with his crucibles, a brazen serpent, and large cabinets cluttering the room, is both Hawthorne and Seymour Kirkup, the Florentine dabbler in spiritualism; or he may just as well be Dr. Etherege or Dr. Grimshawe taken bodily from the English romances.[7] Pansie is highly colored by Hawthorne's daughter Una, for both children are sportive gardeners who make no distinction between flowers and weeds. Colonel Dabney—"powdered, finely dressed, but old, old"—is just one more in Hawthorne's galaxy of stock villains like Ethan Brand or Judge Pyncheon.[8] And lastly there is the grandsir's housekeeper, Martha, who is Crusty Hannah taken from *Grimshawe*.

Only the moral idea or theme is new. Having failed to bring any logic into *Septimius Felton*, Hawthorne returned to a notebook entry of 1848 for the heart of his fragmentary romance, "A man, arriving at the extreme point of old age, grows young again, at the same pace at which he has grown old; returning upon his path, throughout the whole of life, and thus taking the reverse view of matters."[9] In Study "F" Hawthorne rephrased the same idea and made it apply to Dr. Dolliver: "As he returns down the road of life, he meets all mankind full in the face coming towards him . . . ; he is reluctant to leave a baby, entrusted to him, friendless in the world, and therefore avails himself of this secret, which he had discovered in the course of his researches. . . ."

Therefore, in his last treatment of the theme of immortality, Hawthorne came full circle to the initial belief he had held many years before: the indefinite extension of life is a reward for the man who will use his gifts wisely. Herein lay the substance of the "sunshiny book" and had Hawthorne lived to complete it—or at least to write more than the three fragmentary chapters—he might have left an enduring monument to his last meditations on a theme which had haunted him throughout his life.

5

It is no doubt useless to regret that Hawthorne did not live to complete the romance; yet most of the critics have looked with kindly

---

7. Frank P. Stearns suggested that Dr. Dolliver may have been modeled on "an old apothecary in Concord, named Reynolds, a similar man to, but not so aged as, Hawthorne's Doctor Dolliver." *The Life and Genius of Nathaniel Hawthorne* (Philadelphia and London, 1906), p. 412.

8. Stearns further states that "There also lived at Concord in Hawthorne's time a man with the title of Colonel, a pretentious, self-satisfied person, who corresponded fairly to his description of Colonel Dabney . . ." *Idem*, p. 413.

9. *American Notebooks*, p. 125.

eyes on these fragments and have been saddened by an old man's inability to bring them to any conclusion. Oliver Wendell Holmes, whose brief obituary essay prefaced the first chapter when it appeared in the *Atlantic Monthly*, established a critical opinion which has been echoed by the older writers of his day. To the Autocrat, this single scene was an excellent finale to his friend's great career which, so far as he knew, had been concluded with *The Marble Faun* and *Our Old Home*. It had all the ingredients of one of Hawthorne's finest achievements; its graceful style, its sharp delineation of the principal characters, and its gentleness were, for Holmes, rarely found even in the excellent work of the early years.[1]

When the three chapters were finally published together in 1876, this critical opinion remained unchanged. The reviewer in the New York *Tribune* considered the series "an exquisite fragment. . . . That it would have been a much superior work, if Hawthorne had lived to complete it," the writer concluded, "we think there can be no doubt."[2] The biographers of Hawthorne have, for the most part, added little to these appraisals. James was content with a brief generalization, "The author strikes, with all his usual sweetness, the opening notes of a story of New England life, and the few pages which have been given to the world contain a charming picture of an old man and a child."[3] Lathrop believed that his father-in-law had achieved a perfection of "matter and style" which would argue that his literary skill had improved after the ill success of *Septimius Felton*.[4] Woodberry in 1902 was laudatory in similar terms[5] and Stearns likewise considered the romance as an exquisite conclusion to Hawthorne's great career.[6]

Later critics have not, however, cherished Hawthorne's memory with equal reverence. Concentrating as they are bound to do on the four novels of the major phase, they, like Stanton, have grouped these chapters with the other ineffectual works of the last years.[7] Herbert Gorman, writing about 1927, would grant that ". . . the function of these chapters was to repose upon his coffin as a symbol of the creative thread snapped short."[8] Newton Arvin, on the other hand, returned to the opinion which Holmes set forth a few weeks after Haw-

1. O. W. Holmes, "Nathaniel Hawthorne," *The Atlantic Monthly*, xiv (July, 1864), 102.
2. *The New York Tribune*, xxxvi (July 7, 1876), 6.
3. Henry James, *Hawthorne* (New York, 1880), pp. 171–2.
4. G. P. Lathrop, *op. cit.*, p. 370. See also Lathrop, *A Study of Hawthorne*, p. 282.
5. G. E. Woodberry, *Nathaniel Hawthorne* (Boston, 1902), p. 289.
6. Stearns, *op. cit.*, p. 413.
7. Theodore Stanton, *A Manual of American Literature* (New York and London, 1909), p. 138.
8. H. S. Gorman, *Hawthorne; A Study in Solitude* (New York, 1927), p. 161.

thorne's death.[9] It would seem that he, together with Lathrop, Stearns, and Woodberry have seized joyfully upon *The Dolliver Romance* after the tragically unfulfilled promise of *Doctor Grimshawe's Secret* and *Septimius Felton.*

There is much to be said in their favor. At least the first chapter may well rank with the excellent sketches in *Twice-Told Tales* and in *Mosses from an Old Manse.* But the novelist of 1863 had four great books behind him and he could return, neither in his workshop high in his tower nor in the opinion of his peers, to the kind of writing he brought to such perfection in his early years. He had already made his name and established his reputation; he could not go back to Salem and to the twelve years of solitude and meditation. Sometime during the long reach from *The Scarlet Letter* through *The Marble Faun* he had lost his way and worked himself dry.

9. Newton Arvin, *Hawthorne* (Boston, 1929), p. 283.

VI

The Keen Edge and the Blunt

1

HAWTHORNE so often called himself a romancer that the name has become almost synonymous with the man. Perhaps in the Preface to *The House of the Seven Gables* he gave the clearest expression of his position; he had "more to do with the clouds overhead than with any portion of the actual soil of the County of Essex."[1] Yet this admission is only the end of the account. Where did Hawthorne obtain his peculiar bias which made him neither a "romancer" like Fenimore Cooper and his great favorite, Sir Walter Scott, nor an allegorist like his other favorite, John Bunyan? What, in short, made him a combination of the two, an allegorical romancer?

Many critics have investigated Hawthorne's Puritan bias. They have revealed his reading in sermons, in Cotton Mather, in New England histories and legends; they have similarly emphasized the twelve years of isolation from the world and the long apprenticeship in short stories which are in themselves little sermons and capsules of romanticized New England history.

It is perhaps sufficient to say that Hawthorne had inherited a Puritan's and an allegorist's preoccupation with sin; he may have found that interest coursing in his blood stream when he was born, the heritage of a witch judge and the generations of Hathornes in Salem, or he may have obtained it from his reading. Whatever its origins, we know that Hawthorne had this Puritan bias and a strong preoccupation with the effects of sin on men and women, both dead and living. Therefore, when he made studies of those people, he wrote allegories —the representation of abstract vices and virtues in recognizable terms which all men understand.

A definition of Hawthorne the romancer is more difficult than that of the allegorist. In general, we may say that he was "romantic" in his interest in the past, in his use of timeless subjects rather than those of contemporary interest, and in his concern with the damaged souls of men rather than with their faces and clothes. As an allegorist, he was primarily concerned with morals—the operations of laws of right and

---

1. *Seven Gables*, p. 16. Miss Jane Lundblad has made an interesting study of Hawthorne as a "Gothic Romancer." See *Nathaniel Hawthorne and the Tradition of the Gothic Romance* (Upsala, Sweden, and Cambridge, Harvard University Press, 1946).

wrong in the world; and as a romancer he merged the moral with the strange, crepuscular world which was not of this daily earth but of his own strange imagination.[2]

Yet I should like to advance the theory that Hawthorne, as an allegorical romancer, was not *personally* interested in the operation of moral laws. In his own life he exhibited none of the violent concern with good and evil which would have led him to outspoken condemnation of wrongs in his fellow men. Throughout the whole range of his fiction, essays, and notebooks, his private moral tone is strangely dispassionate.

If Hawthorne was not personally interested in the moral world, he was passionately concerned with it *as an artist*. Caring as little as he did about the ravages of sin in the nation and abroad, he was, however, vitally interested in the effects of good and evil on his creatures of imagination. And as an artist he wrote always within the framework of Puritanism: the operation of moral laws, laws of right and wrong in the tightly confined New England world he knew so intimately. Yet with Hawthorne we are seldom concerned with the eternal verities which men throughout all ages have agreed are true; instead, we often find ourselves facing moral laws which are mere conventions of an age. An obvious example is *The Scarlet Letter;* Hawthorne in no wise championed the Puritan code which visited such a retribution on Hester Prynne that for seven years she stood defamed in men's eyes. Certainly he did not believe that the reformers at Blithedale were heralds of a new age of man.

So dispassionate was Hawthorne's personal interest that he usually turned his thought on fundamentally trivial moral laws. True, *The Scarlet Letter* is not based on a subject of slight human worth but *The House of the Seven Gables* has a weak moral—"that the wrong-doing of one generation lives into the successive ones."[3] *The Blithedale Romance* is a study not so much of the operation of a moral law as its lack of operation. And *The Marble Faun* treats the least serious of any of his moral truths: the effects of sin on a primitive, unblemished innocence. One might well conclude that Hawthorne's four great romances show a steady decline in the importance of moral laws.

The triviality or importance of a moral law has nothing to do with Hawthorne's artistry or success. What is of prime importance is that his mind was forever ranging over all possible variations of morals in

2. It is interesting to note at this point a cogent remark of Hawthorne's sister-in-law, Miss E. P. Peabody, "He loved best to take some incident ready made to his hand, and to work out in thought the generation of it from eternal principles, or the consequences of it in the spiritual experience of those concerned with it, either actively or passively." "Hawthorne's Marble Faun," in *Last Evening with Allston* (Boston, 1886), p. 296.

3. *Seven Gables*, p. 14.

which, as an artist, he was interested. The notebooks testify to the number of moral themes which constantly stirred in his imagination. He was forever playing with correspondences and differences between good and evil and with the "effects," as he called them, of right and wrong on human lives. Quiet as was his outward demeanor, his watchful eyes were ready to catch the briefest glints of light and shadow which played through his imagination. He obviously spent days and months in apparently idle speculation while he sat in his writing room or walked along the streets of Salem or over the hills of Lenox. Then, suddenly, a theme would strike him with such force that the secret fires of his imagination were touched and he could produce a romance. What I wish to stress is that every circumstance had to be just right; the abstract moral had to meet some clearly visualized object and, when that union took place, the romance could nearly write itself.

What were the proper circumstances which Hawthorne, the romancer, had to discover before he could compose a novel? Why did he fail in the last years? The second question I shall withhold but the first I shall try to answer.

2

In the germination of a romance, Hawthorne's mind seized two things: the first was a moral law and the second a romantic image or episode. The moral need not have been of great human value; it was generally a provisional truth with which his mind began to play: a woman taken in adultery, a family wronged through several generations, a man who goes back to England in search of his ancestry, or a youth defying the rules of mortal life by concocting a brew of immortality. The second—the image or episode—is "romantic" because Hawthorne was concerned not with a realistic study of life, such as he found in Dickens or Trollope, but with men's souls; and for an investigation of secret hearts he must have a focus, a visual representation of the abstract moral he was seeking to demonstrate. The images may be best illustrated by his use of a letter A, a faun with furry ears, a bloody footstep, or a magic elixir shimmering in the sunlight. Then there were the romantic episodes which struck his imagination: a man lying dead in a parlor with the blood oozing from his mouth, the drowning of a girl in the Concord River, or the slaying of a young soldier on the hill behind the Wayside.

These "germs"—moral idea and image or episode—need not occur in the order I have given them. While *The Scarlet Letter* demonstrates that "the old colony law" came first and the image of the letter afterward, *The Marble Faun* illustrates that the image of the Faun of Praxiteles preceded the image of the innocent man who does a great wrong.

What came next was a symbol, which I shall define as the fusing of the image and the moral so that one became the visual representation of the other. The symbol was the fixing of the moral idea in concrete terms. Afterward, as the studies in this book are witness, Hawthorne projected characters and scene.

When this magical event or moment took place, some hidden reservoir was tapped. One might well employ James's figure in the Preface to *The American* which Lowes used so effectively in *The Road to Xanadu:* a "deep well of unconscious cerebration"[4] was stirred and there poured forth the complete pattern of plot, characters, and scene which Hawthorne made into his four great romances. What is significant for Hawthorne is that the process worked superbly from 1849 to 1860 and then failed him in the last phase. Perhaps even more significant than the strange magic of the process is the speed with which, once Hawthorne had planned his novels, he could write them. *The Scarlet Letter* was composed in about six months,[5] *The House of the Seven Gables* in five.[6] The most arduously written of the four romances was *The Marble Faun*,[7] but when we reach 1858 or 1859 we are approaching the crack-up.

The fact that Hawthorne appears seldom to have made any revisions in his final drafts of the 1850's further reveals how thoroughly he had outlined in his mind and provided for all the necessities of fiction. There is, of course, the legend that Hawthorne intended to have Hester confess to a Catholic priest at the end of *The Scarlet Letter*;[8] whether Hawthorne was uncertain of the conclusion he finally gave his novel is relatively unimportant when we realize how thoroughly his tale organized itself when once the secret springs of his imagination had been tapped.

4. *The Novels and Tales of Henry James* (New York ed., New York, 1907–17), II, vii; J. L. Lowes, *The Road to Xanadu* (Boston and New York, 1927), p. 56 ff.

5. *The Scarlet Letter* was begun in June, 1849, and completed on February 3, 1850. Cf. *American Notebooks*, p. 304; *Hawthorne and His Wife*, I, 340. Hawthorne was unable to work during July, 1849, owing to the last illness of his mother. *Hawthorne and His Wife*, I, 340–2.

6. *The House of the Seven Gables* was composed between August, 1850, and January 26, 1851; *American Notebooks*, p. 308; *Hawthorne and His Wife*, I, 364, 381. It might be well to note that Hawthorne was at work on *The Blithedale Romance* from August, 1851, until May 1, 1852. *American Notebooks*, p. 335. Julian Hawthorne states that the actual writing was "between the first of December and the last of April of the next year [1852]." *Hawthorne and His Wife*, I, 431.

7. Julian Hawthorne states that his father wrote a "first sketch" for *The Marble Faun* in Italy and afterward "rewrote and elaborated" it in Redcar. *Hawthorne and His Wife*, II, 199. Perhaps this novel is the first one in which Hawthorne used a sketch or study but no such manuscript has survived.

8. According to Julian Hawthorne, this anecdote referred not to *The Scarlet Letter*, but to "Rappaccini's Daughter." *Hawthorne and His Wife*, I, 360–1.

Before we glance backward to the novels of the major phase, we might well summarize this organic growth of Hawthorne's romances.

In Hawthorne's mind were lodged many themes and subjects which would illuminate what he called the "moral nature" of the universe. Any one of them might be the wind on which his imagination took wing when once the moral idea was joined with a vivid image. The romantic image or episode might come before the moral idea, but whatever their order they became one in the symbol he erected from those two beginnings. When everything was just right, when the theme was one exactly suited to his curiously introspective nature, and when the image or episode brought with it enough dramatic force to let him see his story in rough outline from beginning to end, then he began to evolve what were, to him, matters of secondary importance, such as characters, scene, and plot. They were secondary because, when the keen edge of his artistic hand was working well, they came with complete and unswerving logic. It is this secondary level of artistry that we reach when we read the preliminary studies of the last phase. Hawthorne has already defined, however hesitantly and tentatively, what his moral idea will be and what is the generative image or episode. In the studies for *Grimshawe*, for example, he has resolved that the American tourist will remove a taint from his family and he has decided that the image will be the bloody footstep at Smithell's Hall. Thus the studies begin to sketch the plot, project generalized characters, outline the scene, and erect the point of view from which the story will be told.

We might now glance back to the 1850's and see how this theory of the keen edge worked in the four great romances.

3

For years Hawthorne had brooded over the "old colony law" which had stated that a woman taken in adultery should wear a badge in token of her shame.[9] Perhaps during the dull hours of the Salem Custom House he had meditated on the moral implication of this law. Sometime in the long germination he had hit upon the idea of the scarlet letter; he had mentioned a woman's wearing that token in "Endicott and the Red Cross."[1] And perhaps even before he came home in June, 1849, to inform his wife that he had lost his place, he had pondered and planned his romance; certainly Mrs. Hawthorne's words that he could now write his book suggest that he had discussed

9. G. P. Lathrop, *A Study of Hawthorne*, p. 212 and note; E. L. Chandler, "A Study of the Sources of the Tales and Romances Written by Nathaniel Hawthorne before 1853," *Smith College Studies in Modern Languages*, vii, No. 4, July, 1926, pp. 43–4; *American Notebooks*, p. 299.

1. *Twice-Told Tales*, p. 487.

the project with her.[2] Then he considered his idea and his image throughout the summer of 1849 and finally came to actual composition in September of that year. By that time the magical transformation of the theme and image into a symbol had taken place; and that symbol was Hester Prynne, the subject of the moral idea and the representation of the image in the streets of Boston. Thereafter, the characters and narrative episodes came with beautiful logic. An adulterous woman must have a child and there must be the lover. Perhaps at this point—and we can surely trust the studies of the last phase—Hawthorne struggled hardest. What manner of man must this lover be? Should he be a lawyer, a governor, a medical man, or a minister? He needed someone who should feel the moral shame in secret and the minister was his best choice. Finally, there must be the evil leech on these peoples' lives and it would surely not take Hawthorne long to make Chillingworth the former husband of Hester. With these characters carefully planned in his head, Hawthorne need only choose his scene and then begin to plot a few actions of his narrative.

It was Hawthorne's constant practice throughout his career to keep his dramatis personae to about four leading figures. It was likewise his habit to arrange his narrative in a few well-developed scenes which, far separated as they might be in time, would be joined by a group of intercalary chapters.[3] Actually in *The Scarlet Letter* there are only four major scenes: Hester on the scaffold with her infant; Hester and Pearl at the Governor's mansion; Hester and Dimmesdale on the forest walk; and Hester, Pearl, and Dimmesdale on the scaffold together.

This first and greatest of the novels demonstrates one singular device which Hawthorne used throughout his fiction and for which he sought desperately in the drafts of the last years and that is what he called the "central event" or the "central scene." In fact, this element might also be the focal episode of which I have spoken. Before he had even begun writing the novel, he had well in mind not only his central symbol and a few illustrative events but one dramatic moment toward which the whole narrative should move. At that point would be the climax of the events and the resolution of the moral idea. In *The Scarlet Letter* this central event takes place on the scaffold. One of the beauties of the romance is that it is fully rounded by an anticipatory scene of penance in the public place and a concluding scene of retribution and expiation on the same spot. But for Hawthorne's purposes, this moment in the narrative must always come late; generally it was the last main action in the book. All subsidiary scenes

2. *Hawthorne and His Wife*, 1, 340.
3. See Matthiessen, *American Renaissance*, p. 203.

and action worked toward that focus. Thus, if not at the beginning of composition, at least by the time he was partly under way, Hawthorne knew where he was going. The deep well had been struck and the energy of creation gushed forth with unabating vigor.

The House of the Seven Gables illustrates the same organic pattern as *The Scarlet Letter*. Here again the moral idea undoubtedly came first: what was the result of a crime, festering through two centuries, on men and women of the nineteenth century?[4] Secondly, there was the image, the seven-gabled house in Salem. The two, image and idea, fused in the Pyncheon-Maule feud and the evil of old time working into the present. In the notebooks lay the germ for his central scene: the picture of a man lying dead in a room with the sunshine streaming through the windows.[5] The magical fusion of all three took place in 1850 and in August of that year he sat down to write his second romance.[6]

The pattern of narrative action is quite similar to that of *The Scarlet Letter*. Again Hawthorne uses the device of a few leading characters —Phoebe and Hepzibah Pyncheon, the Judge, Clifford, and Holgrave. Likewise there are only a few major scenes: the death of Colonel Pyncheon in the seventeenth century, the dramatic entry of Judge Pyncheon to take Clifford away, the death of the Judge, the railway journey of Hepzibah and Clifford, and finally the discovery that Clifford was free of the terrible bondage in which he had so long been held. The book is rounded by two deaths, just as *The Scarlet Letter* was balanced by the two scenes on the scaffold. Again it is important to remember that the central event—Judge Pyncheon's death—is late in the romance.

The creative forces which shaped *The Blithedale Romance* are very similar to those which produced the two preceding novels. Here again the moral idea may well have antedated the image. This theme took the form of a question: what would happen to a reformer who so ardently devoted himself to the cause of man's improvement that he sapped the vital juices which made him a human being? And, secondly, what would be that reformer's influence on the lives about him?

The image was Brook Farm. It is noteworthy to mention at this point that Hawthorne denied that he was picturing any lifelike group of socialists; the fact is important because Hawthorne preferred to make his way less along the path of recognizable facts and more along the way which his imagination led him. It led him to Blithedale,

4. Cf. *American Notebooks*, p. lxxvi ff.
5. *Idem*, pp. 130, 306.
6. See note 6 above. Julian Hawthorne mentions that his father did not begin *The House of the Seven Gables* until he had "sufficiently digested the plan" of it. *Hawthorne and His Wife*, I, 364.

modeled only slightly on Brook Farm. Yet these two—idea and image —were blended in Hollingsworth, the symbol; from him grew the other characters: Priscilla, the innocent and loving; Zenobia, the voluptuous and the intellectual; and Coverdale, the whimsical spectator. The central scene of Zenobia's drowning is, for the first time in Hawthorne's novels, a significant levy on his own notebooks and on his memory.[7] Yet the very borrowing illustrates how brilliantly Hawthorne had passed a recollection through those magical transmutations, had clothed it in credible artistic colors, and had made it an integral part of the romance. Somewhere, as we shall see, between the drowning of the girl in the Concord River and the visit to Smithell's Hall a wondrous mirror had broken.

Nowhere better than in *The Marble Faun* do we find the precedence which the image had over the moral theme. Hawthorne's visit to the Villa Borghese in 1858 and his view of the Faun of Praxiteles gave him the young man of innocence. The idea came second and again it may have been in the form of a question: what would be the effects of a crime for the sake of love on a pure heart? These two became fused in Donatello.

Most readers have recognized that *The Marble Faun* is a weaker romance than the other three.[8] The tentative reason I should like to assign for this weakness is that Hawthorne was already beginning to show the decline which became a precipitous descent to the romances of the last phase. By his very admission in the Preface that Italy offered so many more exciting elements of romance than could a new country like the United States,[9] he was trying to break the pattern of Essex County, Boston in the seventeenth century, and Lenox and open new horizons for his craftsmanship. But, because he was attempting things hitherto foreign to his mind and art, he nearly failed; he relied too heavily on his Italian journals, a reliance which resulted in the "guide-book" quality of the work which so many commentators have noticed; and he almost split his book into many sections by focusing his attention on too many people and not on his symbolic, central character, Donatello.

Yet despite his near failure, Hawthorne did succeed. He had a moral idea in whose artistic and human importance he deeply believed. His theme was a "grand one," as Fields was later to remark of *Septimius Felton*.[1] It was not great nor grand, perhaps, from any large human truth which it illustrated; it was great because Haw-

7. See *American Notebooks*, pp. 112–15, 300–01; *Hawthorne and His Wife*, I, 296–303. *Blithedale*, pp. 579–88. See also Oscar Cargill, "Nemesis and Nathaniel Hawthorne," *PMLA*, LII (September, 1937), 848–62.

8. *Hawthorne and His Wife*, II, 238 ff.; Arvin, *Hawthorne*, pp. 256–62.

9. *Marble Faun*, p. iii.

1. *Yesterdays*, p. 96.

thorne artistically believed that it was. In his meditations in Rome and later in Redcar, Yorkshire, where he finished the romance, he could keep his eye on his subject; he was able to believe in the artistic worth of his theme and when that faith was strong in him, and when he was properly moved by his subject, he could tap those secret springs; the journals and his recollections of Rome were happily blended into the pattern of true romance. For the last time, when the moral idea was the right one and the romantic image sprang into view, the fires of Hawthorne's imagination burned brightly; nearly everything fell into proper order; the pattern of organic growth was complete. Now we may look at the last phase and to the shattering of the successful pattern of the 1850's.

4

I shall now undertake to answer a question often raised in this book: why did Hawthorne fail in the last years? The question has a corollary: how do the fragments of the last phase illuminate the romances of the major phase?

Numerous critics have essayed to solve the mystery of these last years but they have been content to summarize the failure merely in one sentence or a paragraph.[2] Since there is seldom any chance that an investigator may penetrate the mind of a literary artist and see why he failed, as did Thackeray and Conrad, to maintain in his last years the greatness he had achieved in his major period, a solution may be beyond the power of any critic.

Certainly there are obvious reasons for Hawthorne's collapse. His own health deteriorated and, for a man not yet in his sixties, he aged with astonishing rapidity. An equally obvious reason for the declining powers is that Hawthorne wrote too much. Throughout a period of four years he completed the essays which were gathered in the volume *Our Old Home;* and he penned the thousands of words which were partially published in the posthumous romances.

A third reason for his failure takes us to the fringes of Hawthorne's curious mind. As it is for every artist, no matter what his medium and no matter how happy he may be in his daily life, there always exists a tension between him and the world he knows. His interpretation of that world is a reaching out for expression, in Robert Frost's phrase,[3]

2. W. C. Brownell, *American Prose Masters* (New York, 1929), p. 101; V. L. Parrington, "The Romantic Revolution in America," *Main Currents in American Literature,* II (New York, 1927), 449–50; John Erskine, "Hawthorne," *The Cambridge History of American Literature* (New York, 1917–21), II, 21; F. L. Pattee, *The First Century of American Literature, 1770–1870* (New York and London, 1935), pp. 545–9.

3. From Robert Frost's definitions of poetry, printed on the dust jacket of *West-Running Brook* (New York, 1929). See Lawrance Thompson, *Fire and Ice* (New York, 1942), pp. 18, 233.

and an attempt to resolve those differences and tensions between the artist and the world. The successful interpretation is an artistic resolution of that "reaching out," of that tension. But sometimes in the course of literary history the tension is too great and the gap between the artist and society becomes far wider than he can ever bridge. The English romantic poets are apt examples of men who lived in times which were inimical to their minds and understanding. They spent their youth in battering against that tough wall of the times in which they lived (witness Shelley), or fled to the past (as did Keats), or took refuge in their own introspective broodings in a countryside which best suited their temperament (as did Wordsworth).

The temper of an age may be against a school of poets; similarly a violent rift in the pattern of life may wreck a single artist while it gives strength to another. (If Hawthorne became lost, Whitman matured in the Civil War.) When Hawthorne returned from England, he believed that he could resume the spinning of tales with the artistic success of the 'fifties; in short, he believed that he would find life as he had left it and the tensions no greater than those he had known in Salem and Lenox. But the Civil War was a disaster to Hawthorne. The tight world of New England society, together with its moral themes, was gone and he discovered that his artistic world was in ruins.

His first effort on his return was to write an English romance but, as he admitted wryly, a country at war was little interested in the connections between the New and the Old World.[4] He abandoned *Doctor Grimshawe's Secret* just as the war broke out in the South. Then as a partial attempt to bridge the gap between the life he had known and that of a country at war, he undertook the romance of immortality, set at the outbreak of the Revolution. But it was the kind of compromise which Hawthorne could not effect; his mind was baffled by the times in which he lived and he had no sympathy with Septimius' infatuation with elixirs of life. In *The Dolliver Romance* he made no compromise with the days of struggle and set forth bravely to write a romance in the old vein. By this time, unfortunately, he had aged so much that he could hardly grasp a pen.

There may be a fourth reason for Hawthorne's failure after 1860, one which may go deeper into his mind than the effects of the Civil War. I have made much theoretical use of Hawthorne's artistic, not necessarily personal, interest in the operations of moral laws. Perhaps in the last phase he completely lost interest in right and wrong which had moved him so profoundly in the decade before. When a man, even like Hawthorne, grows old, he loses interest in causes (if he has dreams of reforming society) or in matters of morals, whether they

4. Cf. Caroline Ticknor, *Hawthorne and His Publisher*, p. 259.

are eternal or temporary. He has, for himself, faced most of the questions and given all the answers to the riddle of the universe he knows.

For Hawthorne, this theory means that he had lost the artist's preoccupation; he could no longer be stirred to the core of his artistic nature by a new light he might play over the tense surface of life. The old problems still remained but the mind had lost the keen edge to be profoundly interested in them or work them out in terms of well-motivated human character. He was tired physically, and mentally he was exhausted. He had been granted only a limited budget of moral themes and subjects and an equally limited roster of men and women and these he had used in a series of moral exempla which revealed certain facts in human life.

We can postulate a fifth reason for Hawthorne's failure in the last phase. It was that Hawthorne was unable to fuse image and moral in a symbol. The bloody footprint never became a workable symbol, as had the letter A or the Faun of Praxiteles, because neither the moral idea nor the image sank into the "deep well"; they remained always on the surface of conjecture and planning. They were not usable, not because they were fantastic—nothing was too fantastic for Hawthorne's peculiar nature—but the circumstances of the times in which he lived and his fundamental inability to take either the bloody footprint or the elixir of life as serious and important images forced Hawthorne into the hasty improvisations which he substituted for the tough mental labor of years gone by. Thus the answer to the problem of Hawthorne's failure lies somewhere in the misty regions of fancy and imagination, as Coleridge differentiated them. For Hawthorne, the imagination reflected vivid lights and worked with incredible coherence when a moral or an image touched the smoldering fires. The moral had to be fresh and important, the image exciting. Whether Hawthorne was merely tired of the kind of problems which had once moved him or he had no more answers to give, we shall never know. My theory depends on the latter reason: Hawthorne could no longer be stirred, as he had been four times set afire, by any usable truth in human nature; when his enthusiasm and interest were gone, his craftsmanship fell to pieces and he experimented with a novel set in England and with a wholly new technique of outlining his tales.

In the studies for the posthumous romances, as well as in the long unfinished drafts, we find Hawthorne so often striving to set down a forceful statement of the "central thought." What he implies is that he did not have clearly in mind the meaning of his tale. In *Grimshawe* he did not know at the beginning nor at the end whether his main character, Etherege or Redclyffe, should be a hero or a dupe; in *Septimius Felton* he began with an attractive young man and contrived a fool at the conclusion of both drafts. Thus when neither the focalizing moral nor the central image was fused in his imagination, he could expend his efforts only in artless contrivings.

At this point it is illuminating to contrast Henry James's projects for his later novels with Hawthorne's preliminary sketches. The project which James dictated for *The Ambassadors* demonstrates that he had clearly in mind not only Strether's discovery of a new life in Paris but also the chief incidents and the main characters to illustrate that theme.[5] There is a clear and almost ruthless logic about James's projects. Hawthorne, on the other hand, planned in no such logical fashion; he was a "romancer" because he relied on his imagination alone, whereas James, with his revisions in story-telling technique over a period of nearly thirty-five years, wrestled with problems which appealed to his rational intelligence. For James, the preliminary draft was a complete picture with all the colors, overtones, and meanings harmoniously blended; he was working from intelligence and with a considerable store of inventive power. Hawthorne depended on the mystical operations of his imagination to fuse moral and image and then to evolve the whole panoply of romance; and while he had intelligence of a very high order, he did lack invention, especially when nothing went well for him. Therefore, for Hawthorne, the preliminary study was an exercise in conjecture, a chance to offer two or three suggestions and to choose the one which best suited his purpose.

This comparison between James and Hawthorne is not intended to be taken as an unhappy reflection on Hawthorne. There was a time when Hawthorne's imagination worked supremely but it was an imagination, like that of a romantic poet, which failed at the end, whereas James's intellect and invention served him quite well throughout a long career. The two may be a world apart but each serves to illuminate the other's craftsmanship.

5

Having established the importance of the moral idea and the romantic image or episode in Hawthorne's fiction, we may now turn to what I have termed the "secondary level" of his craftsmanship. The main theme or image occupied such a large place in his mind that he seldom bothered, in the initial stages of his work, with what other novelists have usually considered a very important aspect of their fiction, namely, the characters and the roles they will play. For his part Hawthorne never cared about his men and women until he had proceeded far beyond the preliminary studies and had his romance well in hand. They remained abstractions to exemplify the moral;

5. F. O. Matthiessen and Kenneth B. Murdock, eds., *The Notebooks of Henry James* (New York, 1947), pp. 372–415.

their relation to that moral must be definitely and finally established before he dared allow them to assume any distinguishing marks of individuality. Thus the hero of *Grimshawe* is, throughout the first two sketches, only the young American who goes to England; in Study "C" he temporarily acquires the name "Chatsworth" but he may as well be anonymous. The earliest sketch of Dr. Etherege describes only "an old gentleman"; Lord Braithwaite begins as "a nobleman" and Pearson of the hospital is merely the old pensioner. Whether he planned the romances in his mind while roaming through Salem or over the hills of Lenox, or fashioned them on paper in the Wayside tower, the process was the same: characters were first puppets in a pageant of allegory; afterward they could become individuals, living and breathing.

But the "afterward" in the last phase was a long time away. As late as the middle of Draft "G" Hawthorne had no idea what shape the pensioner, Lord Braithwaite, or the English girl would take. Then, perhaps when the time was growing short and many pages had been wasted, he attempted to particularize. Of the pensioner he wrote in an aside, "I must hit still upon some picturesque peculiarity to distinguish this man, and embody and symbolize his creed; that done, I think I should have hold of the right clew."[6] Two-thirds of the way through the narrative he had no conception of the villain, "Shall he be preternatural? . . . A monkey? A Frankenstein? A man of straw? A man without a heart, made by machinery . . . A worshipper of the sun? A cannibal? a ghoul? a vampire? a man who lives by sucking the blood of the young and beautiful?"[7] If Hawthorne proceeded from the abstract moral to its clear development in the narrative scheme of his romances, he moved from the abstract to the real in creating his characters; and when he could not fictionally demonstrate his moral, his characters forever remained wraithlike. I shall attempt to show later the one way in which Hawthorne tried to vitalize them as people.

Once he had sketched the general plan of his narrative—unresolved as the moral might be—and had projected a few allegorical characters, Hawthorne would then begin to plan the scene in which the action moved. Yet it is important to note that, in the germinal stages of a romance, the scene had few recognizable connections with any place Hawthorne knew or intended to picture; it would consist of colors or effects which he would throw over the action. These would form the airy substance of romance:

Endeavor to give the effect of a man's leaving England 200 years ago, and coming back to see it so changed. . . .[8] His researches shall produce

6. Grimshawe "G," 34[b].
7. *Idem*, p. 52[b].
8. See above, p. 3[2].

effects, by bringing to light facts, which neither he himself nor anyone else expected. . . .[9] The story of the Bloody Footstep must be made wild, shadowy, and mythical, and yet be so handled that the story shall have all the advantage of its effect. . . .[1] [and] this interview with the dying soldier, whom he has shot, has an influence on all this story.[2]

These "effects" and "influences" are touchstones for an understanding of Hawthorne's fiction. Rather than rough out the actual scene and place his allegorical characters on a special plot of earth, he tried always to discover shadowy meanings and colors to be woven into the texture of his romances, whereby the simple might be rendered complex and the trivial become significant. Except as the plot was a veil behind which clustered a host of cloudy witnesses to the moral he wished to reveal, a narrative and its scene were unimportant to Hawthorne throughout his whole career. In *The Scarlet Letter,* to take the most famous example, there are numerous twists of the narrative which are shot through with the strange half-light of Hawthorne's temperament; Dimmesdale stands on the scaffold with Hester and Pearl and, during the long vigil, a flaming letter A appears in the heavens to warn him that he may no longer conceal his sin. Or again, when Hester casts away the richly embroidered letter as she walks with the minister through the forest, a strong ray of sunshine picks out the emblem and makes it vivid. Always Hawthorne melded these symbolic meanings with every development of his plot. The essential point to remember, after one has examined these sketches and studies, is that Hawthorne never saw his way easily to fit these incidents into the romance unless he had clearly erected a unifying symbol from his moral and image. Symbolism was the hooks and eyes which joined all things together; the moral idea or the image was first and the action, the characters, and the scene to illustrate it came afterward.

I have left to the last a summary of one aspect of Hawthorne's craftsmanship which has occupied a large place in this study: Hawthorne's dependence on his earlier romances and on his own notebooks. When he sat down to compose the last drafts, he must have known that the preliminary studies gave him no complete view of his narrative nor of the central meaning of the romance. But he felt that he must push on and, perhaps by patching and filling, set down seventy or eighty thousand words and then see what he had accomplished. Temporarily, to solve his difficulties, he retraced old paths which had long been familiar to him. In the period of his greatest achievement he had plundered his notebooks for details of character

9. See above, p. 32.
1. Grimshawe "G," p. 9[a].
2. See above, p. 82.

and plot, but the disparate elements had been so carefully stirred in his imagination that they came forth with only the slightest resemblance to the notebook entries. So far as one can tell, *The Scarlet Letter* and *The House of the Seven Gables* would admit of no such minute investigation of sources to which these last romances have been subjected. Perhaps the drowning of Zenobia in *The Blithedale Romance* bears the closest resemblance to an actual event in Hawthorne's own experience that can be found in the whole range of his work; there may likewise be numerous reflections of the Italian notebooks in *The Marble Faun,* but Hawthorne had worked them over so carefully and fashioned them with such artistry that the charge of plagiarizing his own work can hardly be tenable.

After 1860 Hawthorne's greatest difficulties came when he endeavored to fill in his tentative sketches of characters and to give them some breath of life. This task he left to the last, long after he had worked those abstract figures into the major action of his romances. At the moment of creation they were mere shadows of men and women; but when he came to portray them in the last drafts, he retraced his steps to the days of the *Twice-Told Tales* and borrowed liberally from himself. Hardly a character in these unfinished novels was born in Hawthorne's imagination. Dr. Etherege (or Grimshawe) was closely modeled on Seymour Kirkup; Ned was traced from the orphan boy in the West Derby Workhouse; George Bradford lived again in Pensioner Pearson; Aunt Keziah recalls all the witches who had grimaced in many of the early tales; and little Elsie and Pansie are straight from the Italian journals, with a few touches of Hawthorne's own daughter Una.

Hitherto Hawthorne had sketched his men and women by utilizing details which he had scattered through numerous volumes of his journals or stored away in his retentive memory. They were composite portraits and were painted with colors which he had hoarded for a long time. In the last phase he modeled his characters on people he had met in England or Italy. Yet when he came to refresh his memory by consulting his notebooks, the vivid pen sketches had grown dim and blurred and he never could breath a new life into them when he placed them in a framework of romance. Perhaps a symbol of his collapse lies in Study "F" for the English romance, wherein he mechanically drew up a list of items, including several men he had met in his travels outside the consulate, by means of which he hoped to garner enough material to fill the lacunae in his tale.

Hawthorne's literary career from *Fanshawe* to *The Dolliver Romance* covered a period of thirty-six years. His literary output was by no means small and especially during the last phase did he seem driven by a passion for putting words on paper and writing that "crowning achievement" of his life. Doubtless the fragments of that phase are unworthy of the man who had accomplished so much, but they have been of the utmost value in allowing us a backward glance over many well-traveled roads. With the exception of Hawthorne's attempt to write a romance set in England, the pathways and scenes along the trail have been very familiar. Characters nearly identical with figures of another day, scenes from the journals, and ideas for tales have been brought from the closet, freshened with a few touches of the palette and paintbrush and allowed to stand in their new, ill-fitting clothes.

Yet in the years of failure have come gleams from the magician's workshop of another day. The road back may be like a celestial railroad journey into the past, but it has located the milestones along the way of a great novelist's journey from experimentation to success and then to dissolution. It has shown us Hawthorne's strange artistic preoccupation with moral ideas—ideas in which he himself may not have been personally interested but from which he could spin effortlessly those marvelous tales of a world no other man has ever made. It has demonstrated that the moral idea met head-on an image, the two fused into a symbol, and from that merging automatically came characters, scene, and plot. But all circumstances and themes had to be just right; the romancer's hand must sense the artistic worth of his theme and his eye catch the shimmering lights from his image before the transformation took place. When the process worked in those inner recesses of his imagination, the novel wrote itself; when he found that his artistic world was shattered to bits and that he could no longer be vitally interested in old moral themes in a new Civil War and when he had grown too old really to care about the impulses which once moved his creatures of imagination, he dropped the pen and, in Longfellow's phrase, "left the tale half told."

APPENDIX

Julian Hawthorne's Edition of "Doctor Grimshawe's Secret"

1

The "Grimshawe" manuscripts, together with the rest of Hawthorne's literary effects, passed into the hands of his widow. When she died in 1871, these papers were divided among her children. The larger group, consisting of the "Grimshawe" drafts, went to Julian Hawthorne and the earlier manuscript journal, later published as *The Ancestral Footstep*, was bequeathed to Rose, who had married George Parsons Lathrop. About this time Lathrop induced Julian Hawthorne to allow him to read the letters and unpublished material in preparation for a study of his father-in-law which he was planning to write.[1] Shortly thereafter he had read one of the "Grimshawe" drafts, for in a review of *Septimius Felton*, which he wrote in 1872, he alluded to ". . . a sketch found among the author's papers, the date of which it is impossible to determine with precision, though both its matter and form indicate that it must have been written subsequently to the journal above mentioned [i.e., *The Ancestral Footstep*]."[2] He then proceeded to outline Grimshawe "H" in such detail that there can be no doubt that he had read the unfinished, revised draft. Yet he could not have been acquainted with the whole of the narrative as it was later published, for he stated: ". . . he [Redclyffe] soon makes his way to the old hall, but just as his connection with it and its inmates begins, the manuscript terminates."[3] Thus the later and revised Draft "H" was all that was known to exist in 1872.

After Lathrop published his *Study of Hawthorne* in 1876, Julian Hawthorne precipitated an uncomely family quarrel which may have brought down on his head numerous questions concerning his editing of his father's drafts.

Angered by the "revelations" in his brother-in-law's book, Julian Hawthorne sent a long letter to the New York *Tribune* which was printed on July 8, 1876. He charged Lathrop with seizing the unpublished papers and letters immediately after Mrs. Hawthorne's death while he, Julian, was unavoidably detained in America, with

1. See *The New York Tribune*, xxvi (July 6, 1876), 2.
2. G. P. Lathrop, "History of Hawthorne's Last Romances," *The Atlantic Monthly*, xxx (October, 1872), 453–4. See also Lathrop, *A Study of Hawthorne*, pp. 277–8.
3. *Idem*, p. 280.

keeping the material long after Una and he had begged for its return, and with using private information in a "biography" which Nathaniel Hawthorne had earnestly enjoined his family against publishing.[4] Lathrop defended himself by stating that the Hawthorne papers were left jointly to the three heirs and that he had revealed nothing of a private or confidential nature in his *Study*.[5]

At any rate Julian Hawthorne soon received the papers from Lathrop and, doubtless owing to these "revelations" on Lathrop's part, began a transcription of the one "Grimshawe" manuscript known to exist at that time—Draft "H." In 1877 or 1878 he lent his *copy* of the draft to an English friend, Keningale Cook and, while he admitted that he had no intention of publishing it, he confessed sadly that he had mislaid the original of "H" and was at a loss to know what he would do with such an incomplete tale.[6] Therefore, because the narrative was in an incomplete state, he decided to publish the fragment as an appendix to a life of his father which he had in preparation.[7]

Then in the summer of 1882 Julian Hawthorne discovered Draft "G." He realized that he could complete the young American's adventures in England and thereby produce a fairly consistent book. After transcribing "G," he drew up an agreement with the Boston publisher, James R. Osgood, who, in August, 1882, announced that a posthumous romance by Nathaniel Hawthorne would be issued in November.[8] Immediately there arose numerous questions concerning the authenticity of the book and the statement that the manuscript had been "recently discovered" among Hawthorne's papers.[9] A few acute critics recalled that, as early as 1872, Lathrop had substantially outlined this fragmentary romance.[1] Julian Hawthorne was then forced to make the explanation which stands as the preface to the published *Doctor Grimshawe's Secret*—with one significant remark which he chose to omit from his preface. The body of the work, he said, was practically complete but there were ". . . fragmentary notes containing indications of the elaborate work, and there is the elaborate work itself."[2] When he so much as admitted that there were two separate drafts or that the one draft contained notes as well as narrative, some critics promptly suggested that the two fragments should be

---

4. *The New York Tribune, loc. cit.*

5. *Boston Daily Advertiser*, cxxviii (July 19, 1876), 2.

6. Julian Hawthorne further admitted to Cook that he had not transcribed the whole draft owing to the faintness of the ink and to the difficulties of the handwriting. See *Athenaeum* (London), No. 2878 (December 23, 1882), 847–8.

7. *Grimshawe*, p. xiii.

8. *The Publishers' Weekly*, xxii (August 19, 1882), 204; "News and Notes," *Literary World*, xiii (August 12, 1882), 271.

9. *Literary World*, xiii (September 9, 1882), 296.

1. *Ibid. The Publishers' Weekly*, xxii (August 26, 1882), 231.

2. *Literary World, loc. cit.*

printed together as a study of Hawthorne's method of work.[3] This editorial policy Julian Hawthorne chose not to follow, for, by the autumn of 1882, he had decided to print the narrative and notes as separate units. *Doctor Grimshawe's Secret* was published on December 18[4] and the "Notes to a Posthumous Romance" were issued in the *Century Magazine* for January, 1883.

Not until 1884, when Julian Hawthorne published the biography of his father, was the editorship of the two drafts finally made clear. Julian briefly outlined Draft "G" and then turned to discuss his treatment of the revision "H."

He [Hawthorne] consequently turned back, and began the book again, importing new scenes and characters, and continuing until the hero is finally landed in England, and has come into relations with the English personages of the tale. Here the revised first part overlaps the second, and connects itself with it, the last sentence of the former being identical with a corresponding one in the latter. In printing the story under the title of "Dr. Grimshawe's Secret," I ignored so much of the original as is covered by the revise, and omitted the intercalary studies, some parts of which were afterwards printed in a New York magazine [i.e., the *Century*].[5]

First, I shall submit a brief analysis of how Julian Hawthorne patched the two drafts together to form the published *Doctor Grimshawe's Secret:*

Grimshawe, chaps. i–x, pp. 1–129	Draft "H," pp. 1–36
Grimshawe, chap. xi, pp. 130–8	Draft "G," leaves 73–4
Grimshawe, chaps. xii–halfway through xiv, pp. 139–77	Draft "H," pp. 37–47. The last words of this draft are, " 'My cheeks would not have been so very pale,' said Edward, laughing, 'if an English shot had not deprived me of a good deal of my American blood.' "
Grimshawe, latter half of chap. xiv, and chaps. xv–xxv pp. 177–343	Draft "G," leaves 18–31, 36–7[a], 44–51, 54–8[a], 60[b]–7

Anyone can easily see that there are large sections of Draft "G" which were not included in the published text. Throughout the portions of "G" which Julian did publish the hand of the editor is everywhere apparent. Quite properly he corrected his father's rare misspellings; he changed the punctuation to suit his own taste and he omitted words which would have been repetitious or clumsy. But set

3. *Ibid.*
4. See *The Publishers' Weekly,* xxii (December 23, 1882), 899, 901; *Boston Evening Transcript,* lv (December 18, 1882), 5; *The New York Tribune,* xlii (December 18, 1882), 6.
5. *Hawthorne and His Wife,* ii, 302.

against these fairly understandable liberties are the following rather extraordinary licenses: (1) in order to make the tale coherent, he revised and made consistent his father's careless naming of characters (as we have seen, Hawthorne did not give identical names to characters in both drafts); (2) he omitted whole paragraphs in the narrative itself and supplied transitional phrases or sentences to render the omission unnoticeable; (3) he shifted one whole sequence (chap. xi) from the end to the middle of the draft; and (4) he completely neglected the long meditative passages which belong with the rest of the draft and which would have supplied vivid glimpses of Hawthorne in the workshop of the last phase. In short, what we have today as *Doctor Grimshawe's Secret* is hardly recognizable as the romance Hawthorne wrote in the latter months of 1860 and into the early months of 1861.

2

I have described the sale history of "G" in the Bibliography but it might be worth mention here that Julian split the draft into two fairly equal sections: the narrative he disposed of to Stephen H. Wakeman, from whom it was acquired by the elder Mr. Morgan. The meditative passages, which were easily lifted from their context, he sold to W. K. Bixby of St. Louis, Mo.; the Henry E. Huntington Library acquired those pages in the Bixby sale of 1904. Yet as late as 1930 several leaves of this draft were still unaccounted for. In that year the late Mr. W. T. H. Howe bought, for an unknown sum, a few sheets of "G," which are now deposited in the Berg Collection of the New York Public Library. Unfortunately, even at this late date two leaves are still lost.

The various disconnected segments of "G" can at last be brought together in the following table:

MS. Leaves	Publication	Present Owner
1–6	Unpublished, except for several paragraphs in *Grimshawe*, Appendix, pp. 345–7, 347–8	Huntington (HM 1699)
7–8	Unpublished, except for several paragraphs in *Grimshawe*, Appendix, pp. 349–50	Berg
9–18	Unpublished, except for one paragraph, *Grimshawe*, p. 177	Huntington
19–31	*Grimshawe*, pp. 180–239	Morgan
32–5	Unpublished	Huntington
36–7[a]	*Grimshawe*, pp. 239–45	Morgan
37[b]–8	*Grimshawe*, Appendix, pp. 358–64	Morgan

39–43	*Century*, xxv (January, 1883), 434–9	Huntington
44–51	*Grimshawe*, pp. 245–81, and Appendix, pp. 365–6	Morgan
52–3	*Century*, pp. 439–42	Huntington
54–8[a]	*Grimshawe*, pp. 282–303	Morgan
58[b]–9	*Century*, pp. 442–4.	Morgan
60–7	*Grimshawe*, pp. 304–43 (60[a] unpublished)	Morgan
68–9	Unpublished	Lost
70–2	*Century*, pp. 444–8	Huntington
73	*Grimshawe*, pp. 130–5 (first half of chap. xi)	Huntington
[74]	*Grimshawe*, pp. 135–8 (second half of chap. xi)	Berg

BIBLIOGRAPHY

Preliminary Studies and Manuscripts

The following manuscript drafts are to be found in three major collections of Hawthorne's works. The sale history of each item in the Huntington Library or in the Berg Collection of the New York Public Library is noted at the conclusion of the bibliographical description of that manuscript. One draft of *The Dolliver Romance* is deposited in the Concord Free Public Library, Concord, Mass. With one exception (the complete autograph of *The Ancestral Footstep*) all of the manuscripts now in the Pierpont Morgan Library were first the property of Julian Hawthorne, who sold them to the late Mr. Stephen H. Wakeman; at the sale of the Wakeman Collection in April, 1924, they were purchased by the elder Mr. Morgan and are now permanently deposited in the Pierpont Morgan Library, New York City. These manuscripts will be identified briefly in the following bibliography by the caption "Morgan." The present owners of the other items will be noted as "Huntington," "Berg," etc. All dimensions of the MSS. are in inches.

The Ancestral Footstep. Complete Autograph MS.
88 pp. 4to (7¾ x 9¾). Closely written, recto and verso, on ruled pages of a paper-bound notebook. Paginated continuously in the author's hand from "1" through "88." Composed in the form of a journal, with each entry bearing a date beginning April 1 and ending May 19, 1858. Enclosed in a red cloth portfolio and contained in a red morocco case. (Morgan)
The MS. item was sold by George Parsons Lathrop to the late George H. Williamson of Brooklyn, New York; it was purchased from the Williamson Collection in 1915 by Mr. J. Pierpont Morgan, Sr. W. H. Cathcart was mistaken in stating that this MS. was formerly in the Wakeman Collection. See W. H. Cathcart, compiler, *Bibliography of the Works of Nathaniel Hawthorne* (Cleveland, Ohio, The Rowfant Club, 1905), p. 62.
Grimshawe "A."
4 pp. 8vo (4⅞ x 7⅞). Written in smooth hand, perhaps in England before Hawthorne's return to Concord. This MS. was acquired from Julian Hawthorne by W. K. Bixby and was purchased by the Huntington Library in a private transaction. (Huntington—HM 2862)
Grimshawe "B."
2 pp. 8vo (4⅞ x 7⅞). Written over both sides of a single leaf, probably shortly after Hawthorne's return to Concord; there is a reference to Mrs. Harriet Beecher Stowe, who came from England on the same boat with the Hawthornes. For sale history, see "A." (Huntington—HM 2862)

Grimshawe "C."

2 pp. 8vo (5 x 7⅞). Unnumbered. For sale history, see "A." (Huntington—HM 2862)

Grimshawe "D."

4 pp. 12mo (4¾ x 7⅝). Numbered "2" on recto of second leaf. Written on both rectos and versos. For sale history, see "A." (Huntington—HM 2862)

Grimshawe "E."

2 pp. 8vo (6⅜ x 7½). Unnumbered. Written on only the recto of each leaf. The MS. has been slightly damaged so that several words are blurred. One of Hawthorne's signatures has been cut off, possibly from a letter, and pasted crudely at the conclusion of the draft. The early history of this MS. is unknown. (Massachusetts Historical Society, The Washburn Papers, Vol. XIX)

Grimshawe "F." Subject Index to the English Notebooks.

2 pp. 12mo (5⅜ x 5½). Written over both sides of a single sheet of note paper. One notation—"Musicians, June 20, '54"—has been written twice.

This MS. is the only one of all the preliminary studies which has been mentioned by any of Hawthorne's heirs. G. P. Lathrop noted in his Introduction to the *English Notebooks* (I, 408), "Among the papers left . . . bearing on 'Septimius Felton' [*sic*] was a list of references, with dates, to passages in his English journals, containing matter which he probably thought would prove suggestive and useful when he should come to that part of the completed romance which was to enact itself among English surroundings." It was purchased from Julian Hawthorne by William K. Bixby and sold in 1916 to the Huntington Library. *Rare and Fine Books . . . Consigned by W. K. Bixby*, Anderson Galleries, New York City, March 30, 1916, #538. (Huntington—HM 1401)

This index was first reproduced in Elizabeth Shortill Walters's "A Study of Hawthorne's Theory of Romance and His Creative Method" (M.A. dissertation, Tulane University, 1940), p. 52. I am deeply indebted to Miss Walters (now Mrs. Robert S. Heath), who relinquished her prior rights to the index and allowed me to include it in this book.

Grimshawe "G." Original Autograph MS.

117 pp. 4to (7¾ x 9¾). 4 pp. (leaves 68 and 69) are lost. This extensive draft was dispersed in three portions which are now in the Morgan, Huntington, and Berg Collections. The three segments will be described separately:

1. 61 pp. (not consecutive) 4to (7¾ x 9¾). Consists of 31 leaves, numbered in Hawthorne's hand on the rectos only: 1–6, 9–18, 32–5, 39–43, 52–3, 70–3. Written on white, unruled paper, on both sides of the leaf, except 43ᵇ, which is blank. For the sale history of leaves 9–12, 32–5, 39–43, 52–3, and 70–3, see "F" above and *Rare and Fine Books . . . Consigned by W. K. Bixby*, #585. Leaves 1–6 and 13–18 were purchased in 1922 from Julian Hawthorne. (Huntington—HM 1699)

Leaves 9–12, 32–5, 39–43, and 70–3, while in the Bixby Collection, were exhibited at the Grolier Club, New York City, in 1904 on the centenary of Hawthorne's birth. See *First Editions of the Works of Nathaniel Hawthorne Exhibited at the Grolier Club* (New York, 1904), p. 63. Portions of this draft were published by Julian Hawthorne as "A Look into Hawthorne's Workshop," *The Century Magazine*, xxv (January, 1883), 437–52.

2. 76 pp. (not consecutive) 4to (7¾ x 9¾). 38 leaves, paginated in the author's hand on the rectos as follows: 19–31, 36–8, 44–51, and 54–67. Bound in a red morocco binding with "H" below. (Morgan)

Although a few pages remain unpublished, the major portion of these leaves has been published in the second half of *Doctor Grimshawe's Secret* and in "A Look into Hawthorne's Workshop," pp. 437–52.

3. 6 pp. (not consecutive) 2 leaves, 4to (7¾ x 9¾), and 1 leaf (5 x 8). Unbound. The first two leaves are numbered in Hawthorne's hand on the rectos, "6" and "7." A few paragraphs were included in the Appendix to *Grimshawe*, pp. 349–50. The third leaf, unnumbered, belongs at the very end of the draft. The ink is badly faded and the paper brown with age. It immediately follows the last leaf (73ᵇ) and may thus be numbered "74." It begins abruptly in the middle of a sentence, "curiosity in his face as he struts toward him" and thus constitutes the latter half of *Grimshawe*, chap. xi, pp. 135–8. In 1930 these six pages were purchased by the late W. T. H. Howe in a private transaction with Julian Hawthorne; at Mr. Howe's death they were purchased for the Berg Collection of the New York Public Library. (Berg)

Grimshawe "H." Unfinished Last Draft.

49 pp. 4to (7¾ x 9¾). Written smoothly on white paper and bound in a modern red morocco binding. Paginated irregularly in the author's hand on the recto and verso of each leaf from "1" through "47." Two pages repeat the pagination "34" and "35." Bottom of leaf bearing pp. 35 and 36 has been cut off and lost. The last page breaks off abruptly with the words, " 'My cheeks would not have been so very pale,' said Edward, laughing, 'if an English shot had not deprived me of a good deal of my American blood.' " *Grimshawe*, p. 177. (Morgan)

This draft was used by Julian Hawthorne as the basis for his text of *Grimshawe*. In his edition it constitutes pp. 1–177.

Septimius "A."

4 pp. 4to (7¾ x 9¾). Unbound. Closely written on both sides of each leaf. It was purchased in 1930 by Mr. Howe from Julian Hawthorne. (Berg)

Septimius "B."

2 pp. 12mo (4½ x 7¾). No pagination. Written over both sides of a single leaf. Inlaid to quarto size in a modern red morocco binding. (Morgan)

Septimius "C."

2 pp. 8vo (5⅛ x 8). Unbound, no pagination. Written over both sides

of a single leaf in a large hand. Paper brown and torn in several places. For history, see "A" above. (Berg)
Septimius "D."
    2 pp. 8vo (5 x 8). Unbound, no pagination, except for "XIX" at the top of p. 1. For sale history, see Grimshawe "A." (Huntington—HM 12131)
Septimius "E."
    3 pp. 8vo (5¼ x 8¼). Written over a letter from James T. Fields, dated November 5, 1861. The first three sentences of Hawthorne's notations are written between the paragraphs of Fields's letter; the remainder is composed in the blank spaces. Inlaid to quarto size in a modern red morocco binding. (Morgan)
    Following is Fields's letter:

Boston, Nov. 5, 1861

My Dear Hawthorne,
    I think you had better allow me to put your story into my prospectus for 1862. And these are my reasons.
    1ˢᵗ !!! of course I want your name as a leader to my list of attractions.
    2ᵈ I think you will get more money out of the story, handling two sums instead of one.
    Tell me you allow me to name a forthcoming story by N. H. on the Decʳ. cover. I must hear by return mail.
    I could not let you do anything that could in the slightest degree dull the edge of your fine genius. So you must trust me in this case as acting not wholly from selfish motives.

Yours ever,
J. T. F.

Write me at once please.

Septimius "F."
    4 pp. 8vo (4¾ x 7¾). Unnumbered loose sheets, written over both sides and inlaid to quarto size in a modern red morocco binding. (Morgan)
Septimius "G."
    2 pp. 12mo (4 x 5¼). Unnumbered. One leaf torn from a small pocket notebook and written over both sides. Inlaid to quarto size in a modern red morocco binding. (Morgan)
Septimius "H."
    4 pp. 8vo (4½ x 7¼). Two loose sheets torn from a small pocket notebook, closely written over both sides. Inlaid to quarto size in a modern red morocco binding. (Morgan)
Septimius "I." Complete Autograph MS.
    92 pp. 4to (7¾ x 9¾). Written in a careful but very small hand. Paginated in the author's hand on the rectos and versos from "1" through "94." The verso of 94 is blank. Page 38 is misnumbered "37"; on the next page the numbering is resumed in order. Pages 67 and 68 are missing (see *Septimius Felton*, p. 364). One paragraph at the top of p. 69 is unpublished. There are frequent jottings in the margins and at the tops of pages which, for the most part, have been faithfully reproduced in the

published version of the romance. Bound in a modern red morocco binding. (Morgan)

Included in the MS. is the following note from Julian Hawthorne to Stephen H. Wakeman, "He [Hawthorne] made two versions of this story, one of which was posthumously published, while the second [Draft "K"] has never been in type, with the exception of some parts which were published in Lippincott's Magazine about 1885."

Septimius "J." Complete Scenario of the Plot.

4 pp. 4to (7¾ x 9¾). Unnumbered and written closely over both sides of 2 leaves. Bound in a modern red morocco binding. (Morgan)

Septimius "K." Unfinished Revised Draft.

57 pp. 4to (7¾ x 9¾). Written in a very small hand. Paginated in the author's hand on rectos and versos continuously from "1" through "57"; 57ᵇ is blank. There are numerous marginal notations and suggestions for the development of the tale. Bound along with "I" and "J" in a modern red morocco binding. (Morgan)

Julian Hawthorne published a summary and a few paragraphs from this draft as "Nathaniel Hawthorne's 'Elixir of Life.' How Hawthorne Worked," *Lippincott's Magazine,* xlv (January–April, 1890), 66–76, 224–35, 412–25, 548–61.

There is a separate leaf, 2 pp. (7¾ x 9¾), which Hawthorne has marked "25 (Additional)"; this item is a revision of a colloquy between Septimius and an old man of Concord which occurs in Draft "K" on p. 25. (Morgan)

Dolliver "A."

2 pp. 12mo (4 x 7¾). Unbound. A single leaf torn from some other larger sheet of paper, perhaps from a letter; part of a signature appears along one side of the MS. Both recto and verso are numbered "1," either in Hawthorne's or some other hand. For sale history, see Grimshawe "A." (Huntington—HM 2862)

Dolliver "B."

3 pp. 8vo (5¼ x 6¾). Unbound. The paper is brown with age, the ink is badly faded, and the edges slightly torn. Written over a letter from Ticknor and Fields, dated June 16, 1863, and enclosing a cheque for $150 for the article "Civic Banquets" to be issued in the *Atlantic Monthly* for August, 1863. For sale history, see Septimius "A." (Berg)

Dolliver "C."

4 pp. 8vo (5 x 8). Unnumbered. Written over a letter, dated July 6, 1863, requesting Hawthorne's autograph. Hawthorne has written over four pages of the letter; the last words of the study are written upside down on p. 3 of the letter. Inlaid to quarto size in a maroon levant binding.

This MS., together with "G" and "H" below, was acquired from Julian Hawthorne by Frederick Lehmann and was purchased at the Lehmann sale in December, 1930, by W. T. H. Howe. See *Library of Frederick W. Lehmann,* Anderson Galleries, New York City, 1930, #567. After Mr. Howe's death, it passed to the New York Public Library. (Berg)

Dolliver "D."

2 pp. 8vo (5¼ x 6). Unnumbered. Written over both sides of a single, unbound leaf. For history, see Grimshawe "A." (Huntington—HM 2862)

Dolliver "E."

2 pp. 8vo (4⅞ x 7¾). Unnumbered. Written over both sides of a single leaf. Inlaid to quarto size in a modern red morocco binding. (Morgan)

Dolliver "F."

4 pp. 8vo (3⅞ x 6). Two leaves, unbound. Written over a letter, dated July 22 [1863], from J. T. Fields, regarding printer's proofs of Hawthorne's article "Civic Banquets." For history, see Grimshawe "F." (Huntington—HM 2863)

Dolliver "G."

2 pp. 8vo (5 x 8). Unnumbered. Written over a brief business note to Hawthorne and dated August 27, 1863. Inlaid to quarto size in modern maroon levant binding. For history, see Dolliver "C." (Berg)

Dolliver "H."

2 pp. 12mo (4¾ x 7½). Unnumbered. Written over a note, dated September 18, 1863, from Hawthorne's friend, David Roberts, on receiving a presentation copy of *Our Old Home*. For history, see Dolliver "C." (Berg)

Dolliver "I." Complete Autograph MS. of Chap. I.

24 pp. 4to (7¾ x 9¾). Written in a large hand on the rectos and versos of 12 single leaves. Paginated continuously in the author's hand from "1" to "24." The handwriting is so badly faded on pp. 1–3 that it is almost illegible. Thereafter it is quite clear. At the top of the first page Hawthorne has written, "Fragments of a Romance/Chapter 1./The Brazen Serpent." (Concord Free Public Library, Concord, Mass.)

On a separate sheet of paper is an inch-square picture of Hawthorne and underneath J. T. Fields has written the following note, "Presented to The Concord Library by James T. Fields June 17, 1875, The First Chapter of Hawthorne's Unfinished 'Dolliver Romance.' This MS. was laid on his coffin the day he was buried in Concord."

Dolliver "J." Complete Autograph MS. of Chap. II.

10 pp. 4to (7¾ x 9¾). Written in a large hand on single sheets of white paper. Paginated continuously in the author's hand on the rectos and versos from "9" through "18." Bound in a modern red morocco binding. (Morgan)

Dolliver "K." Complete Autograph MS. of Chap. III.

15 pp. 4to (7¾ x 9¾). Written in a large hand on single sheets of white paper. Paginated continuously in the author's hand on rectos and versos from "11" through "25"; 25ᵇ is blank. Bound with "J" in a modern red morocco binding. (Morgan)

INDEX